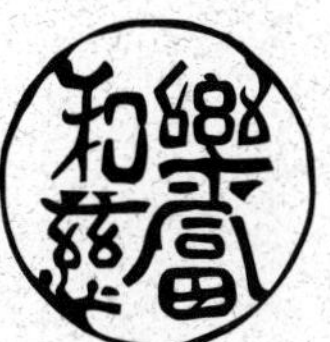

ISBN 0-943651-24-7

Design: Bob Stern

Printing:
The Printmore Press, New York, NY

On the cover is an enlarged detail of, "*the seal designed by Rizio Awoki for John La Farge and cut in ivory for him when he was in Japan in 1886. It embodies his surname in Japanese characters.*"
Royal Cortissoz, *John La Farge: A Memoir and a Study* (Boston and New York, 1911).

JOHN LA FARGE: Watercolors and Drawings

The Hudson River Museum of Westchester

This book was published to accompany the exhibition
JOHN LA FARGE: Watercolors and Drawings

THE HUDSON RIVER MUSEUM OF WESTCHESTER, Yonkers, NY
October 28, 1990 through January 6, 1991

THE MUNSON–WILLIAMS–PROCTOR INSTITUTE, Utica, NY
February 23 through April 21, 1991

THE TERRA MUSEUM OF AMERICAN ART, Chicago, IL
June 15 through August 11, 1991

This exhibition and catalogue are funded in part by
the New York State Council on the Arts and the John Sloan
Memorial Foundation, Inc.

CONTENTS

INTRODUCTION

Barbara Bloemink

The current exhibition offers an in-depth, intimate examination of the works on paper of John La Farge, considered to be one of the most significant and innovative nineteenth century American artists. In a 1910 obituary, the *New York Tribune* declared La Farge to be "... one of the greatest geniuses this country ever produced ... a universal genius who belongs to all time."[1] With the advent of abstract art in the 1920s, however, La Farge's work temporarily fell out of favor with art critics and the general public. The very elements that had won him praise during his lifetime—his eclecticism, fascination with multiple techniques and media, interest in exoticism and so-called "minor" and decorative arts—were dismissed as old-fashioned and retrograde.

During the regionalist and nationalist tendencies of the 30s and 40s, La Farge's work, in contrast with that of his friend and contemporary Winslow Homer, remained out of favor, appearing too sophisticated and European to the American public. As Guy Pene du Bois noted in a 1931 review, La Farge was "a sophisticated personality in a country whose men boasted of their manliness, who voted as their fathers had voted, and thought with an equal amount of versatility."[2]

However, during the last decade, La Farge's reputation as one of the most inventive and fascinating artists of the nineteenth century has resurfaced, largely through scholarly articles and increasing art market interest confirming his significance as an artist and an innovator. Since 1910 there have been two retrospectives of La Farge's work. One, at The Metropolitan Museum of Art in 1936, emphasized the artist's oil paintings and murals. A second, more comprehensive exhibition, was mounted by the National Museum of American Art in 1987. It included a selection of the artist's best work in painting, mural design, watercolor, and stained glass. The current exhibition is the first to investigate the artist's works on paper, from early school drawings copied after Old Masters to the fully realized designs for secular and religious interiors and richly evocative watercolors of the South Seas.

To a much greater extent than with another medium, drawings and watercolors offer clues into their creator's mind. For many artists, including La Farge, works on paper are often forms of visual thinking or note taking for work in other media and as such, allow us to view the artist's thinking process over time, the elaboration

1
"John La Farge Dead," *New York Tribune*, November 15, 1910, p. 7.

2
Guy Pene du Bois, "The Case of John La Farge," *The Arts* 17 (Jan. 1931), p. 277.

between initial and progressive "thoughts." Unlike with oil or acrylic paint, it is much more difficult for an artist working in watercolor or ink to completely eliminate "mistakes" and rework images on paper. The media are fugitive, offering washes of color and line which, if not properly handled and preserved, will fade with time. The awareness of their relative fragility often gives works on paper a special character and freshness. Because of their nature, drawings and watercolors are often intimate, contemplative viewing experiences. Generally smaller than paintings or sculpture, they require viewing from close proximity.

As James Yarnall demonstrates in the following chapters, works on paper can be found at every significant stage of John La Farge's career and reveal his continuing experimentation with unusual subject matter and techniques. In addition to his works on paper, La Farge was responsible for considerable innovations in a myriad of different endeavors in various media. Contemporaries regarded La Farge as a Renaissance man, a brilliant conversationalist, with an insatiable curiosity and encyclopedic mind, ". . . there was probably no subject of interest to man which was not of interest to him. He drank of civilization as one drinks from a bubbling spring . . . out of [his intellect] poured his paintings and his other works, for he was ever the artist, the maker, the man who must put his ideas in tangible form."[3] He numbered among his intimate friends some of the most advanced thinkers of his time, including H. H. Richardson, Stanford White, Augustus Saint Gaudens, William and Henry James and Henry Adams.

La Farge's work is astonishing in its variety of forms, techniques and subject matter. He worked in paintings, sculpture, drawing, watercolor, illustration, architectural design, wood engraving, murals, stained glass, and photography. He is credited with inventing a new school of wood engraving, initiating the use of opalescent glass in stained-glass design, collecting and incorporating motifs and compositional elements from Japanese art prior to his European contemporaries, painting plein-air landscapes before the Impressionists, working in Tahiti and the South Seas a year before Gauguin's arrival, and creating a new form of art criticism using psychology and physiology to analyze meaning.[4]

One of the most salient features of La Farge's work is its conflation of influences. Throughout his life, La Farge preferred to work independently. His earliest drawing lessons given by his grandfather, an accomplished miniature painter, provided the artist with a sense of precision and attention to areas of pure unadulterated color. While still in grammar school, La Farge studied briefly with an English watercolorist, learning to work with luminous washes of transparent color. On an early trip to Europe, the artist furthered his knowledge of medieval painting methods through discussion on encaustic painting with Henry Le Strange, decorator of the Ely Cathedral. He studied stained glass in the cathedrals of France and met with Pre-Raphaelite painters while in England. After only a few weeks in the studio of painter Thomas Couture, La Farge left, choosing instead to pursue an independent study by copying Old Master drawings and Rembrandt etchings in the Louvre which he found ". . . a logical method of learning and learning very seriously . . . In the Master's drawings and studies for given work I met him intimately, saw into his mind, and learned his intentions and his character, and what was great and what was deficient."[5]

In Newport, Rhode Island, beginning in 1859, La Farge forged his own style of landscape painting. In a manner which anticipated the working methods of the Impressionists, he worked largely out-of-doors, creating a series of sketches and paintings that are far in advance of most of his American and European contempo-

3
Royal Cortissoz, *John La Farge: A Memoir and a Study* (Boston and New York, 1911), pp. 262-3.

4
Henry Adams, "The Mind of John La Farge," *John La Farge*, (New York, 1987), p. 71.

5
Autobiographical fragment, quoted by Cecelia Waern, *John La Farge, Artist and Writer* (New York and London, 1896), p. 11; quoted in H. Barbara Weinberg, "John La Farge—The Relation of His Illustrations to His Ideal Art," *American Art Journal*, 5, (May, 1973), p. 58.

raries in terms of topographical and atmospheric realism. Believing the study of nature to be as important as the study of art, La Farge avoided past formulas of landscape painting and composition. Instead in works from this period, such as the painting *Paradise Valley*, he chose to paint modest landscapes from commonplace vantage points with no narrative or literary content. He made numerous sketches of natural light, land and cloud formations which he often inscribed with notes on local color and atmospheric effects. In these so-called "plein-air" works, La Farge moved away from the detailed factual recording of nature practiced by most of his American contemporaries. Instead, his landscapes are evocative compositions of nuance and subtlety, combining generalized landscape elements with moods reflective of inner experience and states of mind.[6] The same sense of inner life manifested itself on outer surface appearance can be found in his painted floral still lifes from this period, considered by many to be among his finest works. Unlike earlier depictions of the subject, La Farge was less interested in accurately capturing every botanic detail of the flowers than in suggesting their fragility and transience.[7]

Another area in which La Farge was in advance of both his American and French contemporaries was his interest in Oriental art and culture. His earliest exposure to Far Eastern art probably dates from his trip to Paris in 1856 where he encountered Japanese Ukiyo-e, several years in advance of Whistler's first recorded interest in these brightly-colored woodblock prints. La Farge began collecting Japanese prints upon his return to the United States where, in 1860, he married Margaret Perry, granddaughter of the commodore credited with opening up international trade with Japan.

Throughout his life, La Farge remained interested in Oriental philosophy and imagery. Its influence can be seen in much of his work after 1860—in particular through the use of asymmetrical compositions with large expanses of white and brilliant flat areas of color. By the end of his life he had written numerous books and articles on Japan and his travels in the South Seas, and created over 200 works of art in various media relating to the Far East. His early drawings for wood engravings combine Japanese and gothic motifs to create eerie imaginative fantasies. Rejecting the traditional hard-edged line of his contemporaries, La Farge used a Japanese brush to give his illustrations a fluid character. The resultant tonal washes with subtle gradations of form taking the place of traditional modeling earned the artist critical acclaim and consideration as the father of the first new "American" school of illustration.[8]

As James Yarnall notes, photography played an important role in La Farge's art. Most of the artist's illustrations were destroyed through the process of cutting the woodblocks. La Farge photographed the woodblocks before they were cut and later painted over the photographs with watercolor and gouache, creating "new" colored versions of his illustrations.[9] The artist constantly experimented with media. In addition to his extensive use of photography, in 1860 La Farge turned to the French technique of reproduction called *cliché-verre* in which the artist drew with a sharp stylus on sheets of glass which one could then make contact prints on photographic paper.

Probably La Farge's greatest influence can be traced to his view of the artist as craftsman, thereby blurring the line between so-called "fine" arts such as painting and sculpture and the decorative or "minor" arts such as wood engraving, murals, glass working, interior design, etc. By the 1870s La Farge had largely abandoned oil painting to concentrate on large decorative projects such as interior decoration of Boston's Trinity Church which earned him national recognition on its completion in 1877. In the interior of the church, La Farge created a complex interplay between his pictorial painted effects and the existing architecture. The result was hailed for the

6
Adams, "The Mind of John La Farge," pp. 20-4.

7
Ibid., p. 21.

8
Ibid., pp. 31-6.

9
James Yarnall, essay following.

10
Henry La Farge, "John La Farge's Work in the Vanderbilt Houses," *American Art Journal* 16, (Autumn 1984), pp. 30-70.

11
Adams,"The Mind of John La Farge," p. 40.

12
du Bois, "The Case of John La Farge," p. 270.

13
Adams,"The Mind of John La Farge," p. 44.

sensuality of the painted mural decorations and the romantic subject matter, heralding a new era in American mural decoration.

La Farge received a number of commissions following the acclaim for his work on Trinity Church. Among the projects for which he was hired were the Union League Club dining room and the Manhattan homes of William and Cornelius Vanderbilt II. For William Vanderbilt, he created a triptych stained-glass window, commemorating in allegorical form the rise of the Vanderbilt fortunes, over the grand staircase and another stained-glass window in the Japanese parlor for the house located at 640 Fifth Avenue. Cornelius Vanderbilt II paid La Farge $100,000 to oversee all interior decoration of his house located on the corner of Fifth Avenue and 57th Street, including the stained glass, embroidered hangings, sculpture and painted murals. Although he hired other artists to carry out specific projects within the interiors, the end result was clearly under La Farge's direct supervision. Through surviving photographs and La Farge's watercolor design renderings of the Vanderbilt homes, as well as from extant stained-glass windows and sculptural panels, the interior design scheme of the Vanderbilt houses can be surmised.[10]

La Farge's innovations in stained glass have been traced to a day when he was ill and lay watching sunlight stream through a tooth powder jar on a windowsill. The jar was intended to look like porcelain and cheaply manufactured, which caused the light coming through the glass to look streaky rather than clear. La Farge recognized that because of the coarse nature of its manufacture, particles were suspended in the glass, modulating the degree of opacity and translucency and scattering the incoming light in various directions. He quickly realized that this principle could be applied to stained glass and began to design and manufacture stained glass introducing a variety of new pictorial effects through the blending and layering of different colored glass within a single sheet.[11]

In 1889 he was awarded the Legion of Honor and first class prize for stained glass at the Paris Exposition Universelle with the following tribute, "He is the great innovator, the inventor of opaline glass. He has created all its details, an art unknown before, an entirely new industry, and in a country without a tradition he will begin one and be followed by thousands of pupils filled with the same respect that we have ourselves for our own masters. To share this respect is the highest praise that we can give to this great artist."[12] Although he soon had a number of imitators, La Farge is credited with being the greatest innovator in the history of modern stained glass in the variety of pictorial and expressive effects he made possible.

A second innovation La Farge brought to the stained-glass tradition was to expand the traditional subject matter to include Japanese motifs. While today our generic conception of stained glass often includes such motifs as peacocks, cherry blossoms, peonies and other exotic flowers, these were all introduced into the medium by La Farge, who was the first to create large-scale floral images in glass.[13] As with his monumental mural projects, La Farge exploited illusionism and ornament within the stained-glass medium through the use of layered opalescent glass, combining these effects with a reintroduction of pictorial subject matter. For most of his major stained-glass commissions, La Farge first made studies in watercolor, the medium that best approximated the effects of sunlight through the translucent glass.

As Kathleen Foster has noted, watercolor was the first medium of La Farge's youth and the preferred medium of his old age, and it assisted him in realizing his finest achievements in other media. Although previously considered a "minor art", "a pretty material for lady amateurs to use in flower painting or vase decorating," La

Farge was quickly attracted to the calligraphic qualities of the medium which he associated with Japanese art. As he noted, "Yet the painter of watercolor exercises far more skill, must be far more resourceful, and, in the end, with his simple means, often suggests more than the oil painter is able to represent."[14] La Farge played a significant role in the watercolor movement in America. His interest in and use of the watercolor medium paralleled that of other artists of the time, as during the latter half of the nineteenth century there was an unprecedented growth of watercolor societies across the United States. He used the medium increasingly after the 1870s, preferring it to oil paint because of its greater ease of use and fluidity, its facility for capturing quick sketches with translucent, brilliant colors.

La Farge's work in watercolor varied considerably in intent, subject matter and technique. He published a number of watercolor designs for embroidery in *Art Amateur* magazine which are noteworthy for their naturalism. These designs had a strong influence on American needlework of the following decades and differed considerably from the prevalent English manner of embroidery which was characterized by highly stylized and geometric designs. During the 1870s La Farge's watercolor production included a number of exquisite floral studies, unique in their evocative, lyrical qualities. Gradually he shifted from exhibition flower pieces to decorative designs, using watercolors to give patrons a sense of proposed schemes for interior decorations. He adapted his technique according to his subject. Some of his watercolors are highly finished with areas of brilliant opaque color characteristic of the precision of miniature painting reminiscent of his grandfather's teachings. Others are characterized by loose, painterly washes of transparent color and handling more in keeping with the British tradition of watercolor.

Among La Farge's best known and most popular watercolors are those painted with imagery from his trips to Japan in 1886 and the South Seas in 1890-91. In each country he visited, La Farge chose his subject matter carefully. In Japan he focused on landscape and Buddhist temples and sculpture, in Hawaii on landforms and tropical scenery. In Samoa, La Farge concentrated on depicting native activities. Seizing the opportunity to paint the nude in true sunlight as opposed to the artificial conditions of the studio, he painted numerous figural studies. In Tahiti, where the native culture had been largely destroyed, he concentrated again on the tropical vegetation and on Fiji, where he and his companion Henry Adams were able to travel extensively, he painted the rugged and uncultivated landscape of the island's interior. Adams described his technique in the tropics, "He splashes in deep purples and deep green til the paper is soaked with a shapeless daub, yet the next day, with a few touches, it comes out a brilliant mass of color and light. Of course it is not an exact rendering of actual things he paints, though often it is near enough to surprise me by its faithfulness; but whether exact or not, it always suggests the emotion of the moment."[15]

Around 1886 La Farge began to devote a large amount of his time to writing. By his death he had completed seven books on art history and theories of perception, and three dozen essays, various travel accounts, and aesthetic studies. Because he was both an artist and was unusually well-read on a number of different topics, La Farge was able to write on art from a number of unusual vantage points including science, philosophy and art history. He had an easy, informal writing style and included various anecdotes and descriptions which made his writing accessible to a large audience. His books had a wide circulation, and his vivid literary style had an influence on fellow writers of the time.

La Farge's works on paper outnumber all other individual parts of his artistic

14
John La Farge quoted by W. A. Rogers, *A World Worth While* (New York, 1922), p. 142; quoted in Kathleen A. Foster, "John La Farge and the American Watercolor Movement: Art for the 'Decorative Age'," *John La Farge* (New York, 1987), p.125.

15
Worthington Chauncey Ford, *The Letters of Henry Adams 1858-1891* (Boston, 1930), p. 407.

production. In contrast to the 250 oil paintings, a dozen mural projects and 400 extant stained-glass windows, there exist roughly 4,000 drawings, many in the original sketchbooks, and 1,200 watercolors. Works on paper give a comprehensive perspective on all aspects of La Farge's career. Since the artist's death, few exhibitions have explored La Farge's works on paper in any depth. In addition to two retrospective exhibitions mentioned earlier in this essay, which each included a selection of watercolors and drawings, the majority of exhibitions have been organized by art galleries offering works for sale. The most significant exhibition which featured works on paper was organized by the Peabody Museum in Salem, Massachusetts in 1978. Focusing entirely on the South Seas materials, it included forty-eight watercolors and is considered to have been one of the best watercolor shows to date.

The idea of organizing an exhibition of La Farge drawings originated in conversations between guest curator James Yarnall and Maureen O'Brien in 1986. When Maureen left the Parrish Art Museum, she offered the show to The Hudson River Museum where it was enlarged to include watercolors as well as drawings. From the beginning, it was decided that the focus of the exhibition should be scholarly and educational. Rather than just sampling the "best" and most "important" works, it was decided to offer a comprehensive view of La Farge's work on paper by including works which bracket all stages of his career and demonstrate points of technique, working methods, stylistic developments and unusual subject matter. The current exhibition includes both familiar works and works which have not previously been shown having remained among the descendants of the original purchasers since La Farge's lifetime.

Throughout his career, John La Farge exhibited an extraordinary curiosity about art making and materials and the latter's effect on the formulation of a concept. His innovative and elegant use of a variety of media and technique to develop exquisite surfaces through every stage of his career can be seen through the viewing and thoughtful examination of his works on paper.

JOHN LA FARGE: Watercolors and Drawings

James L. Yarnall

I

Juvenilia and early works

The scandal hit the front page in late May 1885: "MR. LA FARGE'S ARREST. The Unhappy Climax to a Long Series of Disagreements."[1] On May 19th, John La Farge received a summons at his New York studio to appear in court on charges of grand larceny. Later the same day, a judge at the Jefferson Market Court listened to a complaint filed by his business partners that the artist had appropriated valuable drawings and studio photographs belonging to the La Farge Decorative Art Company. "What we say, Judge, is that Mr. La Farge has concealed or given away our property and all we wish is to get it back," the lawyer for the company stated. "I have delivered up all the property I had belonging to the company," replied La Farge, "the Sheriff came in and took all there was."[2]

1
"Mr. La Farge's Arrest," *New York World*, 21 May 1885, p. 1.

2
"Artist La Farge Arrested," *New York World*, 20 May 1885, p. 2.

At the time of his arrest, La Farge was fifty years old and at the apogee of his career. He had decorated the mansions of millionaires, gained recognition as an inventor of opalescent stained-glass windows, received critical acclaim for his oil and watercolor paintings, and developed a reputation as a genial writer and conversationalist. His life had been anything but difficult. Raised in aristocratic surroundings, educated in good schools, independently wealthy, and married into a prestigious family, he was genuinely privileged. Yet, with all that he had going for him, La Farge was continually plagued by personal and professional turmoil. Creditors had hounded him for the better part of his adult life. Many considered him a hopeless hypochondriac, prone to complaining and attacks of irascibility. His relationship with his family had grown so remote that La Farge regarded himself as a virtual bachelor. In business, he had the reputation of being unable to balance his books or keep to a schedule. His lax management of commissions led to a string of legal entanglements that drained his finances and ruined his peace of mind. La Farge's ignominious arrest was simply the most unpredictable twist in a life marked by serendipity, personal eccentricity, financial instability, professional acrimony, and familial discord.

La Farge's troubles are particularly ironic given the magnitude of his achievement. As a stained-glass designer, he stood at the head of his profession, creating a revolution in glass technique. As a watercolorist, he had few equals in his time. He inspired the American mural movement and broke ground for the appreciation of Japanese art in this country. His voluminous writings included art

3
Royal Cortissoz, *John La Farge: A Memoir and a Study* (Boston and New York, 1911), p. 45.

4
Cortissoz, *John La Farge*, pp. 56-58; cf. Henry Adams, "John La Farge, 1830-1870: From Amateur to Artist" (unpublished Ph.D. dissertation, Yale University, 1980), pp. 17-23.

5
Ibid., p. 50; cf. Adams, "Amateur to Artist," pp. 25-26.

6
Ibid., p. 66.

7
Ibid., pp. 66-67.

8
Ibid., p. 67.

9
Ibid., p. 67.

criticism, art history, and travel writing. Few American artists of the nineteenth century rivalled him for imagination, sophistication, intellectual accomplishments, or personal charm. Critics have compared La Farge to Leonardo da Vinci for his universal talents, to Hokusai for his gift for illustration, to Michelangelo for the heroic proportions of his decorative endeavors, and to Confucius for the sagacity of his words.

John Frederick Lewis Joseph La Farge was born on March 31, 1835 at 40 Beach Street, mid-way between the Battery and Washington Square in New York.[3] He was the eldest of nine children of a distinguished French Catholic family. His father, John Frederick La Farge (1786-1858) was an emigré; his mother, Louisa Josephine Binsse de Saint-Victor (1813-1895), was born in this country, the daughter of emigrés. John Frederick La Farge made a fortune dealing real estate in New York State. In the affluent family residences, the artifacts of European culture surrounded the young John La Farge. Paintings and engravings graced the walls, and La Farge recalled spending hour after hour perusing extensive libraries of illustrated books.[4]

La Farge's maternal grandfather was Louis Binsse de Saint-Victor (1773-1844), a successful miniaturist. "My grandfather took to painting miniatures and giving drawing lessons and learned his art as he went along," La Farge later reminisced. "I dare say some of his miniatures may still exist. On a small scale he was an exquisite painter. He was also a good teacher and started me at six years old in the traditions of the eighteenth century."[5] These early lessons struck La Farge in retrospect as "sadly prosaic." They seemed to be mere training in the mechanics of drawing.

After having learned thoroughly how to sharpen crayon, how to fasten paper, how to cover large surfaces with parallel lines so as to make a tint, I was gradually allowed to begin to copy things that represented something. I was given engravings to copy, which engravings were made on purpose to imitate the touch of the crayon.[6]

Within a couple of years after he began to copy under his grandfather's supervision, La Farge also began to work from nature, at times in the medium of watercolor.

Gradually the work became more interesting, and by the time I was eight years old, I could begin to do something that had a certain amount of careful resemblance to an original. I still have some of these very early pieces of work. Then came more liberty and I copied right and left, beginning even to paint in water color by myself. And the boy's little studies from nature have some amount of something, both in drawing and color.[7]

During this period, La Farge's formal education dovetailed with his grandfather's training. He attended the Grammar School of Columbia in New York from 1840 to 1848. At first, the art training he received there was uninspiring. La Farge complained that he did "no more natural study of anything" and admitted "even a hatred of the miserable teachings of the drawing master."[8] Fortunately, at some point, "for a little while, broke a slight opening into the blue by my finding an English water color painter, who gave me thoroughly English lessons."[9] These lessons evidently consisted of learning to lay down watercolor in thin washes on dry paper over graphite underdrawing, using the white of the paper for highlights, the borders for color testing, and the bottom of the page for written annotations. The importance of this exposure to English techniques cannot be overemphasized. At all stages of La Farge's career, these methods surfaced in his works, particularly in landscape or travel painting.

Only one watercolor study from nature survives from the years when La Farge would have been in grammar school. This is a strikingly realistic depiction of a dead bird, inscribed "my first bird *shot*" (Yale University Art Gallery). Dated 1845, La Farge would have been only ten years old at the time and yet he already showed a very capable handling of the medium. Although the inanimate bird was not particularly difficult as a subject of study, La Farge depicted it with notable precision and control.

The earliest surviving examples of La Farge's work as a copyist date from several years after this. On New Year's Day, 1849, La Farge's father gave him an unusually large sketchbook consisting of pages in an 8 x 10 inch format with elaborately embossed borders (Yale University Art Gallery). During the months that followed, La Farge filled it with copies in brown and black ink after engravings of works by Jean-Baptiste-Siméon Chardin, Edwin Landseer, Paul Potter, and others.[10] Although La Farge was prone to dismiss summarily his early training, these early copies reveal that he was proficient as a draughtsman who could emulate with great precision serious works of art. The crisp lines and cross-hatching of the drawings so faithfully duplicate the originals that the drawings themselves have been mistaken at times for engravings.

From 1848-1850, La Farge attended the newly-founded French Catholic college of St. John's, the present Fordham University. In October 1850, his parents had him transferred to the college's parent school, Mount Saint Mary's College near Emmitsburg, Maryland. A year later, La Farge was back at St. John's where, in March 1852, he was expelled after a violent fight with another student. His uncle, Louis B. Binsse, defended La Farge to the president of Mount Saint Mary's, blaming the young man's parents for the troubles. He claimed that their leniency and religious differences threatened to destroy La Farge's character.[11] The president readmitted La Farge to Mount Saint Mary's. He went onto complete its rigorous curriculum, graduating with a class of six in June 1853.[12]

La Farge dismissed his college courses and teachers as neither stimulating nor imaginative.[13] Compared to grammar school, he called college "a still greater extinguisher of art, at least in the way of the use of the eye and hand."[14] He reserved his enthusiasm for a professor of English at St. John's, an "Oxford man" who took him "suddenly into the literary and historical side of art."[15] This teacher exposed La Farge to the recent writings of John Ruskin (1819-1900), the English painter, essayist, and art critic who had rebelled against Victorian standards. The study of Ruskin instilled in La Farge a lively appreciation of the medieval ideal of beauty. "But all of this was literature and history and archaeology at bottom," La Farge noted, "rather than the study of art."[16]

Despite his statements to the contrary, La Farge continued to pursue artistic endeavors throughout his college years. During walks in the Catoctin Mountains around Mount Saint Mary's, he filled a sketchbook with studies of trees, flora, and fauna (Yale University Art Gallery). As La Farge's grandson, the late Henry A. La Farge, aptly noted, drawing at this time "became for him as natural as writing, and as useful for jotting down ideas and impressions."[17]

La Farge also drew portraits of his professors at Mount Saint Mary's, and at times made engaging caricatures that left an indelible mark on his classmates. One particular incident, that also illuminates La Farge's early involvement with photography, provides some insight into his youthful artistic personality.

[La Farge] has been for years an enthusiastic amateur photographer, and he was one of the

10
About ten leaves in the sketchbook date from 1849. The remaining are later additions, including a few leaves in the hand of La Farge's son, Bancel. The sketchbook descended through the artist's wife, remaining in the family until 1985.

11
Letter, Louis B. Binsse to Rev. John McCaffrey (Mount Saint Mary's College), 15 Aug. 1852, Archives, Hugh Phillips Memorial Library, Mount Saint Mary's College, Emmitsburg, Maryland. Cf. Robert I. Gannon, S.J., *Up to the Present: The Story of Fordham* (Garden City, New York, 1967), p. 45; James L. Yarnall, "The Role of Landscape in the Art of John La Farge" (unpublished, Ph.D. dissertation, University of Chicago, 1981), pp. 14-18; and Adams, "Amateur to Artist," pp. 32-40.

12
"John La Farge: Flame of Inspiration," *Mount Alumnus* 1 (Spring 1952), pp. 8, 27-28.

13
H.P. La Farge, "Schoolboy Letters between John La Farge and his Father," *United States Catholic Historical Society Historical Records and Studies* 18 (Mar. 1928), p. 87.

14
Cortissoz, *John La Farge*, p. 68.

15
Ibid., p. 68.

16
Ibid., p. 69.

17
Henry A. La Farge, "The Early Drawings of John La Farge," *American Art Journal* 16 (Spring 1984), p. 5; cf. Adams, "Amateur to Artist," p. 27.

first to attach the photographic heads of prominent persons to bodies of his own invention, and create comical environments for them. One of his first pictures, and one which his classmates remember to this day, was of a brilliant room attached to a bar. The venerable president of the college and the professor of Latin were playing billiards, while the professor of Greek lolled in a huge chair, drinking soda and brandy. Copies of this masterpiece of La Farge's early years were handed about with great secrecy for fear the college authorities would get hold of them. But the existence of the work of art leaked out, and the faculty finally obtained copies and enjoyed the good-natured caricatures quite as much as did the students.[18]

After graduation from Mount Saint Mary's in 1853, La Farge found himself in the position of having to decide upon a profession. Pressed by his father to pursue a career in law, La Farge apprenticed with a law firm in New York City beginning in 1854. By 1855, he had completed the necessary requirements to earn a general master's degree from Mount Saint Mary's. At that time, the college awarded such a degree after an alumnus devoted two years of practice in the field to some aspect of "scientific and literary pursuits."[19] In La Farge's case, this was evidently the study and practice of law.

In the meantime, La Farge did not give up on his artistic interests. In 1854, he had the opportunity to study under "a French artist" who badly needed pupils.[20] In a studio setting, La Farge sketched from the nude, copied from the work of old masters as well as contemporary artists, and made his first attempts at illustrating poetry.[21] The most accomplished drawing from this period is a copy after Gericault's *Start of the Race of the Barbieri Horses* (Fig. 1). La Farge evidently worked from a lithograph, but he effectively infused the copy with a vigorous handling and animated spirit that recalls the original painting.[22] Many years later, he discussed the importance of lithographs as an introduction to works by other artists.

Then came the acquaintance with pictures that were just showing their faces in this country, the French school of 1830. I remember the delight of buying a Diaz and a Troyon and a Barye for a few dollars that I had intended for books instead. The lithographs from these men beginning to be famous in Europe came into our market and affected many of us.[23]

At this same time, photographic reproductions of European works of art became readily available in the United States. La Farge was quick to appreciate that photography, with its potential to reproduce art that he might otherwise never see, could be a great learning aid.

We do not realize sufficiently the enormous change of the early middle of this century in giving us, for the first time, a sense of responsibility in the copying of works of art of the past. The lithographs were beginning to help in that way and in a few years the photograph was to change the entire question. What one would have given at that time for a photograph from an old master such as we have by thousands every day, can hardly be guessed at.[24]

La Farge's perceptive response to these varied opportunities to become familiar with contemporary art of Europe far exceeded the whim of mere youthful artistic dilettantism. Yet even at this point La Farge adamantly claimed that he did not consider pursuing art as a career. An opportunity to pass a year in Europe in 1856 contributed to a change in his thinking.

18
"Inspired by Faith, Catholic and Colorist, John La Farge, Heralded by Puritan Boston, a Type of Catholic Imagination in Art," *Republic* 24 (5 Mar. 1904), p. 5.

19
Mount Saint Mary's College, *Catalogue of the Officers and Students of Mount Saint Mary's College, Emmitsburg, Maryland, for the Academic Year 1854-1855*, p. 16.

20
Cortissoz, *John La Farge*, p. 17. The identity of this teacher is uncertain. H. Barbara Weinberg, *The Decorative Work of John La Farge* (New York, 1977), p. 23, proposes this was Régis Gignoux. Cf. Adams, "Amateur to Artist," p. 49.

21
The only recorded illustration with this date, now lost, was exhibited in 1890 at Reichard and Co. in New York (cat. no. 52): "From a Poem by Wm. M. Praed. Illustration. Dated 1854. Crayon." The poems of William Macworth Praed (1802-1839) were popular during the 1850s.

22
La Farge, "Early Drawings of John La Farge", p. 9. Henry A. La Farge notes the probable source of this drawing as Eugène Le Roux's lithograph published in *Les artistes anciens et modernes* (Paris, 1851).

23
Cortissoz, *John La Farge*, p. 70.

24
Ibid., p. 69.

On April 7, 1856, just a week after his twenty-first birthday, La Farge boarded the steamer "Fulton" with his brothers, Henry (1839-1906) and Alphonse (1840-1889), bound for Le Havre, France.[25] According to La Farge, the trip was "a manner of amusement . . . and of taking up also some family connections."[26] The brothers arrived in Le Havre around April 17th and proceeded directly to Paris. There, La Farge found himself suddenly thrust into a thriving mecca for artists and writers of many nationalities, brimming with the cross-currents of Romantic and Classical thought.

Comte Jacques Benjamin Maximilien Binsse de Saint-Victor (1772-1858), La Farge's granduncle on his mother's side, was a renowned author and critic and a close acquaintance of many older artists. Saint-Victor's son, Jacques Paul Raimond (1825-1891), who went by the name Paul de Saint-Victor, was a literary, drama, and art critic and defender of Romanticism. He was conversant with the younger generation of artists and celebrities. Through the entree afforded by his relatives, La Farge gained privileged access to the most important salons and studios in Paris. He particularly recalled visiting the ateliers of the then-popular salon painters Jean-Léon Gérôme and Théodore Chassériau. He also mingled with leading literary lights of the day, including the champions of French Realism, the Goncourt brothers, and the great poet Théophile Gautier.[27]

Sometime in May, La Farge left Paris alone to tour Belgium in order to study medieval architecture and stained glass, his first significant exposure to the medium that would later become his specialty. He traveled up the picturesque Meuse River, visiting tourist sites such as Dinant, Namur, and the castle of Crèvecoeur. Early exhibition records of La Farge's work indicate that he sketched town and castle views in watercolor, pastel, and charcoal, but all of these pictures are now unfortunately lost.[28] Arriving in Antwerp, La Farge registered admiration for what he termed "early oil painting," evidently Flemish altarpieces of the fourteenth century.[29] Proceeding southward to Brussels, he met Henry Le Strange, a renowned decorator and restorer of medieval architecture. The young American traveler must have impressed Le Strange, for the latter commenced to provide La Farge with an education in the "manners of painting" found in Belgian altarpieces. La Farge learned "about painting in wax, for instance," and was "led to read various documents of information with regard to the questions of the early ways of painting."[30] This encounter whetted La Farge's appetite to undertake formal instruction in oil painting.

After his return to Paris in June, La Farge followed the recommendation of an American friend to enter the studio of Thomas Couture, a highly acclaimed salon painter and popular teacher.[31] La Farge explained to Couture that he had enrolled in order to get "a practical knowledge of painting, as practiced by him" and that he "was doing this as a study of art in general and had no intention of becoming a painter."[32] Couture required the most elementary students to master drawing before picking up a brush, and refused to exempt La Farge from this regime.[33] As a result, La Farge drew in Couture's atelier for a couple of weeks, producing a handful of competent drawings. La Farge soon grew restless with the studio routine, realizing that this instruction was not advancing his ambition to paint in oils.

I was impatient to paint according to school ways, for which I had come, but the routine of the school demanded drawing in the Couture way, and as I unfolded my plan to him he thought I might wait till the next year, and meanwhile go on studying the variations of drawing by the old masters, many of which, as you know, are in the studio.[34]

25
"Passengers Sailed . . . in the Steamship Fulton," *New York Times*, 7 Apr. 1856, p. 8.

26
Cortissoz, *John La Farge*, p. 73. Mary Gay Humphreys, "John La Farge, Artist and Decorator," *Art Amateur* 9 (Jun. 1883), p. 12, relies on an interview with La Farge when terming this "wanderyear" orchestrated by the artist's parents.

27
Cortissoz, *John La Farge*, p. 84-85; cf. Adams, "Amateur to Artist," pp. 84-88.

28
Moore's Art Gallery, New York, *Catalogue of a Collection of Oil and Water Color Paintings by John La Farge*, 26-27 Mar. [1885], cat. nos. 77, 83, and 84. Reichard and Co., New York, *Catalogue of Drawings, Water Colors, and Paintings by Mr. John La Farge*, 15 Apr.-1 May 1890, cat. no. 3.

29
Cortissoz, *John La Farge*, p. 89.

30
Ibid., p. 89; cf. Adams, "Amateur to Artist," p. 123.

31
Cecelia Waern, *John La Farge, Artist and Writer* (London and New York, 1896), p. 11; cf. Adams, "Amateur to Artist," pp. 100-09.

32
Cortissoz, *John La Farge*, p. 91.

33
Albert Boime, *The Academy and French Painting in the Nineteenth Century* (New York, 1971), pp. 450-51.

34
Cortissoz, *John La Farge*, p. 92; Albert Boime, *Thomas Couture and the Eclectic Vision* (New Haven, Connecticut, 1980), p. 571, proposes that the annual summer vacation probably contributed to this stoppage of La Farge's training.

At Couture's urging, La Farge set off to copy old master drawings by obtaining a card of permission to work at the Louvre, an activity that he found to be very stimulating.[35] He explained that, whereas copying an easel painting was essentially mimicry of forms, copying drawings provided insights into the working processes of great artists.[36]

La Farge continued copying drawings during a tour of northern Europe that began in late June 1856. Departing from Paris with his brother Henry, he made his way through Germany. He worked in museums at Munich and Dresden, at one stop rendering an animated copy in red chalk after a drawing for Michelangelo's mural of the *Crucifixion of St. Peter* (Fig. 2). La Farge effectively delineated the complex anatomy and musculature of the nude figure, and captured the spirit of anguish in the eyes of the saint. Like many of La Farge's drawings, the precise source of the copy cannot be pinpointed. The artist inscribed it "From original in Dresden? Munich? collection," reflecting his own failing memory during the last years when he placed such inscriptions on his drawings.

La Farge traveled on to Copenhagen, casually sketching from nature along the way. Around the middle of July, he began a watercolor copy of Rembrandt's *Christ and the Disciples at Emmaus* (Fig. 3) in the Copenhagen National Gallery (then the Royal Gallery). He later described this experience fondly:

I had plenty of time to do it in. The summer days are endless. I was alone and the guardians treated me as a spoiled child, bringing me lunch and allowing me to sponge out the surfaces of the great master, whose work, fortunately, had not been varnished or retouched. As I did not consider that I knew enough about oils to copy anything of importance, I painted in water color, in the English way, as I had been taught. I was enabled to learn a great deal of the methods of Rembrandt and to connect them with my studies, outside of any idea of practice as yet.[37]

This picture, which La Farge said that he finished on July 15, 1856, has only recently resurfaced after being lost since 1911.[38] He employed a variety of mixed media, primarily gouache applied thickly and meticulously. The sketch betrays weakness in drawing and proportion, but effectively captures the moodiness and spirituality of Rembrandt's masterpiece. The overall impression is one of significant artistic potential as yet inhibited by faltering technique in the handling of complex media.

La Farge apparently stayed in Copenhagen until mid-August. He had planned to continue on to Russia with his brother Henry, who suddenly was called back to the United States. Instead, La Farge returned to Paris to rendezvous with his brother Alphonse, and together they set out on a tour of Brittany to visit relatives.[39] By late August, they had reached the town of Morlaix, home of their mother's brother-in-law, Pierre Antoine Auguste, comte de la Barre de Nanteuil. They stayed in Brittany for some time, traveling to the surrounding towns such as Berven, Goulven, Lanmeur, Roscoff, St. Pol de Léon, and Arras. Along the way, La Farge sketched Breton types and sites in graphite and watercolor. One sketch from this stay in Brittany shows a de Nanteuil house at St. Pol de Léon, with its rooftops, yard, and trees (Mead Art Gallery, Amherst, Massachusetts). Although faded by time, this study has the picturesque feeling of an English travel sketch of the 1830s.

It is unclear just how long La Farge stayed in Brittany or whether he returned to Paris after his Breton sojourn. A year later, he was back on the road. On August 9, 1857, he wrote to his Breton relatives from Switzerland about his flirtations with a bar-

35
Repertoire des Cartes d'Artistes, d'Élèves, et Permissions 1853-1858, Book LL19, Archives du Louvre, Paris. The application for permission is undated.

36
Cortissoz, *John La Farge*, pp. 94-95.

37
Ibid., pp. 94-95.

38
American Art Association, New York, *Catalogue of the Art Property and Other Objects Belonging to the Estate of the Late John La Farge*, 24-31 Mar. 1911, lot 643. The picture was bought-in for the estate and subsequently lost. In 1987, records at Vose Galleries disclosed that the picture had entered the collection of George Breed Zug sometime before the 1920s. Subsequent research at Dartmouth College, where Zug had taught art history since 1913, led to the location of the picture at the Hood Art Museum.

39
Letter, John La Farge (from Copenhagen) to a member of the de Nanteuil family, 13 Aug. 1856, Private Archives, Ploujean, Finistère, France; cf. Adams, "Amateur to Artist," pp. 110-18.

maid.[40] The next day, La Farge noted to them that he was "at Bâle, studying the Holbeins there."[41] Nearly a month later, on September 5th, he wrote from Switzerland one last time, discussing the news of his father's illness that had just reached him.[42] Many years later, La Farge explained how this illness had required his return to New York in October 1857.

Whatever I wished or intended or thought of was put aside by my return home, determined by my father's wishing me back on account of his illness. I returned in the winter of 1857-8, having spent a part of the autumn in England on my way home. I had plenty of time to give to looking at paintings, because almost every one for whom I had letters was away from London.[43]

La Farge evidently crossed the English Channel to debark from Liverpool. On the way across England, he visited Manchester to view the Manchester Art Treasures Exhibition. This assemblage of paintings from private owners and the royal collections included both old master and contemporary works. The canvases of the British Pre-Raphaelites impressed La Farge most profoundly:

They made a very great and important impression upon me, which later influenced me in my first work when I began to paint. But of that I had no warning.[44]

When La Farge arrived back in New York in late 1857, he resumed the life he had left. "I knew that on my return I should go back to reading law; which I accordingly did," he noted, "though stealing as much time as I could for visits to some of my new friends, the painters and the architects. They made a manner of link with Europe, at least the architects did, Richard Hunt and his two or three students, George Post and Van Brunt, and William Ware and Richard Gambrill."[45] La Farge's life changed abruptly when his father died suddenly on June 25, 1858 on the family estate at Glen Cove, Long Island.[46] This death marked a dual liberation for La Farge who found himself independently wealthy under the terms of his inheritance and freed from any pressure to pursue a career in law.[47]

40
Letter, John La Farge to a member of the de Nanteuil family, 9 Aug. 1857, Private Archives, Ploujean, Finistère, France.

41
Letter, John La Farge to a member of the de Nanteuil family, 10 Aug. 1857, Private Archives, Ploujean, Finistère, France.

42
Letter, John La Farge to a member of the de Nanteuil family, 5 Sept. 1857, Private Archives, Ploujean, Finistère, France.

43
Cortissoz, *John La Farge*, p. 97.

44
Ibid., p. 98. Aside from what La Farge called the "miles of old masters" at this exhibition, La Farge could study 969 watercolors by artists such as Turner, Sandy, Cotman, J.D. Harding, and William Henry Hunt, along with 689 oils by contemporary painters such as Turner, Constable, Bonington, and Wilkie. Cf. Adams, "Amateur to Artist," pp. 129-30.

45
Ibid., p. 109.

46
"John La Farge" [obituary], *New York Times*, 26 Jun. 1858, p. 5. Cf. Adams, "Amateur to Artist," pp. 130-31.

47
John La Farge the elder's will (Surrogate Court, New York City) was executed on 8 Jul. 1858. The will gives one-third of the sizable estate to his wife, with the remaining two-thirds divided equally among six of the eight children, including the artist.

II

The Newport period

1859–1873

Not long after his father's death, La Farge realized that parental objections and money were no longer obstacles to a career in art.

I began to be a little freer of myself. I saw a little more of the few artists, and even took a room at the Studio Building in Tenth Street, where occasionally I made some little drawings, and even tried to paint on a small and amateurish scale, but I recognized that I needed training in the practice of painting.[1]

He contemplated a return to Europe for formal studies in an academy or atelier. He settled for an option closer to home that promised to provide the same type of training.

Talking of this one day to Richard Hunt, merely because his French training had made him acquainted with and respectful of the artists of France whom I especially liked, he suggested that I might like to be with his brother, William, who thought of taking some pupils, who was settled in Newport, and with whom I could continue the practical teachings that I had almost begun at Couture's studio; Hunt being, of course, a favorite and brilliant pupil of Couture's. I met thereupon Bill Hunt, saw some piece of his work, and was pleased with what he did and said, and with all of that very charming character, so that in the spring of 1859, I came to Newport to try the experiment, and began in a little more serious way than before.[2]

La Farge's decision to move to Newport and study with Hunt soon met with a setback. "But a disappointment was in store for me, and it was this,—that Hunt had abandoned the practice of Couture, which was what I wished to continue."[3] La Farge nonetheless learned a great deal from Hunt, particularly in the area of portraiture. He remained in the collegial atmosphere of Hunt's studio for over two years, until Hunt himself relocated to Boston. Notwithstanding this contact, La Farge also distanced himself from Hunt. Within just several months after his arrival in Newport, La Farge had developed an independent program to paint landscape and still life from nature.

La Farge's main focus during the Newport period was on oil painting, and particularly what he called his "programme" to depict weather conditions and lighting effects. His subjects were humble

1
Cortissoz, *John La Farge*, pp. 109-10. Cf. Adams, "Amateur to Artist," pp. 133-34.

2
Ibid., p. 110.

3
Ibid., p. 111.

and ordinary, ranging from flowers placed on a window sill to the rocks and pastures of the surrounding Newport landscape. Except for several major landscapes, these works were usually small in scale and modest in intention, but today connoisseurs praise their subtlety of color and evocative mystical quality. Also greatly admired today are La Farge's oil portraits of family and friends, executed under the influence of Hunt and Couture.[4]

In a nominal sense, La Farge's agenda during the Newport period prefigured the later efforts of the French Impressionists who so ardently observed the effects of nature. La Farge's moody oil landscapes and still lifes, however, are stylistically far more reminiscent of the French Barbizon school or of English Pre-Raphaelite painting of the 1850s.[5] La Farge's actual reasons for remaining in Newport once he suspected the limitations of Hunt's instruction complicate any analysis of La Farge's work during the 1860s. He didn't stay on for artistic reasons as much as for personal ones. Shortly after arriving in Newport, he fell in love with Margaret Mason Perry (1839-1925).

Margaret Perry belonged to an illustrious Newport family. Her grandfather was Commodore Oliver Hazard Perry, the hero of the Battle of Lake Erie in the War of 1812. Her great-uncle was Matthew Calbraith Perry, who had opened Japan to the West during the early 1850s. Margaret was attractive, fashionable, well-educated, and intelligent. She evidently first came to know La Farge through her brother, Thomas Sergeant Perry (1845-1928), who also studied in Hunt's studio. By late 1859, La Farge and Margaret Perry were romantically involved, but their budding relationship faced obstacles presented by religious differences. Margaret's Episcopalian upbringing stood in sharp contrast to the Roman Catholicism of the La Farge family. The dilemma played itself out during the following year. In December 1859, Margaret went south to the Bayou Teche in Louisiana with her family for the winter. After corresponding with Margaret for several months, La Farge heard rumors that she had a number of ardent suitors. In April 1860, he went to Louisiana to propose marriage, and Margaret accepted. In the months that followed, she received religious instruction before finally deciding to convert to Catholicism. To avoid the appearance that the purpose of the conversion was only to expedite their marriage, Margaret married La Farge in Newport on October 15th, 1860, three weeks before joining the Church in New York City.[6]

In March 1861, the La Farges purchased a stately residence near Kay Street in downtown Newport, not far from Hunt's studio. La Farge paid $9,000 for the home, the equivalent of nearly $400,000 today, a price that gives some idea of the extent of La Farge's wealth at the time.[7] Margaret gave birth to their first son, Christopher Grant, in January 1862, and other children were born on almost an annual basis for the next decade. Seven children survived to adulthood, the last one born in 1880, the twentieth year of the marriage.[8] As might be expected, maintaining a large family in a privileged manner proved beyond La Farge's capabilities. He depended heavily upon both his inheritance and money from Margaret's family, with his only other income from the occasional sale of oil paintings or sporadic commissions for book illustrations. Not surprisingly, this financial basis proved to be tenuous and led to monetary crisis. In early 1864, the La Farges, hounded by unpaid creditors, fled Newport under the cover of night, "leaving prodigious debts behind them, and one silver spoon in the side-board drawer; the servant's wages unpaid, the house dismantled of its richest ornaments."[9]

In October 1864, after a short period of residing in Roxbury, Massachusetts, just

4
On the Newport paintings, see Henry Adams, "The Mind of John La Farge," pp. 19-31 and James L. Yarnall, "Nature and Art in the Painting of John La Farge," pp. 81-95, in *John La Farge* (New York, 1987); cf. Henry A. La Farge, "John La Farge and the 1878 Auction of his Works," *American Art Journal* 15 (Summer 1983), pp. 4-34.

5
Cf. Waern, *John La Farge*, p. 16: "In the painting of still-life and flowers he followed a method of his own, based on the principles of the pre-Raphaelites."

6
Cf. Weinberg, *Decorative Work*, pp. 42-45, for a more detailed discussion.

7
Land Evidence Book 35, p. 652, Newport Town Hall, Newport, Rhode Island. The deed is dated 23 Mar. 1861 and gives the price of the house.

8
See James L. Yarnall with Mary A. La Farge, "Chronology," *John La Farge* (New York, 1987), pp. 240-41, for a complete listing of children.

9
Letter, Henry James to Thomas S. Perry, 18 Apr. 1864, cited in Leon Edel, *Henry James Letters*, (Cambridge, Massachusetts, 1974), vol. 1, p. 52.

10
Land Evidence Book 39, p. 99, Newport Town Hall. The sale was transacted on 10 Oct. 1864 to Ann M. Wood for $18,000 (the equivalent of nearly $800,000 today).

11
On Stephen Barker, see James L. Yarnall, "John La Farge's *Paradise Valley Period*," *Newport History* 55 (Winter 1982), p. 21, note 7. La Farge had visited Paradise frequently prior to his move there; he even seems to have rented summer houses on Paradise Avenue before 1864.

12
John La Farge, S.J., *The Manner is Ordinary* (New York, 1954), p. 28, notes that houses were rented in Newport during the winter. He also suggests that La Farge established "a lifelong pattern of living and moving half in and half out of his own household" even during the 1860s. During the summer of 1865-1866, the family stayed in the house of Margaret's mother on Catherine Street in Newport; see letter, Thomas Sergeant Perry to John La Farge, 16 Nov. 1865, Thomas Sergeant Papers, Colby College, Waterville, Maine.

13
La Farge, *Manner is Ordinary*, p. 28.

outside of Boston, La Farge recovered his financial footing by selling the Newport house for double the price he had paid for it.[10] Even with this great profit, by the time La Farge had paid off creditors, the family could no longer afford a residence in costly downtown Newport. Instead, they rented a house just outside of the city in the picturesque farmlands known locally as "Paradise" (now part of Middletown, Rhode Island). For the next seven years, the La Farges continued to rent different houses along Paradise Avenue from Stephen Barker, who owned many farms in the area.[11] During the winters when rent in downtown Newport was more affordable, the family moved into town. At times, they stayed with Margaret's mother on Catherine Street.[12] They also paid frequent visits to La Farge's mother on the family estate at Glen Cove, Long Island.

The years spent in Paradise were the last genuinely happy years of family life that La Farge would ever know.[13] Even so, they were fraught with financial worries and other problems. In 1865 or 1866, La Farge became gravely ill with a sickness he believed to be lead poisoning. For the next two or more years, the illness essentially incapacitated him.[14] This malady curtailed vague plans to go abroad in order to resume a formal study of art.[15] Instead, La Farge continued his independent regimen of painting from nature in Newport. He was, however, far less isolated than might be imagined. Boston was an easy trip by steamer and train, allowing the artist close contact with his friends from early days in Hunt's studio, William James, Henry James, and Tom Perry. New York was also readily accessible by direct steamer connection, and La Farge maintained a space in the Tenth Street Studio Building throughout the 1860s.[16] In Newport, Winslow Homer, Elihu Vedder, and other artists came to stay with La Farge at times, and he was friends with David Maitland Armstrong and Samuel Colman, two artists who later engaged in decorative work like La Farge. He also exchanged paintings and may have painted landscapes with John F. Kensett.[17] Additionally, Newport itself attracted a sophisticated class of year-round residents and summer visitors. La Farge and his wife were active in Newport's "Town and Country Club," an elite group that combined social and intellectual pursuits.[18]

La Farge's primary focus during the Newport period was on oil painting, but he depended on drawing as a ready means of documenting experiences, for preparatory studies, and even as a form of simple recreation. Portrait drawing was especially important to the artist. It served, in many respects, to substitute for photography as a means of recording family and friends for posterity. La Farge was already accomplished as a portraitist before coming to Newport. A rendering of his brother Frank drawn sometime around the time of their father's death emulates a fifteenth-century Florentine silver-point drawing (The Pierpont Morgan Library, New York).[19] With a few graceful lines, La Farge not only captured a good likeness, but also conveyed his brother's delicate constitution and gentle demeanor.

There is ample evidence that La Farge took great pride in his children and that the early years of his marriage abounded in the simple delights of family life. He filled sketchbooks with the equivalent of baby pictures, capturing his infant children in moments of play, repose, and mischief. The most personal family portrait depicts Margaret La Farge pregnant with their second son, Bancel (Spencer Museum of Art, Lawrence, Kansas). Sketched softly in black chalk on Japanese paper, the portrait is a moving image of maternal solemnity during a late stage of pregnancy. La Farge liked this work so much that he had the drawing reproduced as a lithograph for members of his family, much as a later generation might make copies of a favorite family snapshot.[20]

14
La Farge attributed his illness to lead poisoning in a letter to the editor, "Mr. La Farge's Health," *New York Daily Tribune*, 28 Oct. 1908, p. 7. Waern, *John La Farge*, p. 21, noted the onset of the illness as 1866 and gave its duration as "several years." Cf. Adams, "Amateur to Artist," pp. 258-64, who ascribes the illness to a form of hysteria.

15
La Farge's intention to travel to Europe was noted when he sold the contents of his personal library at Leavitt, Strebeigh & Co., Auctioneers, New York, *Catalogue of the Private Library of John La Farge, esq., (who will shortly depart for Europe)* . . ., 18-19 Dec. 1866.

16
The luxurious steamer and train accommodations between Boston and New York via Newport were available daily during the 1860s and 1870s. See John B. Bachelder, *Popular Resorts and How to Reach Them* (Boston, 1875), pp. 104-07.

17
Kensett summered in Newport in 1863 and 1864, although he probably knew La Farge several years before this through the Century Club in New York. Kensett owned a seascape by La Farge by 1867 when he loaned it to the annual exhibition of the National Academy of Design (cat. no. 352). He loaned the picture again in 1871 (cat. no. 353). In 1873, the picture was sold at Kensett's estate sale and has never again surfaced.

18
Information on this club and its formation is provided in the writings of several founding members. See Thomas Wentworth Higginson, "Julia Ward Howe," *Outlook* 85 (26 Jan. 1907), p. 169; Julia Ward Howe, *Reminiscences 1819-1899* (Boston and New York, 1899), pp. 401-09, and records of the club preserved in the Newport Historical Society that served as the basis for Virginia Galvin Covell, "A Critical Examination of the Town and Country Club of Newport, Rhode Island" (unpublished Master's Thesis, University of Rhode Island, 1964). Cf. Adams, "Amateur to Artist," pp. 158-61. La Farge evidently lectured on the South Seas at a meeting of the club at an uncertain date; see Laura E. Richards and Maud Howe Elliott, *Julia Ward Howe 1819-1910* (Boston and New York, 1916), vol. 1, p. 50.

19
La Farge, "Early Drawings of John La Farge," p. 23. An 1856 portrait of Auguste de Nanteuil (Private Collection) is also a very accomplished and expressive work (see La Farge, "Early Drawings of John La Farge," ill. p. 14).

Another touching portrait shows Margaret La Farge in prayer with the baby Bancel beside her (Fig. 4). This likeness can be linked to La Farge's determination around 1865 to paint a monumental oil of a secularized Madonna and Child in an open-air setting. La Farge portrayed Margaret and Bancel many times, making a number of different composition studies of the pose from different angles.[21] La Farge then outlined the figures in oil on a large canvas but, inexplicably, gave up on the work before filling in the underpainting.[22] Notwithstanding, the notion behind the projected Madonna painting suggests the depth of La Farge's affection for his family at this time.

La Farge also recorded likenesses of members of his extended family and friends. His brother-in-law, Thomas Sergeant Perry, frequently visited the La Farge home. In 1865, La Farge drew him sitting, his head turned to the right, chatting with a companion not shown in the composition (Redwood Library, Newport). An inscription at the bottom of the drawing indicates that Perry was "Talking to Bancroft at Paradise Farm." John Chandler Bancroft (1835-1901), son of renowned historian George Bancroft, was an aspiring artist who lived on Purgatory Road, several blocks away from La Farge's home on Paradise Avenue.[23] La Farge had known Bancroft well before moving to Paradise Avenue in 1865. In 1863, he drew two informal portraits of Bancroft that captured spontaneously the young artist's Bohemian appearance (Redwood Library, Newport, and Worcester Art Museum, Worcester).[24]

Another welcome visitor to the La Farge home was a priest who played an important role in various aspects of La Farge's life, Father Isaac Thomas Hecker (1819-1888). La Farge had known Hecker since the late 1850s when the priest founded the Paulist order.[25] In 1860, Hecker had instructed Margaret on her conversion to Catholicism. He later obtained several commissions for La Farge, including two altarpieces and the interior decoration of the Church of St. Paul the Apostle in New York.[26] La Farge sketched Hecker's portrait while the priest was reading Goethe during a visit to Paradise in 1866 (Fig. 5), endowing him, as one critic has described, with "the appearance of a Biblical prophet, like one of those with which La Farge would later decorate the spandrels of Trinity Church in Boston."[27]

More formal in spirit are La Farge's portraits of Father Francis Aloysius Baker (1820-1865), one of Hecker's favorite young priests. His premature death in 1865 caused great mourning for the artist and his family. The most incisive sketch shows Baker in three-quarter profile gazing to the right, a solemn expression on his face (Fig. 6). The portrait is drawn with a firm hand and judicious use of shading that effectively captures the intensity of the young priest. La Farge probably used photography as an aid in rendering this portrait, as he clearly did in another portrait made after the cleric's death.[28] In fact, La Farge routinely consulted photographs during the 1860s and can be considered a great innovator in the creative use of photography as an aid to his work.[29]

Many of these portrait drawings originally formed pages of the artist's sketchbooks. Over thirty sketchbooks survive more or less intact from the Newport period, although almost all lack one or more leaves.[30] Near the end of his life, La Farge extracted the best drawings from his sketchbooks in order to mount them as individual works of art. He stamped many of these drawings with his red Japanese seal as a means of authentication. At this later time, he also frequently added marginal notes to describe the subject or give the date of execution, at times providing inaccurate information due to a faulty memory. La Farge intended to use these mounted works for a proposed book on his drawings. When this failed to materialize, he placed the mount-

20
The lithograph was evidently made around 1895, and copies today are owned by a large number of La Farge's descendants.

21
The subject appears in sketchbooks at the Yale University Art Gallery, the Addison Gallery of American Art, and the Bowdoin College Art Museum.

22
The painting in question is *Paradise Valley* (Private Collection). During its conservation at Harvard's Fogg Art Museum around 1933, X-rays revealed the underlying outlines of the figures. Henry A. La Farge recognized the outlines as those of the madonna grouping. He explains this discovery in his unpublished "Catalogue Raisonné of the Works of John La Farge" (Henry A. La Farge Papers, New Canaan, Connecticut), entry P1866.5.

23
La Farge claimed that he and Bancroft studied color theories together, and applied them to the painting of landscape. See Cortissoz, *John La Farge*, p. 122; John La Farge, "Son of Bancroft" [Letter to the Editor], *New York Times Saturday Review of Books and Art*, 17 Aug. 1901, p. 581; and Louise Siegel, "John Chandler Bancroft (1835-1901)" (unpublished manuscript, Curatorial Files, National Museum of American Art, Smithsonian Institution, Washington, D.C., 1969).

24
Adams, "Amateur to Artist," p. 202.

25
Weinberg, *Decorative Work*, p. 43.

26
The patrons refused both altarpieces after La Farge worked extensively on them during the early 1860s. La Farge worked on the decorative scheme of the Church of Saint Paul the Apostle sporadically from 1875-1899. Disputes with the patrons over cost ultimately led to his dismissal, and another artist took over the commission. See Weinberg, *Decorative Work*, pp. 211-39.

27
Adams, "Amateur to Artist," p. 202.

28
James L. Yarnall, "New Insights on John La Farge and Photography," *American Art Journal* 19 (1987), p. 58.

29
James L. Yarnall, "John La Farge's *Portrait of the Painter* and the Use of Photography in his Work," *American Art Journal* 18 (1986), pp. 4-20; Yarnall, "New Insights on John La Farge and Photography," pp. 52-79; La Farge, "Early Drawings of La Farge," p. 26.

ed drawings in portfolios for sale or gave them away to family and friends.[31]

La Farge's sketchbook drawings number in the thousands, many depicting the landscape of Paradise. He frequently ventured into the Paradise Hills, located just to the east of Paradise Avenue. He developed a particular fondness for Bishop Berkeley's Rock and the so-called Last Valley, craggy protrusions of rock just off the beaches of the nearby Atlantic Ocean. La Farge jotted down almost anything of interest that he observed on his jaunts around the island. He delineated the barest outlines of clouds whirling through the sky, stylizing the forms with linear flourishes that recall the calligraphic handling of Japanese prints (Fig. 7). He sketched the landscape with layers of heavy charcoal and graphite outlines, endowing Newport with a ponderous feeling that Henry A. La Farge compared to a Rembrandt etching, a comparison the artist would have appreciated.[32] Few subjects in the natural environment escaped him. Cecelia Waern, La Farge's first biographer, summed up their range of subject matter and style: "The sketch-books of this time are many in number; they contain first thoughts and careful finished studies; slight, but comprehensive, records of pose and gesture; rocks and sea, plants and animals, imaginative vagaries and ornamental fancies."[33] The last part of her statement refers to the fact that La Farge filled entire sketchbooks at times with studies for book illustrations, a significant accomplishment of the Newport period.

La Farge had dabbled in illustration since at least his college days, inspired by the books and periodicals in the family libraries. He reserved his greatest enthusiasm for the designs of William Blake and other English artists, but was nonetheless familiar with French and German schools of illustration. He grew serious about illustration as a significant form of expression during the year before he came to Newport.[34] An elaborate coin design represents his earliest attempt to render an imaginary subject in the tight, realistic style initially associated with his illustrations (Fig. 8). The coin depicts a classically-featured bust with the back of the coiffure in the shape of a hag-like witch's face, an allusion to the corruption of Tammany in New York, then a debated political topic.[35] La Farge next designed illustrations for Robert Browning's *Men and Women*, experimenting with the technique of *cliché verre*. Literally translated "glass negative," *cliché verre* took advantage of recent photographic advances by using a design drawn with a stylus on a coated glass plate as a negative to make contact prints on sensitized paper. The control and precision of line obtained by *cliché verre* are similar to that in La Farge's earlier coin design, but the technique additionally lent the illustrations an appropriate murky and moody appearance.[36]

Illustration assumed an important dimension in La Farge's work in 1864 when he received a commission for nine plates in a Christmas gift-book edition of Tennyson's *Enoch Arden*.[37] For this project, he drew with ink washes directly on prepared woodblocks that were sent out for engraving. La Farge indulged his fancies in composing these illustrations. He copied motifs from Japanese prints, emulated the style of Pre-Raphaelite illustrations, incorporated the contours of the Newport landscape, and employed the visages of friends. The success of *Enoch Arden* led the publisher Horace Scudder to ask La Farge to be a regular contributor to *The Riverside Magazine for Young People*, founded in 1866.[38] Over a five-year period, La Farge prepared a variety of woodblocks to illustrate arcane episodes drawn from history, mythology, legend, and fiction.[39] *The Wolf Charmer* (Fig. 9), the best known of the series, is based on a medieval Breton folk story of a piper who tamed a pack of wolves with the music of his flute. La Farge merged a composition and figure derived from a now-lost painting by Titian with wolves drawn to a scale larger than life.[40] He used a

30
Most of the sketchbooks descended in the family and are now in the Yale University Art Gallery, New Haven, Connecticut. Other repositories include: Bowdoin College Museum of Art, Brunswick, Maine; Museum of Fine Arts, Boston; David and Alfred Smart Gallery, University of Chicago, Chicago; Winterthur Library, Henry Francis duPont Winterthur Museum, Winterthur, Delaware; and a Private Collection, Rhode Island.

31
Weinberg, *Decorative Work*, pp. 7-8. Many of these portfolios were sold in the artist's estate sale. Portfolios that have remained more or less in their original state are found in the following repositories: Addison Gallery of American Art, Phillips Academy, Andover, Massachusetts; Bowdoin College Museum of Art, Brunswick, Maine; and Yale University Art Gallery, New Haven, Connecticut.

32
La Farge, "Early Drawings of John La Farge," p. 27. La Farge noted his particular fascination with Rembrandt's etchings in Waern, *John La Farge*, p. 11.

33
Waern, *John La Farge*, p. 21.

34
La Farge's first study for Browning's *Men and Women* was dated 1858 in the La Farge Estate Sale, cat. no. 723.

35
La Farge, "Early Drawings of John La Farge," p. 23.

36
Ibid., pp. 23-25.

37
Charles F. Richardson, "A Book of Beginnings," letter to the editor, *Nation* 91 (1 Dec. 1910), pp. 520-21; James L. Yarnall, "Tennyson Illustration in Boston, 1864-1872," *Imprint, Journal of the American Historical Print Collectors Society* 7 (Fall 1982), pp. 10-16; Weinberg, *Decorative Work*, pp. 58-60.

38
Weinberg, *Decorative Work*, pp. 59-60.

39
Letter, John La Farge to Horace Scudder, 22 Oct. 1869, Scudder Papers, Houghton Library, Harvard University, Cambridge, Massachusetts. In this letter, La Farge noted that the idea was to avoid familiar subjects. Among the subjects he proposed were fairies, witches, mermaids, sea serpents, giants, centaurs, Argonauts, Amazons, Hadrianic processions, Druidic sacrifices, Christian Crusades and martyrdoms, Nordic mythology, and medieval chivalry.

thick Japanese brush in applying ink to the block. During his visit to Japan in 1886, La Farge took it as a great compliment when a Japanese artist who had recognized the technique called him the "Wolf-Man."[41]

All of La Farge's illustrations of the Newport period similarly meld disparate elements from different artistic traditions. In fact, the study of La Farge's work can easily become an exercise in identifying sources of both motifs and styles. For *The Island Home* in *Enoch Arden*, La Farge cloaked the Paradise Hills and Second Beach in Paradise with pronounced Japanesque stylizations. In *The Giant*, designed for the *Riverside Magazine*, he wrought the opposite transformation, taking a print from Hokusai's *Mangwa* and rendering it into contemporary western realistic terms. *The Halt of the Wise Men* for the *Riverside Magazine* used the reaches of Paradise for a setting but derived its stylistic treatment from the work of Delacroix and Chassériau. This eclecticism, at times derided as derivative, was extremely inventive in its application. It reflected the encyclopedic knowledge of artistic sources that La Farge had acquired from the time of his youth. Until the end of his life, the pleasure he derived from the study of art of many cultures, styles, and periods continued to enliven his work.

La Farge's eldest son, C. Grant, gave a detailed description of the artist's methods for preparing and executing these illustrations.

His studies used to be made largely in sketch books, and I recall that at a very early date he liked to draw on Japanese paper and had sketch books made up of such paper. He used a crayon pencil. When it came to the wood, the surface of the block used to be prepared with what I take to have been some form of Chinese white. I can remember that this material came on a sort of thin pasteboard card, which he used to moisten and rub on the surface of the block until it was evenly, and, I think, rather thinly whitened. I am pretty sure, but not entirely so, that he then laid in the outline of his drawing with lead pencil as a guide. After this the drawing was made in wash with camels' hair brushes, using India ink as a medium.[42]

This technique created problems for engravers who, C. Grant recalled, "wanted lines to engrave, not wash."[43] One of several woodblocks that remained uncut due to the collapse of *The Riverside Magazine for Young People*, *In the King's Garden* (Fig. 10), indicates the reasons why an engraver might complain. La Farge placed the design on the block with painterly abandon. Rich effects of shadow compete for attention with subtle, minute details. The engraver had to devise a way to reduce the painterly rendering to linear terms. Invariably, La Farge found fault with the decisions that the engraver made.

During the 1860s, drawings on woodblocks were, of necessity, destroyed by the engraver in the cutting process. La Farge photographed his woodblocks before their cutting in order to retain an image of the design for use in evaluating and criticizing the final product. The photographs of uncut woodblocks later would prove to be an additional boon for La Farge. Around 1873, he had them reproduced at various scales in different colored inks on tinted paper. He then gathered groups of these reproductions into portfolios for sale through his Boston dealers, Doll and Richards.[44] Ten years after this, he used many of the reproductions yet again by painting over them in heavy gouache and watercolor, creating "new" colored versions of the illustrations for sale at his exhibitions.[45]

La Farge's illustrations displayed proficiency in the handling of monochromatic

40
The landscape and figure were derived from Titian's *Martyrdom of Saint Stephen*, a picture destroyed in the Renaissance but known from engravings. Russell Sturgis, "John La Farge," *Scribner's Magazine* 26 (Jul. 1899), p. 12, discussed the scale of the wolves.

41
Waern, *John La Farge*, p. 22; La Farge, "Early Drawings of John La Farge," p. 26.

42
Letter, C. Grant La Farge to Frank Weitenkampf, quoted in Frank Weitenkampf, "John La Farge, Illustrator," *The Print-Collector's Quarterly* 5 (Dec. 1915), p. 488.

43
Ibid.

44
Yarnall, "New Insights on John La Farge and Photography:" pp. 62, 78, notes 11-12.

45
Ibid., pp. 61-70.

washes, showing the practical application of his early training in watercolor, received from his grandfather. La Farge also used watercolor episodically during the Newport period to render still life, landscape, and literary subjects. Among the earliest and most satisfying watercolors are several miniature studies painted around the time of his marriage for Margaret La Farge to use as patterns for embroidery (Fig. 11). Laid down in lustrous opaque washes on dry graph paper, these pictures reveal control and deliberation of handling, recalling American Pre-Raphaelite watercolors of the 1850s.

A sudden flurry of watercolor activity took place sometime in 1864 or 1865 when the artist painted around ten watercolors that came to light for the first time in May 1990. These include views of farm buildings on Paradise Avenue (Altman/Burke Fine Arts, New York), studies of the woods and rocks of the Paradise Hills, still lifes of fruit, flowers, and porcelain objects, and a portrait of Margaret La Farge pregnant, seated in a red Japanese kimono with an open book in her hand (all Private Collection). In these works, as well as in a landscape depicting the rocks in the Paradise Hills that has been long known to scholars (Fig. 12), English techniques are pronounced. The pictures are all rendered with thin, transparent washes over light graphite underdrawing, using the white of the paper for highlights. The handling is more restrained and lightly touched than that seen in watercolors that La Farge began to paint during the late 1870s. The primary distinctions between these earlier examples and later works include a sparing use of wet effects, a lack of density in the application of watercolor washes, and the virtual absence of gouache.

La Farge's remaining half-dozen watercolors from the Newport years are figure compositions painted around 1865 as studies for illustrations or oil paintings. Wrought with thick watercolor washes that occasionally appear somewhat muddy, the figure watercolors have been described as belabored or awkward.[46] La Farge began to overcome the difficulties of this genre at the very end of the Newport period. In both his study for and final rendering of *Salome's Dance* (Fig. 13; study in Museum of Fine Arts, Boston), he showed a loosening of technique unprecedented in his figure works. The final version of the subject is in pastel, which La Farge had used in combination with watercolor since the 1850s. Dated 1872, the picture explores the sensuous flesh and drapery in a way that suggests the artist's figure work of the early 1880s.

As the Newport period came to a close, La Farge enjoyed another major success as an illustrator by contributing four plates to Abby Sage Richardson's volume of poetry, *Songs from the Old Dramatists* (published 1873). These designs are more decorative in nature, combining La Farge's knack for realistic representation of the fantastic with unusual spatial arrangements and abstracted forms.[47] The most intriguing illustration is *The Spirit of the Water Lily* (Fig. 14), depicting an allegorical figure emerging from a water lily pad. In the portrayal, La Farge gave tangible form to the lyrical beauty that he himself had always found in the water lily, a subject of his drawing and oil studies since his earliest days in Newport. "Among the many flowers that he studied," noted his first biographer, "water-lilies had for him an especial fascination. In their natural surroundings they afford interesting problems of the combination of different luminous values which make of them almost a grammar of flower-painting. The lotus has always been pre-eminently a flower of the mystic."[48]

The Spirit of the Water Lily ultimately leads to a consideration of a new set of artistic and social relationships that overtook La Farge's life in the early 1870s. The same composition, without the figure of the fairy, formed the basis for the artist's 1872 oil diploma piece presented for membership in an ultra-exclusive New York club called the Lotos Club (Mead Art Gallery, Amherst, Massachusetts). Devoted to the

46
Kathleen M. Foster, "The Still-Life Painting of John La Farge," *American Art Journal* 11 (Jul. [Summer] 1979), p. 26; Kathleen M. Foster, "John La Farge and the American Watercolor Movement: Art for the 'Decorative Age,'" in *John La Farge* (New York, 1987), pp. 130-31.

47
Weinberg, *Decorative Work*, p. 66.

48
Waern, *John La Farge*, p. 21; cf. Adams, "Amateur to Artist," pp. 236-38.

advancement of poetry and fine arts, the Lotos Club derived its name from a poem by Alfred Lord Tennyson entitled *The Lotos Eaters*, a veiled hymn to the opiate state.[49] In 1874, La Farge again adapted the composition for the frontispiece to a volume of poetry dedicated to Tennyson and published by the members of the club, *Lotos Leaves*.[50] La Farge's simple, realistic water lily studies of the early Newport period had evolved into an emblem with symbolic overtones. From this point forward, whenever La Farge painted water lilies, they took on an aspect of mystery and secret meanings derived from the lotus analogy and its use in the circles of La Farge's acquaintances.

This change in La Farge's social life marked a straying from a narrow focus on family life in Newport to a more cosmopolitan outlook. In 1872, circumstances conspired to further the rift that was already underway. That year, Margaret La Farge's grandmother died, leaving her a large inheritance. Margaret purchased a house in downtown Newport in 1873, placing the deed solely in her own name.[51] The family left Paradise to resettle on Sunnyside Place, just a few blocks from their first residence in town. This move marked a shifting of gears in La Farge's life that led to the end of his so-called Newport period.

49
Yarnall, "Role of Landscape," pp. 268-70.

50
John Brougham and John Elderkin, eds., *Lotos Leaves, Original Stories and Essays* (Boston, 1875), frontispiece. The book was entered into the Library of Congress in 1874.

III

Early decorative period 1874–1885

From the relative quiet and seclusion of the Newport years, La Farge emerged as a fashionable decorative artist with a center of operations based in New York. The interior decoration of Trinity Church in Boston (1876-1877) was the most important milestone in his transformation into an artist known for a talent in meeting the desires of wealthy patrons. With the opening of the edifice in early 1877, La Farge's name became a household word. Critics heralded the church as the harbinger of a new decorative age in America. "Mr. La Farge has decorated the new Trinity Church of Boston," noted a reviewer for the popular *Appleton's Journal*, "and after this example we may be sure that churches elsewhere will not hereafter fall exclusively into the hands of plasterers and daubers."[1]

La Farge professed that he had come to decorative art by a combination of chance and necessity when his efforts to earn a living as an oil painter failed. Reflecting back on his career in 1894, he wrote:

I have always been interested in decoration, that is to say the appliance of art in any shape to buildings and objects made for use. I began my artistic studies in a historical and archaeological direction with no intention of becoming a painter . . . I carried out my studies as a painter with some relation in my mind to decorative work, but notwithstanding I made all of my studies that properly concerned painting in a realistic manner.[2]

La Farge's first attempts at decorative work had gone awry. Patrons rejected two altarpieces that occupied him at the start of the 1860s.[3] Five decorative panels painted in 1865 for a dining room in Boston ended up as exhibition pieces at the National Academy of Design.[4] In 1873, La Farge traveled to London in order to escort his important oil painting *The Last Valley* (1867, Private Collection) to an exhibition.[5] The trip gave him the opportunity to visit Edward Burne-Jones and the Pre-Raphaelites in England, as well as to meet Puvis de Chavannes and to view stained glass in France.[6] La Farge credited this trip, along with the realization that he could not support himself by selling oil paintings alone, with his receptiveness to decorative work.[7]

At the urging of the architect William Ware, La Farge proposed designs for windows in Memorial Hall, a building Ware and

1
"Editor's Table," *Appleton's Journal* n.s. 2 (May 1877), p. 473.

2
John La Farge, "[Reply to] the questions asked by Mr. Bing regarding my work and my ideas, so as to include a notice of the same in his report to the French Government" (unpublished typescript, La Farge Family Papers, Department of Manuscripts and Archives, Sterling Memorial Library, Yale University, c. 1894); cf. Weinberg, *Decorative Work*, p. 38.

3
Weinberg, *Decorative Work*, pp. 47-48.

4
Henry Adams, "A Fish by John La Farge," *Art Bulletin* 62 (Jun. 1980), pp. 269-80. The panels were exhibited at the National Academy in 1867.

5
The *Last Valley* was La Farge's only contribution to the *Seventh Exhibition of the Society of French Artists* (cat. no. 18) held in late 1873 at 168 New Bond Street in a gallery directed by the French dealer, Durand-Ruel. Other artists represented in the show included Camille Pissaro, Fantin La Tour, Eugène Delacroix, Charles Daubigny, and Théodore Rousseau. After the closing of this exhibition, La Farge accompanied the canvas to Paris where it was shown at the Annual Salon for 1874 (cat. no. 1039).

6
Waern, *John La Farge*, p. 28. Waern stated that La Farge stayed in Europe "half at least of the year 1873."

7
Weinberg, *Decorative Work*, p. 340.

his partner Henry Van Brunt had designed for Harvard University.[8] La Farge won the commission in late 1874 for a two-lancet window representing the Chevalier Bayard and Christopher Columbus as emblems of Chivalry and Faith.[9] As an experiment, Donald MacDonald, a glass maker then working for the Boston firm of William McPherson, executed one lancet of the proposed window into glass for La Farge.[10] Due to the prevailing glass-making techniques and the limited types of glass available, La Farge found the resultant window unsatisfactory. He destroyed the experimental window, thus ending the commission, but he had set upon a course that would eventually lead to a virtual revolution in stained-glass techniques.

Only a few minor drawings survive from the experimental window, but more complete sketches for several other proposed windows for Memorial Hall give an idea of La Farge's earliest stained-glass designs. A drawing for a window representing the Theban general and statesman Epaminondas (Fig. 15) illustrates the erudite classical repertoire that La Farge employed in figure windows. The design follows traditional English fashions in the disposition of figure, setting, and ornamental frame, but a profusion of naturalistic and decorative details distinguish it as uniquely by La Farge. Overall, it forcibly recalls the work of the Pre-Raphaelites.[11] A similar feeling pervades a color study for the companion to the Epaminondas window, a memorial to Sir Philip Sidney (Private Collection). La Farge employed a photomechanical reproduction of a drawing as the basis for this sketch, painting over it with watercolor. This method of transferring lines eliminated the tedium of redrawing the preliminary design in preparing the color study.[12]

La Farge's next opportunity for decorative work came from the architect Henry Hobson Richardson (1838-1886), an acquaintance of La Farge's since the 1860s.[13] In the summer of 1876, Richardson invited La Farge to submit a plan for the interior decoration of Trinity Church in Boston, then still under construction.[14] La Farge was eager for the commission, agreeing to work for little money and with serious time restrictions. Richardson noted that La Farge took the commission "much less from any hope of pecuniary profit, which he had little reason to expect, than from a true artistic enthusiasm for a work so novel, and affording such an opportunity for the highest exercise of a painter's talents."[15]

La Farge contracted to provide murals with "at least six figures in the arch-spandrels in the tower, and two panels on the nave wall, for the sum of eight thousand dollars ($8,000 [$375,000 today]), all the work excepting the panels of the nave wall to be completed by the 1st day of December, and the panels by the 20th day of December next."[16] The contract provided him with latitude to hire workmen and assistants to execute the work with the understanding that he retained responsibility for the quality and timely delivery of the project as a whole. The difficulties pertaining to the execution of the decoration were monumental. The murals had to be painted directly on the walls using scaffolding from the construction of the church, which was not yet even finished. The work was always rushed, and La Farge not only had to supervise a large number of disparate hands, but also had to paint some of the murals himself in order to get the job done on time. He described the conditions under which they worked as a "jamboree":

> *the windows open, in winter; four of the workmen killed by the tiles dropping down from the roof inside; we working in our overcoats and gloves, unable to use the scaffoldings very often because the other workmen, masons, carpenters, tilers, etc. who were not painters, had them.*[17]

8
Ibid., citing letter, William Ware to Royal Cortissoz, 19 Jun. 1911, Royal Cortissoz Papers, Beinicke Rare Book Library, Yale University, New Haven, Connecticut.

9
Ibid., p. 341.

10
La Farge, "Catalogue Raisonné," entry G1874.1.

11
Foster, "John La Farge and the American Watercolor Movement," p. 145.

12
Cf. Yarnall, "New Insights on John La Farge and Photography," pp. 70-71.

13
Waern, *John La Farge*, p. 30. Waern contended that Richardson became aware of La Farge's work for the first time in 1867 when he exhibited the decorative panels intended for a Boston dining room at the annual exhibition of the National Academy of Design. At that time, Richardson supposedly promised La Farge future decorative work.

14
Weinberg, *Decorative Work.*, p. 91.

15
Ibid., p. 92, quoting Henry Hobson Richardson, *Description of Trinity Church* ([Boston 1877]), p. 10.

16
Ibid., pp. 95-96, quoting letter, John La Farge to Building Committee of Trinity Church, 15 Sept. 1876, Trinity Church Archives. La Farge also designed ornamental windows for the tower and upper nave of the church by a separate contract.

17
Cortissoz, *John La Farge*, pp. 157-58. See further discussion of the difficulties in the execution of the mural in Waern, *John La Farge*, pp. 35-37.

In the end, La Farge found himself on less than friendly terms with the church's Building Committee. In addition to disagreements over working conditions, cost and time overruns created friction that faded only when the overwhelming success of the endeavor became apparent.[18]

Most of the known studies from this project are working drawings for prophets and angels in the central tower (Fig. 16). La Farge sketched his first idea for a mural design on a miniature scale, frequently on a squared grid to permit ready enlargement. His assistants then employed various mechanical and photomechanical processes to enlarge the design. They used full-sized cartoons to trace a design onto a wall or other surface. At times, lantern slides or other projection techniques served a similar purpose. In 1876, La Farge wrote to one of his assistants, the young Augustus Saint-Gaudens:

Mr. Millet is going to try the enlargement on the wall or rather on paper, with the machine to throw up the image to full size.[19]

La Farge also prepared small watercolor studies to guide his assistants in filling the designs with color. For the tower, he sketched an angel in dense watercolor and gouache on coarse buff watercolor paper (Fig. 17). This is one of the earliest watercolors providing evidence of what can be considered La Farge's mature style. The handling of the work is assured and fluid. The strokes are broad and bold, with washes laid down on wet paper, a complicated technique that La Farge learned to handle resourcefully. The colors are vivid and carefully separated into distinct planes to increase the pureness of tone and translucency of hue. The overall effect is spontaneous and effortless.

La Farge's best effort as a muralist at Trinity Church represents *Christ and Nicodemus*. It is one of two nave panels painted after the church opened to the public in early 1877. Numerous preparatory drawings for the panel attest to his effort to find just the right gesture to convey the reverence of the figures. One study for the figure of Nicodemus, executed in charcoal on heavy white Whatman paper (Fig. 18), shows the remarkable effect that La Farge could achieve with an elegant economy. The aesthetic care taken in handling the drawing suggests that La Farge anticipated the commercial value of his decorative studies.[20] In later years, he mounted large exhibitions of such works, offering them for sale as independent pictures with hefty price tags.[21]

In the wake of his Trinity Church success, La Farge's personal life changed rapidly. Before he had even finished up in Boston, the artist had won the commission for a second decorative ensemble for the Saint Thomas Church in New York City.[22] As a result, La Farge began a peripatetic existence, shuttling between New York, Boston, and Newport to juggle the incessant demands of ongoing commissions with the obligations of family life. Initially, the increased professional demands seem to have strengthened La Farge's personal life. In the designs for Saint Thomas Church, the artist's wife served as a model for several figures—the first but only time he chose her to pose for a decorative commission.

La Farge's primary decoration for the church was a large triptych surrounding the altar. On the right wing, the scene depicted the three Marys greeted by two angels as they arrive at the empty tomb of Christ on the morning of the Resurrection. La Farge derived the composition of the three Marys from an ivory miniature now in the Bavarian National Museum at Munich.[23] The female figures all bear the features of Margaret La Farge.[24] The artist worked out the three Marys in small sketchbook

18
Weinberg, *Decorative Work*, pp. 143-44.

19
Letter, John La Farge to Augustus Saint-Gaudens, [1876], Saint-Gaudens Correspondence, Dartmouth College Library, Hanover, New Hampshire; cf. Yarnall, "John La Farge's *Portrait of the Painter*," p. 15 and note 26.

20
This drawing originally belonged to the publisher William Cullen Bryant (1849-1905), who probably purchased it at an exhibition in New York sometime in the 1890s. A nearly identical, now-lost drawing of *Nicodemus* was used as an illustration in Clara Erskine Clement, "Later Religious Painting in America," *New England Magazine* 12 (Apr. 1895), p. 133.

21
La Farge first exhibited several decorative studies at the American Watercolor Society in 1879. He is credited with "inaugurating a category that represented a major new source of energy for the American watercolor movement" by Foster, "John La Farge and the American Watercolor Movement," pp. 144-45. La Farge began exhibiting decorative sketches extensively at the Architectural League of New York in 1887, continuing with some regularity until the end of his career. After 1884, his frequent one-man shows in Boston and New York included decorative works for sale along with still lifes, landscapes, and studies for illustrations.

22
Weinberg, *Decorative Work*, pp. 146-67.

23
Ibid., p. 162.

24
Mabel La Farge, "John La Farge: The Artist," *Commonweal* 22 (3 May 1935), pp. 7-10.

studies while at home in Newport. He used these small studies to prepare a larger cartoon that was squared for transfer to a large size (Princeton University Art Museum). To plan the coloring of the painting, he prepared a large watercolor study (Plate 1). Worked in thin, lustrous washes of transparent watercolor on thick-wove paper, its overall effect is at once delicate and sensuous. The colors resonate in delicate shades of green, blue, and red, giving some idea of the celebrated harmony of the colors in the altarpiece, tragically destroyed by fire in August 1905.[25]

La Farge never again employed his wife's features for a decorative design, turning instead to the use of studio models and New York acquaintances. This seemingly natural evolution reflected Margaret's overall relegation to a lesser role after 1877. La Farge's stature as a decorative artist was rising at a meteoric rate. He realized that his future was in decorative work. He even publicly proclaimed his intentions to leave other artistic pursuits behind in November 1879, when he mounted an auction at Leonard and Company in Boston. The preface to the catalogue of the sale announced:

This collection comprises all the available works remaining in Mr. La Farge's studio. Many of the pictures Mr. La Farge refused to sell last year; but they are offered now to enable him to devote himself entirely to decoration.[26]

There was never any doubt in La Farge's mind that devotion to decoration implied relocation to New York. Beginning in at least 1877, he lived with a guilty conscience about the inevitable schism that this choice imposed on his personal life. His youngest son recalled one attempt that La Farge made to keep the family together by bringing them to Shrub Oak near Peekskill, New York, where the artist's mother had lived since 1870.

[Margaret La Farge] had spent the summer visiting Bonne Maman at her Shrub Oak estate and Father proposed that she should remain there for the winter, make that her headquarters and keep the family there so as to be within easy reach of him while he was working in New York. My mother met this suggestion point-blank. "I refuse," she said, "to have my life spoiled by being imprisoned at Shrub Oak." And that was the end of the proposition.[27]

La Farge became a father figure *in absentia* for the remainder of his life, in many respects leading the life of a bachelor as he dedicated himself completely to his art.[28] He made fewer and fewer visits to Newport as the years passed. His youngest son summed up the dilemma of the situation:

With all his faults, there is one thing with which my father cannot be charged, and that is hypocrisy. He never tried to justify his neglect of his home or his family. His conscience remained clear as to principles. He knew his real responsibility, and he was always uneasy on this matter, and would therefore come back home quite unexpectedly and would be all the more concerned when he was away.[29]

In the midst of the changes in La Farge's personal and professional life during the late 1870s, the artist emerged as a prolific watercolorist. Even though his use of watercolor in recent decorative work had prepared the way for this, this development came as a surprise.[30] The first hint of his growing enthusiasm surfaced in January 1879 when La Farge contributed three still lifes, a landscape, and a figure piece to the

25
Weinberg, *Decorative Work*, pp. 162-166.

26
Preface to Leonard's Gallery, Boston, *The Drawings, Water-Colors, and Oil-Paintings by John La Farge. To Be Sold at Auction*, 18-19 Dec. [1879].

27
La Farge, *Manner is Ordinary*, p. 32. This episode evidently occurred sometime in early 1879. In the fall of 1895, La Farge tried again when he moved the family into a New York house rented to them by the editor Richard Watson Gilder. During the winter of 1896-1897, the family took a "capacious red brick mansion at 22 East Tenth" according to La Farge, *Manner is Ordinary*, p. 4. Both experiments failed.

28
La Farge referred to himself as a "bachelor man" in a letter to Henry Adams, 16 Mar. 1907, La Farge Family Papers (Yale).

29
La Farge, *Manner is Ordinary*, p. 33.

30
Foster, "John La Farge and the American Watercolor Movement," p. 138. Foster points out that La Farge was elected a member of the American Water Color Society in 1868, but did not begin to exhibit with them until 1878. In 1882, he was nominated president of the Society.

annual exhibition of the American Water Color Society.[31] The larger dimensions of the activity became apparent in November 1879 when he offered for sale nearly twenty recent watercolors at the Leonard and Company auction.[32] La Farge had not painted this many new works in such a brief period of time since the early 1860s. This new attention to watercolor appeared to serve both as a liberation from the daily rigors of decorative work and as a sudden resurgence of interest in painting for its own sake.

Most of the new watercolors were studies of flowers such as camellias, roses (Fig. 19), or water lilies. The compositions frequently included vases (Fig. 20) or other oriental *objets d'art* from the artist's personal collection, which included hundreds of pieces at this time.[33] La Farge delighted in contrasting the fragility of petals with the brittle sheen of ceramics, much as he had in his early oil still lifes. He sought close-up perspectives derived from Japanese prints, and indulged to its fullest his calligraphic skill in handling watercolor. "No nearer approach has, probably, ever been made to the freshness, purity, and delicacy of texture of natural flowers," wrote one critic. "To be the painter of these . . . ought to satisfy a modest ambition; and while I am far from saying that Mr. La Farge's other work has been wasted, it is on these modest water-colors that his fame, in the future, promises to rest."[34]

The floral watercolors unexpectedly provided La Farge with something he had sought all his career, a sure-fire formula for selling paintings. "The roses and Oriental wares have, indeed, been selling rapidly," noted a reviewer in 1879. "Mr. La Farge can no longer use the noble boast that he has never sold a picture from an exhibition. The yellow ticket has found out the corners of his small and modest frames, and the artist can congratulate himself in having sold his pictures at full prices without concessions, and on having a mercantile success with a group of works in New York . . ."[35] Although some critics accused La Farge of "selling out" to a subject that was merely popular, the public response to the floral watercolors was nothing short of astounding.[36] Ownership of a La Farge floral watercolor came to be regarded as a veritable status symbol. Not surprisingly, La Farge's friends and colleagues in Boston purchased many of the pictures directly from him before the artist could offer them for public sale.

La Farge's enthusiasm for floral watercolor painting fed into and was fed by his decorative work, particularly stained glass. During the late 1870s, he had developed a novel formula for constructing windows using opalescent stained glass chosen especially for the painterly effects that the glass allowed.[37] By 1880, he had rendered his floral compositions into windows with the same verve and freedom seen in the watercolors. Critics even began to describe La Farge's windows as if they were "paintings in glass," not always favorably. Martin Brimmer, director of the Boston Museum of Fine Arts, wrote that one of La Farge's first floral windows was "a marvel of color—it is like a sketch of jewels, and jewels are not somehow the right material to sketch with."[38] Notwithstanding this criticism, the floral windows created as much a sensation in La Farge's day as his watercolors, earning a following particularly among wealthy private patrons. Today, both the floral windows and the watercolor still lifes remain his most popular works, steadily in demand by an enthusiastic following.

Watercolor also provided the ideal means for developing glass designs, regardless of subject matter. Because he could approximate the translucency and vibrancy of colored glass in a medium that could be handled rapidly and flexibly, La Farge could prepare alternate color studies that would give patrons a good idea of how a window might look when carried out according to different composition schemes.

31
Ibid.

32
Ibid.

33
Leavitt Art Galleries, New York, *The La Farge Collection. Oriental Porcelains, Bric-a-Brac. . . . belonging to John La Farge, Esq., of this City*, 22-23 Dec. [1880], 563 lots; Leavitt & Co., Auctioneers, New York, *Catalogue of Pottery & Porcelain, Japanese Lacquers, Bronzes, Jades . . . from the Collections of Messrs. W.L. Andrews, Sam. Colman, John La Farge, Russell Sturgis, and two other Amateurs*, 31 Mar.-2 Apr. [1879], 584 lots. It is unknown how many lots in the second sale were owned by La Farge.

34
Robert Jarvis, "Pictures by La Farge and Inness," *Art Amateur* 11 (Jun. 1884), p. 13.

35
Earl Shinn, "The Growing School of American Water-Color Art," *Nation* 28 (6 Mar. 1879), p. 172.

36
Foster, "John La Farge and the American Watercolor Movement," p. 138, citing "Studies of the Artists," *New York Times*, 5 Feb. 1879, p. 5.

37
Henry A. La Farge, "Painting with Colored Light: The Stained Glass of John La Farge" in *John La Farge* (New York, 1987), pp. 198-99. Weinberg, *Decorative Work*, pp. 355-67, presents La Farge's patent for the glass and describes his inimicable dealing with Louis Comfort Tiffany over use of the glass.

38
La Farge "Painting with Colored Light," p. 199, citing letter, Martin Brimmer to Sarah Wyman Whitman, 10 Nov. 1881, Archives of American Art, Smithsonian Institution, Reel D-32; cf. Waern, *John La Farge*, p. 58.

When the patrons selected one design over another, they did so with a good knowledge of the intensity of color, the balance of hues, the translucency of the window, and the success of the design in terms of color as well as composition.

Working in stained glass brought about changes in La Farge's watercolor palette. His still lifes and landscapes soon incorporated the ruby reds, emerald greens, and deep blues available in the glass used for his windows. The artist seemed to seek to give watercolor the same translucency and layering of color that came from plating, or the layering of glass, in his stained-glass windows. Another notable aspect of La Farge's stained-glass production at this time is a new-found reliance on, and reworking of, ideas and motifs from his earlier work. When planning windows for the Boston residence of the wealthy financier, Frederick Lothrop Ames, in 1880, La Farge turned to a major floral oil painting of *Hollyhocks* executed in 1863 (Private Collection). The oil painting, then owned in Boston by La Farge's friend John Chandler Bancroft, is a moody, deeply-toned study of hollyhocks in a landscape setting.[39] La Farge copied the composition into a miniature watercolor, greatly heightening the overall tone (Plate 2). The final window then repeated the effects seen in the watercolor study. A critic writing about this evolution noted that the "freshness and exactness of detail" from the original oil were "repeated in the glass with as much freedom as might be shown in a water-color painting, which it, in fact, resembles."[40]

La Farge described another watercolor for a window in the Ames house (Fig. 21) as a "Study in Old Chinese style." This design was based on a Chinese bird and flower painting of the Ming dynasty.[41] The watercolor is applied unevenly to the color study. In places, the washes are thin and transparent; in others, they are almost enamel-like in opacity and color. The window executed from the study (now in the National Museum of American Art, Washington, D.C.) is remarkably similar in effect. It duplicates in glass the fluid transparency of the watercolor, making use of plating pieces of glass one over the other to attain a deep translucent color that contrasts with the vibrancy of single transparent pieces. The window, like the watercolor, achieves a mosaic of tone and texture—indeed it seems almost like a painting rendered in "colored light."[42]

La Farge's maturation as a watercolorist was also evident when he turned to painting landscapes around 1883. He reprised subjects familiar from his oil paintings of the 1860s, including the contours of Paradise in Newport (Fig. 22). But whereas the earlier oil landscapes seemed spare, solid, and stark in color, the watercolors are picturesque, loose, and overtly decorative. La Farge particularly exploited the wet look attained by splashing pigment on the paper to create convincing atmospheric effects. Both the picturesque perspectives and lively handling of the watercolor prefigure a manner of painting landscape that La Farge fully mastered years later in the South Seas.

La Farge also turned to watercolor as a congenial medium to grapple with the challenge of figure painting. Aside from portraits of his family and friends, figure painting had played little role in La Farge's earlier work. His involvement with decoration by necessity changed this. The late 1870s began a period often called the "American Renaissance" in which an enthusiasm for allegory, mythology, and history permeated decorative work.[43] As a result of major commissions for secular murals and windows, La Farge became a primary practitioner of figure subject matter.

In 1879, La Farge won the most grandiose and significant secular commission of his day when he received the contract to oversee the interior decoration of the Cornelius Vanderbilt II residence in New York City.[44] The Vanderbilt fortunes were

39
Bancroft, who lived on Beacon Street, had purchased the painting in 1879 from La Farge's Leonard's and Company auction. It is possible that Frederick Lothrop Ames knew the painting and specifically requested that La Farge translate it into glass for his entrance hall.

40
Humphreys, "John La Farge, Artist and Decorator," p. 14.

41
La Farge, "Catalogue Raisonné," entry W1882.3.

42
La Farge, "Painting with Colored Light," p. 220, citing the artist himself in John La Farge, "Window," in *Dictionary of American Architecture*, vol. 3, col. 1080.

43
The "American Renaissance" began around the time of the American Centennial and was characterized by the emulation of Renaissance prototypes, a concern for the integration of the arts, and a reform in decorative arts. See Richard Guy Wilson, Dianne H. Pilgrim, and Richard N. Murray, *The American Renaissance: 1876-1917* (New York, 1979).

44
Henry A. La Farge, "John La Farge's Work in the Vanderbilt Houses," *American Art Journal* 16 (Autumn 1984), pp. 30-70; Weinberg, *Decorative Work*, pp. 255-70.

immense, permitting what one critic described as undertaking, "on a scale hitherto unattempted, certain decorative works, which must be considered to some degree experimental."[45] La Farge's commission included responsibility for murals, stained glass, sculpture, and tapestries throughout the house, constructed by the architect George B. Post at the corner of Fifth Avenue and 57th Street. Directing a large retinue of artists and craftsmen, La Farge worked on the project untiringly for over three years. The Vanderbilts paid him generously for his efforts: between July 1880 and May 1883, he received payments totaling over $100,000 ($3,000,000 by today's standards), from which he had to pay the cost of materials, labor, and his own salary.[46]

The house featured two major ensembles. The first was a dining room of generous proportions, with a massive ceiling carved in exotic woods and punctuated with life-size bas-relief panels of allegorical figures. It included an ornamental skylight by La Farge, along with tapestries that in part repeated the figure motifs in the ceiling.[47] The second was a Water Color Room lined with murals depicting the seasons, the senses, and allegories of the times of day. The murals included eight life-size figures, along with six monumental painted busts surrounded by festoons of garlands and other decorative flourishes. Sadly, few fragments of the actual decoration have surfaced since the razing of the house in 1927. Photographic albums kept by the Vanderbilt family and the architect, along with early articles on the house, provide the best knowledge of the scheme.[48]

A number of original drawings and color studies for the murals survive that convey at least the monumental conception, if not the ultimate grandeur, of the decorations. The most finished drawing is an allegorical figure of Dawn (Fig. 23). Dated 1880, the figure originally was to serve as the focus of one of two large lunettes found at either end of the Water Color room. Photographs of the house suggest that the design ultimately went unused, but La Farge employed the figure around 1903 as the basis for a stained-glass window in a private residence in Brooklyn (Private Collection).[49]

Most of the figure color studies for the decorations are known today only from photographs taken during the late nineteenth century.[50] Their features spilled over into a number of independent figure works painted around 1883. La Farge's sensuous sketch of Andromache (Fig. 24) is one of several figure studies that may have been related to a stained-glass window project under consideration in 1883, but it seems to have been painted simply for the sake of painting. Exploring lush colors, complex textures, and painterly washes, the picture elevates a simple study of a studio model to a classical presence. Equally striking is a seated female in classical garb that dates from around the same time (Plate 3). Here, the heavy washes of watercolor and gouache are saturated with rich colors that glow like stained glass and enliven the presence of the meditative figure. The technique displays a confident handling and command of figure painting reaffirmed in La Farge's later secular and religious decorations.

La Farge's figure work for secular contexts provided a natural preparation for the flood of religious commissions that came his way beginning in 1881. The innumerable praying and standing saints that he designed for glass from then on carry his figure style into the religious realm. The process of preparing designs for glass was different from that pertaining to murals. These distinctions are important to consider while inspecting La Farge's studies for religious windows.

One of La Farge's early biographers, Cecelia Waern, visited La Farge's glass workshop and made in-depth observations about his process of manufacturing win-

45
Mary Gay Humphreys, "The Cornelius Vanderbilt House. Decorations of the Dining-Room, Water-Color Room, and Smoking Room," *Art Amateur* 8 (May 1883), p. 135.

46
H. Barbara Weinberg, "John La Farge: Pioneer of the American Mural Movement," in *John La Farge* (New York, 1987), p. 185.

47
"La Farge Embroideries," *Art Amateur* 8 (Jan. 1883), p. 49.

48
La Farge, "John La Farge's Work in the Vanderbilt Houses," p. 39.

49
Ibid., pp. 54-56.

50
Ibid., pp. 54-58. Only one watercolor study is known today. An additional four color studies are known from old studio photographs.

51
Waern, *John La Farge*, pp. 56-59.

52
Ibid., p. 56.

53
Ibid., pp. 57-58; cf. Cortissoz, *John La Farge*, pp. 180-81, where La Farge emphasizes the importance of preliminary work in black and white.

54
Ibid., p. 59.

dows.[51] Waern noted that many small preparatory studies were made, "some in colour, others in black and white or pencil."[52] Since these sketches ultimately determined the cutting of the glass and the disposition of lead lines, their design was, in many respects, the most important step in the execution of a window. But such small sketches were only the first of many stages in the process. Waern noted that:

From these studies are prepared full-sized cartoons, often in colour, giving a careful indication of the values in light and dark; and a complete set of enlarged lead lines. From these lead lines are made two transfers on paper and one tracing on glass. This is the so-called "glass frame" which is set up in the wall against the direct light from outside. Meanwhile one of the paper transfers has been cut up into pieces representing the shape of the pieces of the glass. They are carefully numbered and put together again on the wall.[53]

As Waern's description suggests, the larger cartoons and color drawings were generally destroyed as part of the construction process, some for purposes of transferring the design and comparing it to the artist's original sketches, others for actually making patterns to cut glass and plan lead lines. One of the cartoons known today is a study for the figure of the Virgin Mary (Mount Saint Mary's College, Emmitsburg, Maryland), prepared around 1882 for the Barnabas Bates memorial window (Channing Memorial Church, Newport, Rhode Island). Even with her hands clasped in prayer, the figure appears as a simple variation on the type of standing, draped figure that filled La Farge's work in other media at the time.

Surviving full-scale color studies for lead lines are much rarer than cartoons. In fact, although the artist's inventories recorded a dozen of these studies during his lifetime, only one today can be located (The Brooklyn Museum, Brooklyn, New York). This study is in such perilous condition that it cannot travel or be exhibited, a testimony to its use in the making of a window. Waern also described the final steps of this process:

The work in glass now begins. Consulting his colour sketch, the artist decides what passages of colour are to strike the keynote of the harmony, has his glass cut from the corresponding pieces of paper patterns, fastens the pieces of glass to the glass frame by wax, and then proceeds to build his whole scheme of colour on this beginning. The work is thus from the outset a transposition, a painting with glass by an artist in glass. The occasional slightness of the colour sketch is a first thing that strikes the layman; a thin wash of yellow running into purple is enough to indicate a rich drapery of glowing orange with long lines of purple trembling in the shadow of the folds; pale green is translated into a rich opalescence of green and silver and gold, blue into deep modulated sapphire and violet. The slighter the sketch, the better may be the result. There can be no rule. The very incompleteness and suggestiveness of a sketch is sometimes a source of inspiration to the executant.[54]

Waern could well be describing the preliminary sketches for a two-lancet window depicting Saint James kneeling before the Risen Christ installed in 1886 in Trinity Episcopal Church, Buffalo. For this project, both a graphite drawing and a color study dating from around 1884 survive. The drawing (Museum of Fine Arts, Boston) is the artist's early attempt to work out the figures, which are reminiscent of both Renaissance and English Pre-Raphaelite prototypes. The watercolor (Plate 4) is painted over a reiteration of the graphite drawing. Some areas of color are laid in with either opaque or transparent watercolor washes. Others are barely suggested, such as the violet cloak or the pale yellow inner garment covering Christ's chest. The picture is executed on thin tracing paper. Light graphite lines mark the placement of spandrels and mullions. La Farge's assistants probably relied heavily on this design when executing the window, holding it up to light to gauge the balance of colors. The "incompleteness" or "suggestiveness" of the sketch were evidently in no way an impediment for its use by the assistants, as Waern suggested.

Many of La Farge's color studies are highly finished, and probably were intended less as working studies than as presentation pieces for clients. La Farge explained to Waern that the commercial nature of making windows demanded the production of color studies intended for purposes other than making the glass. "The design, the sketch, the cartoon is always better than the completed work. It is again in great part the result of commercial habits. The sketch is made to sell from or to exhibit. The work may take care of itself."[55] A color study for an *Angel of Help* (Plate 5) aptly illustrates this statement. The sensuous handling and vivid characterization of the figure suggest that the artist meant it to stand on its own as an independent work of art. Painted with thick, wet washes of vivid color, the study is as fresh as any of La Farge's figure studies unrelated to a specific decorative context.

The *Angel of Help* is the principal figure in a memorial window that was at the center of a dispute that ultimately would change La Farge's life. The window, a memorial to Helen Angier Ames, fills the wall of the west transept of Unity Church in North Easton, Massachusetts. Allegorical figures of Sorrow and Need flank the angel, while a glittering jewelled sarcophagus held up by a host of angels hovers above these mourning figures. The commission was an expensive one at the time, costing a total of $10,000 (over $300,000 today). The patron was Frederick Lothrop Ames, the brother of Helen Angier Ames. He commissioned the memorial to his sister in 1882 just as La Farge was finishing the windows for the hall of Ames's Boston mansion.[56]

Prior to 1883, La Farge had managed his own decorative projects, at times under contract to then-fashionable New York firms such as the Herter Brothers. A number of talented people worked for him regularly, including Thomas Wright, J.J. Humphreys Johnstone, John Calvin, and a host of artisans, tapestry makers, and painters.[57] By 1883, La Farge had developed a notorious reputation for financial mismanagement of projects. While widely acknowledged an artistic genius, in terms of balancing his books, he came to be regarded as hopelessly inept.[58] The precise circumstances leading to this reputation remain unknown, but one can easily imagine that suppliers had overextended credit and that wages went unpaid for months on end. To improve this situation, in October 1883, a group of businessmen formed a partnership called the La Farge Decorative Art Company.

The partners placed La Farge in nominal control as artistic director of the firm, but it did not take long for the artist to discover the dire consequences of this paternalistic arrangement. From the start, he argued with his partners about designs tendered to prospective clients without his full approval or despite his disapproval. He learned after the fact about work carried out without proper supervision or control over production standards.[59] The conflict over the Ames memorial window became the decisive skirmish in this battle for artistic control. La Farge had received this commission prior to the formation of the company, and he turned it over to his partners with the understanding that he would personally supervise its construction. When he found his role subverted, La Farge decided to communicate the problem to Frederick Lothrop Ames through Henry Hobson Richardson, the architect of Unity Church.

55
Ibid., p. 57.

56
La Farge, "Catalogue Raisonné," entry G1887.1.

57
La Farge, "Painting with Colored Light," p. 200. An interesting insight into the La Farge studio on Seventeenth Street in New York is given in "An Atelier," *Boston Daily Transcript*, 24 May 1883, p. 6. I appreciate the help of Colonel Merl M. Moore, Jr., Falls Church, Virginia, for bringing this article to my attention.

58
"Mr. La Farge's Arrest," *New York World*, 21 May 1885, p. 1.

59
Ibid.

The company then assured Mr. Ames that my undivided time and attention should be given to this work. I demonstrated to my associates that the work could not go on except by my ordinary methods of work, but to this they would not agree. Meanwhile they assured Mr. Ames that the work was going on well under my personal supervision, and would be done in due time. Mr. Ames showed me this assurance and asked me if it was true. I said "no" and gave him a slight explanation of our differences. He notified the company that thereafter he would take nothing but personal assurances from me in regard to the work. Mr. Ames added that he would have nothing more to do with the company.[60]

La Farge's dispute with the company escalated after this incident. Legal maneuvering on the part of the company trapped him into a loss of control over his personal finances. He had to designate an assignee over his affairs, limiting his ability to sell works remaining in his possession except as a means of paying off creditors. In March 1884, La Farge's assignee mounted a large sale of oils and watercolors at Ortgies and Company in New York that included most of the pictures produced by La Farge since 1880.[61] Although La Farge hoped that this sale might pull him back from the brink of financial disaster, the situation only worsened. In October 1884, the artist wrote:

I feel every day more and more the dreadful mistake I have made in a business way. The feeling that I have been swindled grows on me, the sense that what I did these people urged on me, because as they said I could so pay off my creditors, and as you know I am more debarred than ever from so doing.[62]

In order to raise revenues, La Farge needed pictures to sell. Accordingly, he painted numerous watercolors in late 1884 and early 1885. In March 1885, he held a successful auction at Moore's Art Gallery in New York, this time without the control of an assignee.[63] This scramble for solvency collapsed when the La Farge Decorative Art Company filed a civil lawsuit against the artist around May 5, 1885.

The suit alleged that La Farge had appropriated $3,500 (nearly $110,000 today) worth of decorative designs, photographs of nude figures posed for decorative works, and other material belonging to the company.[64] This included photographs and color studies for the Ames memorial and any other projects that had been a topic of dispute during the preceding two years. Following the artist's refusal to answer the civil suit, the allegations expanded to include criminal charges of grand larceny. On May 19, 1885, a sheriff appeared with a summons at La Farge's door in the Tenth Street Studio Building. He also had a warrant to impound drawings and sketches suspected to be stolen. La Farge was arraigned at the Jefferson Market Court in New York and released on $5,000 bond ($155,000 today) posted by his attorney.[65] For the next two days, the story made every front page in New York. As one article noted, the arrest "created a decided scandal in both social and art circles and became the general topic of conversation whenever or wherever artists or connoisseurs met."[66]

The dispute raged for three months, leading to a series of depositions by various artists and artisans central to the case. La Farge ultimately was completely exonerated when the company admitted that the material in question was indeed his property.[67] The lawsuit served La Farge well in at least one regard: it released him from the grip of the La Farge Decorative Art Company. The artist returned to his former independent status. He continued to employ many of the artisans and glass makers that he had used during the preceding years, including Thomas Wright and John Calvin who

60
"Mr. La Farge's Troubles," *New York Commercial Advertiser*, 25 May 1885, p. 1.

61
Ortgies and Co., New York, *Important Collection of Oil and Water Color Paintings, by John La Farge of This City. To Be Sold at Auction*, 14-17 Apr. [1884]. Ortgies and Co., New York, *Supplementary Catalogue of Water Colors, by John La Farge. To Be Sold at Auction*, 14-17 Apr. [1884].

62
Weinberg, *Decorative Work*, p. 383, citing letter, La Farge to Mary W (probably Mary Whitney), 6 Oct. 1884, La Farge Family Papers, New York Historical Society.

63
Moore's Art Gallery, New York, *Catalogue of a Collection of Oil and Water Color Paintings, by John La Farge*, 26-27 Mar. [1885].

64
"Artist La Farge Arrested," *New York World*, 20 May 1885, p. 2.

65
Ibid.

66
"Mr. La Farge's Arrest," *New York World*, 21 May 1885, p. 1.

67
After extensive research, Evelyn Gonzalez of the Municipal Archives, Department of Records and Information Services, City of New York, graciously provided documentation of the case, including the original complaint and police reports, depositions, materials related to other suits occasioned by the lawsuit, and information on the final disposition of the case. Ironically, this suitable disposition of the case was never reported in the press, and what remained most prominently in the public record were the scandalous allegations. La Farge's good name had been badly tainted.

together formed an entity called the Decorative Arts Stained Glass Company.[68] This arrangement suited him well until the end of his life. He later noted:

Ever since I was obliged to give up my former establishment in 1884, at which time I had partners, I have had all my work done by a firm consisting of my two best workmen, than whom there are not better workers in glass in the world. I have my own rooms and reserve stock of my own, and these men serve me both as foremen, and as suppliers of such number of men as I may need.[69]

The disposition of the items that La Farge allegedly took from his company remains unclear, but it appears that he prevailed in holding onto whatever drawings and watercolors he claimed to be his. Sketches for the Ames Memorial window, including the *Angel of Help*, ended up in his possession. He used them to execute the window once Frederick Lothrop Ames reinstated the commission. The completion of the window did not occur until at least 1887, five years or more from the time of the initial order.[70]

La Farge's reputation suffered in a variety of ways due to his involvement with the La Farge Decorative Art Company. He came under particular fire as a result of the exhibitions and sales held during the company's tenure. Critics attacked the 1884 Ortgies and Company sale for being too "hurried,"[71] for including works in condition too poor to sell, and for containing "too large a percentage of rubbish to be overlooked."[72] Some even questioned the authorship of the decorative studies. One critic noted the hands of "Miss Katharine Kidder, Miss Jessie Savage, Mr. Will H. Low and others of Mr. La Farge's former assistants. . . . It was, in short, a collection of odds and ends, but one which nevertheless contained gems as well as rubbish."[73]

To supplement works available in his studio for this auction, La Farge painted about thirty new watercolors in late 1883 or early 1884. Some of the new watercolors were copies of or variations on early flower paintings. Others were studies of figures in classical and contemporary dress. But most were colored versions of his illustrations of the 1860s and early 1870s, painted in heavy watercolor and gouache over photomechanical reproductions used as underdrawings.[74] Criticism ranged from praise for the figure studies to condemnation of the "tracings from photographs colored by Mr. La Farge, academic studies with new backgrounds brushed in."[75]

La Farge fared even worse with critics in late May 1884 when his assignee sold at auction a large selection of small stained-glass pieces. Most of the fragments were what one critic described as

. . . stained-glass misfits, specimen pieces, etc. As a whole, the collection might serve as a warning to those who believe that the present 'movement' in favor of decorative art is likely to result in something great . . . about half the collection, comprising pieces done in the last two years or so, was of an entirely different and much lower quality. Not only the designs, but the very workmanship (little as it counts for in stained glass) and the material itself were inferior. . . . the ruin of the art seems to be only a matter of a little time.[76]

Fortunately, many critics recognized that La Farge's predicament was not under his control. A widely-published sympathetic review noted:

It is a grievous thing that an artist like Mr. La Farge should be compelled to sell the last memento of his atelier in this fashion. It shows how hollow as yet is the feeling for great art in

68
La Farge, "Painting with Colored Light," p. 210.

69
Weinberg, *Decorative Work*, p. 384, citing La Farge, "Reply to Bing," pp. 15, 17-18.

70
Ibid. A late color study for the window is in fact dated 1887-1888 (Private Collection).

71
"The La Farge Sale," *New York Times*, 15 Apr. 1884, p. 5; cf. "Art and Artists," *Boston Evening Transcript*, 16 Apr. 1884, p. 6.

72
Jarvis, "Pictures by La Farge and Inness," p. 12.

73
"The Lafarge [sic] Exhibition," *Critic and Good Literature* 4 (16 Apr. 1884), p. 198. The critic for the *Art Amateur* cited in the previous note also noted the work of La Farge's assistants.

74
Yarnall, "New Insights on John La Farge and Photography," pp. 59-77.

75
"The Lafarge [sic] Exhibition," p. 198.

76
"Art Notes," *Critic and Good Literature* 4 (31 May 1884), p. 258.

this country. Such talents as his ought to be removed from the immediate wants and the cares of business and allowed the freest play, the largest opportunities to do what is in them to do.[77]

La Farge was the ultimate victim of the company originally designed to rescue him from his own bad business sense. The situation clearly damaged many future opportunities for work. Certain architectural firms shied away from the artist as a risky proposition. Near the end of his life, La Farge "dropped a bomb" when he stated bitterly at a testimonial dinner that the firm of McKim, Mead, and White had given him no work for over twenty years.[78] But the debacle of the La Farge Decorative Art Company ultimately proved to have a hidden benefit. For the first time in many years, the artist was free to consider endeavors other than decorative work. In 1886, La Farge shifted into an entirely new activity when he decided to accept an invitation to visit Japan, a pilgrimage that he had anticipated for nearly thirty years.

77
"The La Farge Sale," *New York Times*, 15 Apr. 1884, p. 5; cf. "Art and Artists," *Boston Evening Transcript*, 16 Apr. 1884, p. 6; and "The Fine Arts," *Boston Daily Advertiser*, 19 Apr. 1884, p. 4.

78
"La Farge's Medal Comes Late," *Boston Evening Transcript*, 30 Jan. 1909, p. 2; cf. "John La Farge's Story," *New-York Daily Tribune*, 30 Jan. 1909, p. 7; "Late for a Medal, Says John La Farge," *New York Times*, 30 Jan. 1909, p. 1; "La Farge Shades His Fling at Architects," *New York World*, 31 Jan. 1909, p. 1; "La Farge's Bad Break," *American Art News* 7 (6 Feb. 1909), p. 4. La Farge was speaking at the awards dinner for reception of a medal of honor from the Architectural League of New York. He singled out McKim, Mead, and White in claiming that he had been spurned for over "twenty-two years." La Farge's remarks created a sensation, but he felt that they had been misrepresented and responded in a letter to the editor, *New York Times*, 5 Feb. 1909, p. 6.

IV

Japan 1886

For better or worse, the collapse of the La Farge Decorative Art Company in 1885 changed La Farge's life. By coincidence, one of his closest friends, the historian Henry Adams (1835-1915), also found his world in upheaval at the same time. On the morning of December 6th, 1885, Adams left his Washington, D.C. residence to go to the dentist. When he returned, he found that his wife of thirteen years, Clover Adams (Marian Hooper, 1843-1885) had taken her own life by drinking potassium cyanide, a chemical that she used in her hobby of photography.[1] Marian's unexpected suicide crushed Henry Adams. Not long after her death, he began to plan a trip to Japan to divert his thoughts from painful memories and to seek new meanings to his life.

Adams badly wanted companionship and offered to pay the way for La Farge to accompany him. Given the events of the preceding year, La Farge could take Adams up on the offer. Pulling the artist away from ongoing projects turned out to be easier said than done. Arriving at La Farge's New York studio on Thursday, June 3rd, 1886, Adams literally "dragged poor La Farge, in a dishevelled and desperate, but still determined mind, on board the Albany express."[2] Halfway to Albany in Poughkeepsie, La Farge wired to a publisher his regrets that he lacked time to finish illustrations for Percy Bysshe Shelley's "To a Skylark" (1820), paraphrasing the poem: "The purple evening melts around my flight."[3]

La Farge and Adams set off in style, traveling cross-country from Albany to San Francisco on the Union Pacific Railroad in a special director's car provided for them by Henry Adams's brother, the president of the railroad.[4] After joking with a reporter in Omaha that they were going in search of a "Nirvana" that the reporter prophetically quipped "out of season," the travelers crossed the western plains and mountains and arrived in San Francisco on Thursday, June 10th.[5] Two days later, they embarked to cross the Pacific on the steamer *City of Sydney*. They spent much of the time at sea besieged by seasickness and annoyance. "Four quiet days in sixteen," wrote Adams two weeks into the crossing, "the rest all kick and plunge, shiver and groan. . . . We have been more miserable by linear inch than ever two woe-begone Pagans, searching Nirvana, were before."[6] With great relief, La Farge and Adams docked at Yokohama on July 3rd.

On the dock, Dr. William Sturgis Bigelow (1850-1926), one of

1
J.C. Levenson, Ernest Samuels, Charles Vandersee, and Viola Hopkins Winner, eds., *The Letters of Henry Adams* (Cambridge, Massachusetts, and London, England, 1982) (hereafter *Letters*), vol. 2, p. 640. See a footnote to a letter, Henry Adams to Rebecca Gilman Dodge [6 Dec. 1886]. The trip to Japan is discussed at greater length in James L. Yarnall, "John La Farge and Henry Adams in Japan," *American Art Journal* 21 (1989), pp. 40-77.

2
Letter, Henry Adams to John Hay, 11 Jun. [1886], *Letters*, vol. 3, p. 12.

3
Ibid. This telegram apparently ended the commission for the illustrations.

4
Ibid.

5
Ibid. Cf. John La Farge, *An Artist's Letters from Japan* (New York, 1897), p. 175.

6
Serial letter, Henry Adams to Thomas F. Dwight, 28 Jun.-2 Jul. [1886], *Letters*, vol. 3, p. 13.

Clover Adams's cousins, met the travelers. Bigelow had given up a promising medical career to study Buddhism in Japan.[7] He conducted them through customs and to a hotel in Yokohama. A tour of the city that afternoon was at once fascinating and a letdown. Both La Farge and Adams had come to Japan with expectations of the highest order. Yokohama matched some of what La Farge called the "picture book" images that he had expected to find in Japan, but it also provided ample evidence of dissolute poverty and squalor. With his urbane and at times cynical outlook, Adams complained of "various pervasive smells," the "doll-land" character of the people and architecture, and the endless bric-a-brac that he collected despite its mediocre quality.[8]

On Sunday, July 4th, the travelers began a week of day-long trips to Tokyo, some twenty miles away by train. The highlight of these trips was a visit to the home of Ernest Fenollosa (1853-1908), then the Imperial Commissioner of Fine Arts. Fenollosa had taught philosophy and political economy at the University of Tokyo since 1878. During his residency in Tokyo, he had amassed a personal collection of Japanese art renowned for its quality. This viewing particularly moved La Farge.

I dislike to use analogies, but before these ancient religious paintings of Buddhist divinities, symbolical of the elements or of protective powers, whose worn surfaces contained marvels of passionate delicacy and care framed in noble lines, I could not help the recall of what I had felt at the first sight of old Italian art.[9]

Another high point of the stay in Tokyo occurred when Bigelow took La Farge and Adams to a club theater. There they saw *No* plays, a form of classical Japanese drama incorporating opera and ballet. Although Adams complained of the rigors of having to "sit on your heels all through five hours at the theatre," the spectacle fascinated La Farge.[10]

There was little else in Tokyo of interest to the travelers. Fenollosa had poisoned their thinking about the local architecture, a product of the Tokugawa era named for the family of shoguns that had dominated Japan from 1616-1868. Adams seemed a bit suspicious of Fenollosa's blanket condemnation of the Tokugawa temples, finding them at worst a "trifle baroque."[11] La Farge seems to have simply ignored the architecture of Tokyo. His only renderings pertaining to Tokyo were wash drawings of peasants, tattooed runners (Fig. 25), Buddhist priests, theater performers, and other "types" they encountered daily. La Farge evidently produced these stylized pictures years after the trip as illustrations for his travel writings. They betray strong influences of contemporary travel illustration, and he probably based them on photographs taken or collected during the trip.[12]

A cholera epidemic that broke out with unusual ferocity in July of 1886 curtailed the stay at Yokohama and Tokyo. On Sunday, July 11th, Bigelow and Fenollosa decided to take La Farge and Adams to the mountains of Nikko, where they had summer homes. Heavy rains complicated the journey of some seventy miles, extending the trip to over two days. They arrived at Nikko in an exhausted state at six in the evening on July 12th. They were to remain there for the next six weeks.

At Nikko, Bigelow put up La Farge and Adams in a small house next to his own that belonged to the priest of the nearby temple of Iyeyasu. Behind the house was a Japanese garden with ornamental trees and a small waterfall that became a favorite subject for La Farge to paint. Adams felt less enchanted with the situation than La Farge. He decried the toy-like nature of the house and even complained that the

7
Akiko Murakata, "William Sturgis Bigelow" (unpublished manuscript, Henry A. La Farge Papers, 1972). Cf. Van Wyck Brooks, *Fenollosa and his Circle* (New York, 1962), pp. 15-25; *Letters*, vol. 2, pp. 281, 554; and Yarnall, "Role of Landscape," pp. 331-33.

8
Letter, Henry Adams to Elizabeth Cameron, 13 Aug. 1886, *Letters*, vol. 3, p. 30; cf. letter, Henry Adams to Theodore F. Dwight, 17 Jul. 1886, *Letters*, vol. 3, p. 18; letter, Henry Adams to John Hay, 9 Jul. 1886, *Letters*, vol. 3, pp. 16-17.

9
La Farge, *Artist's Letters*, p. 14. Brooks, *Fenollosa*, is the primary source on Fenollosa; cf. Yarnall, "Role of Landscape," pp. 331-35.

10
Letter, Henry Adams to Elizabeth Cameron, 13 Aug. 1886, *Letters*, vol. 3, p. 18; La Farge, *Artist's Letters*, pp. 21-22.

11
Letter, Henry Adams to John Hay, 9 Jul. 1886, *Letters*, vol. 3, p. 15.

12
Yarnall, "La Farge in Japan," p. 44.

waterfall "splashes a great deal, with very little water."[13] He had trouble occupying his time during the weeks ahead, although finding some useful occupation by borrowing Bigelow's camera to photograph the temples and other sites in the surrounding hills.[14] Otherwise, Adams occupied the hours far less constructively rummaging through interminable offerings of Japanese merchandise such as porcelains, bronzes, and bric-a-brac. Dealers from throughout Japan had heard of the wealthy travelers and brought their wares to Nikko. Adams complained:

. . . the great consumers of time are the bric-a-brac dealers who bring huge cases from Tokio [sic] or even from Ozaka [sic], and consume day after day in opening and displaying stuffs, lacquers, metal-work, books, pictures, crystals, and all the curios of Japan. I buy pretty nearly everything that is considered good by Bigelow and the Fenollosas; but as yet I have seen nothing that seemed necessary to my existence, and my purchases are mostly for commissions or presents.[15]

La Farge passed his time more productively than Adams, dedicating himself alternately to writing and painting. In addition to painting some thirty or more pictures, La Farge wrote about two-thirds of the passages that he eventually incorporated into his travel writings. Although it is often difficult to separate out work done after his return, such a sizable body of work completed in Japan would serve La Farge well as groundwork for many future projects.

Many of the watercolors of Nikko are views of nearby religious monuments. The temple-tomb complex of Iyeyasu Tokugawa (died 1616), the founding shogun of the Tokugawa dynasty, was visible from the balcony of the house in which La Farge stayed. Down an avenue of trees just beyond this were temples and pagodas commemorating Iyeyasu's grandson, Iyemitsu Tokugawa, who ascended to power in 1623. La Farge painted watercolors of the temples with meticulous attention to detail and animated colors, but with less freedom of handling than his watercolors of the years immediately preceding (Fig. 26). The tighter, more controlled surfaces of these pictures likely resulted from La Farge's desire to record his experiences specifically for use in illustrating travel writings at some later time. He painted other watercolors more rapidly, seeking to capture a fleeting impression of a scene to be used later in a more elaborate composition (Fig. 27).[16] These works recall the travel sketches of English and French Romantic painters, particularly J.M.W. Turner and Delacroix. They record views factually, without dramatization or exaggeration. Their feeling is picturesque, but not artificial.

The summer heat and wet weather at Nikko generally prevented La Farge from painting out-of-doors. He executed many of the watercolors during the cool hours of the late evening or early morning while seated in his Japanese house. He obviously used photographs as artistic aids. At one point, Adams observed that "La Farge is trying hard to paint and sketch, but thus far with little result except the taking or buying of countless photographs."[17] This reliance on two-dimensional pictorial aids undoubtedly accounts for the more conventional style of these sketches, conforming so closely as they do to contemporary travel illustration and photography.

The best picture that La Farge executed at Nikko breaks the mold in terms of these works. As the time of their departure from Nikko neared in late August, La Farge painted a portrait of Suzuki or Zenshin San (Plate 6), the Buddhist priest of the Iyeyasu temple who rented out the house that the travelers occupied.[18] He depicted Suzuki sitting casually in a voluminous golden robe on the steps of the clergy house

13
Letter, Henry Adams to Elizabeth Cameron, 13 Aug. 1886, *Letters*, vol. 3, pp. 30-31.

14
Letter, Henry Adams to John White Field, 4 Aug. 1886, *Letters*, vol. 3, p. 27.

15
Ibid.

16
A more finished version of this subject with figures added is in the Worcester Art Museum. See Susan Strickler, ed., *American Traditions in Watercolor* (New York, 1987), p. 74.

17
Letter, Henry Adams to John White Field, 4 Aug. 1886, *Letters*, vol. 3, p. 28.

18
La Farge, *Artist's Letters*, p. 202.

of the temple of Iyemitsu. On Monday, August 30th, the day of their departure, La Farge noted that Suzuki had criticized the picture.

Yesterday he had found fault with my sketching him in his ordinary yellow priest's dress, while he had vestments as beautiful as any painter or clergyman could desire; in proof of which he had rushed into his house and reappeared in those lovely things and moved about the green of the garden as radiant as any flamingo. But I knew not of these possessions of his, and regretted quite as deeply as he could himself of not having painted him in them.[19]

The portrait moved Suzuki deeply, and he returned the honor by "inscribing" the picture on its reverse with ornamental calligraphy applied in silver leaf.[20]

La Farge and Adams returned to Yokohama to spend another week before continuing on to visit Kyoto. On Friday, September 3rd, they traveled to Kamakura, twenty miles south of Yokohama, to view the renowned Daibutsu, or Great Buddha, a colossal bronze statue nearly fifty feet high cast in 1252.[21] Originally housed in a temple destroyed twice by tidal waves, the statue stood open to the surrounding mountains, an exhilarating sight to come upon. Adams delighted in the visit:

I would have given you a present if you could have seen us on our expedition last Friday to what the old books call the Dye boots. This remnant of the vanished splendor of Kamakura is about twenty miles from Yokohama . . . and as La Farge says it is the most successful colossal figure in the world, he sketched it, and I, seizing the little priest's camera, mounted to the roof of his porch . . . [22]

La Farge sketched one watercolor at the site (Private Collection), but he painted his most impressive views (Plate 7 and The Metropolitan Museum of Art, New York) of the statue in his studio after his return from Japan.[23] For these, he seems to have relied upon photographs that the artist noted he and Adams had gone through great trouble to set up.

We took many photographs from new points of view, and we even removed the thatch of a penthouse so as to get nearer and under the statue to the side; and I painted also, more to get the curious gray and violet tone of the bronze than to make a faithful drawing, for that seemed impossible in the approaching afternoon.[24]

On Sunday, September 5th, La Farge and Adams embarked from Yokohama with Bigelow on the steamer *Volga* for Kobe, the port city of Osaka and Kyoto. They spent the next two days at Osaka, visiting the dealer Yamanaka, referred to by Adams as "the great *curio* dealer of Japan."[25] Adams again disgusted himself by purchasing "Tons of porcelain, pottery, and bronze" that he knew he would later not want.[26] On Wednesday, September 8th, the travelers went by train twenty-six miles northeast from Osaka to Kyoto. They took accommodations in a hotel at Ya Ami, on the outskirts of the city. From their veranda, La Farge painted four broad sketches of Kyoto nestled in a valley below, with mountains and trees rising around it (Fig. 28).[27] With an emphasis on atmospheric effects and specific times of day, these pictures are among La Farge's most freely painted works executed in Japan, recalling in mood and treatment his naturalistic open-air oils of the 1860s.

Kyoto offered a frantic change of pace from the relaxed atmosphere of Nikko. La Farge and Adams had only two weeks to spend there before heading back to

19
Ibid.

20
The inscription translates: "Suzuki [illegible], High Priest Gonsho [or Kensho], Chief priest of the Zenchi-in [temple], residing at number four [or fourteen] Yamanouchi, Kami Tuga Kori [district], Nikko-machi [town], Japan, Shimotsuke Province." I am grateful for this translation, given in the most fluent English possible, to Ann Yonemura, Assistant Curator of Japanese Art, Arthur M. Sackler Gallery and Freer Gallery of Art, Smithsonian Institution, Washington, D.C.

21
Adams was quite emphatic that they visited the site on a Friday, meaning that the date would be September 3, 1886. La Farge contradicted this (*Artist's Letters*, p. 224) in claiming to write while "At Sea, Off Izu, September 3," implying that the trip through Kamakura occurred on Thursday, September 2nd. La Farge was clearly in error since the two sailed for Kobe on Sunday, September 5th, not the date that La Farge indicated.

22
Serial letter, Henry Adams to John Hay, 9-15 Sept. 1886, *Letters*, vol. 3, p. 37.

23
Yarnall, "La Farge in Japan," p. 60.

24
La Farge, *Artist's Letters*, p. 225.

25
Serial letter, Henry Adams to John Hay, 9-16 Sept. 1886, *Letters*, vol. 3, p. 37.

26
Ibid., p. 38.

27
Yarnall, "La Farge in Japan," pp. 62-63.

Yokohama to catch a steamer back to the States. In the interim, they were in great demand. Dealers sought them out to sell them curios and artifacts. Their hosts ferried them on sight-seeing tours of Kyoto's historic shrines and monuments, and feted them every evening, beginning with the day of their arrival. Within a week, La Farge complained of an "indigestion of information" that blurred together the events into a single incomprehensible mass.[28] Adams elaborated more graphically their predicament:

The travelling is taking hold of my system. We cannot stand the pace. At our age occasional repose is a benefit. La Farge and I have jounced in kurumas; rattled through temples; asked questions, and talked Japanese, or listened to it, till we cower in fear before every new suggestion. We are nauseated by curios; I detest temples; and he is persecuted by letters of introduction, and I who have delivered only one of mine, pass all my time trying to escape hospitality.[29]

With such an arduous schedule, La Farge found little time to paint. He regretted that this gave a lopsided aspect to his Japanese work, which emphasized the Tokugawa art that he had studied in Nikko.

La Farge and Adams left Kyoto on Monday, September 22nd, to return by a week-long overland route to Yokohama. On the approach to Yokohama on September 28th, La Farge and Adams passed by Mount Fuji, considered the most sacred of holy mountains by the Japanese. Adams, seldom one to express enthusiasm for any aspect of Japan, found the vista breathtaking, noting "it was worth coming to far Japan for this single day."[30]

For La Farge, the mountain marked the end of a specific quest that had lingered in the back of his mind since setting off for Japan in June. Among the unfinished projects he left behind was the commission for a mural of Christ's Ascension for the Church of the Ascension in New York (Fig. 29). He sensed himself at a stalemate in his work on the design, and suspected that in Japan he might find the right setting for the composition.[31] All during his stay in Nikko, the mountains of the region had haunted La Farge, leading him to think on and off again of the Ascension painting. But it was not until he spotted Mount Fuji as he and Adams drove along the road near Kambara Beach that the proper chord struck him.

For a mile now, perhaps, we ran along the sea and the abrupt green wall of hills, so steep that we could not see them and, turning sharply around a corner, beheld Fuji, now filling the entire field of sight, seeming to rise even from below us into the upper sky, and framed at its base by near green mountains; these opened as a gate, and showed the glittering streak of the swollen Fujikawa, the swiftest river in Japan. . . . A[dams] and myself stopped at the place where we had had our view of Fuji, to make a more careful sketch. You can have no idea how much closer the clearer mind worked out the true outline of the mountain, which my excitement had heightened at least a couple of thousand feet; . . .[32]

The sketch of Mount Fuji painted near the Fuji River on September 28th (Fig. 30) served, with some later improvisations, as the basis for the background of the Ascension mural, shrouding Christ and the host of angels in the mists of Japan as they float above the sacred mountain. In and of itself, the watercolor prefigures in breadth of treatment La Farge's later mountain landscape watercolors of the South Seas.

The next day, La Farge and Adams went back to Yokohama to await the steam-

28
La Farge, *Artist's Letters*, pp. 237-38.

29
Serial letter, Henry Adams to John Hay, 9-16 Sept. 1886, *Letters*, vol. 3, p. 39.

30
La Farge, *Artist's Letters*, p. 266.

31
Cortissoz, *John La Farge*, pp. 164, 170. On the Ascension mural, see Weinberg, *Decorative Work*, pp. 177-83; Yarnall, "Role of Landscape," pp. 335-41; Patricia Jean Lefor, "John La Farge and Japan: An Instance of Oriental Influence in American Art" (unpublished Ph.D. dissertation, Northwestern University, 1978), pp. 125-27; and Adams, "Mind of John La Farge," p. 48.

32
La Farge, *Artist's Letters*, pp. 265-69.

33
Serial letter, Henry Adams to John Hay, 22-31 Aug. 1886, *Letters*, vol. 3, p. 34.

er that would take them home. On Saturday, October 2nd, they boarded the *City of Peking* bound for San Francisco.[33] After a voyage that was less difficult than the journey to Japan, they arrived in the States on Wednesday, October 20th. By November, La Farge was back in New York, picking up the projects he had left hanging by his departure four months earlier.

V

The South Seas 1890–1891

In the years immediately following his return from Japan, La Farge resumed decorative projects and other ventures. He soon found himself as busy as he had been during the early 1880s, but without the intense pressure or strife that had characterized the earlier years. He and Henry Adams remained frequent correspondents, often exchanging books on Japan or other exotic lands. During the summer of 1888, they began to discuss the possibility of an extended tour of the Pacific. La Farge jestingly wrote to Adams in August of that year:

[I understand] you wish to go off to the Fijis to drink enemy's blood & generally find peace. I wish I could join you in both delights, but I fear that I am to be detained yet awhile. Meanwhile my enemies may die—undrunk.[1]

Two full years of procrastination and negotiation followed as La Farge and Adams bartered for a mutually agreeable departure date. Both were involved in large publication projects: Adams was finishing his ten-volume *History of the United States*; La Farge was occupied with the illustrations and text for a series of ten articles on Japan to be published in *Century Magazine*.[2] They finally agreed to leave on Saturday, August 16th, 1890. The appointed day came and Adams found himself in the familiar position of having to drag La Farge away from his commitments. He wrote wryly to one of his closest friends, Elizabeth Cameron (1857-1944), that La Farge still had "three pictures to paint, two windows to lead, and his packing to do" between nine in the morning and four in the afternoon.[3]

With La Farge's Japanese servant, Rioza Awoki, in tow to serve as a porter, valet, and all-around handyman, the travelers departed on time early that evening. They went by train up the Hudson to Albany, and thence via Chicago and Omaha to San Francisco. While crossing the country on the Central Pacific railway, La Farge gave Adams watercolor lessons.[4] On August 21st, they arrived in San Francisco and, two days later, boarded the steamer *Zealandia*. They departed at 2 P.M. on August 23rd for Hawaii, the first stop on a tour that ultimately would take them around the world.

The trip to Hawaii was not arduous and took just one week. On Saturday, August 30th, the *Zealandia* docked at Honolulu on

1
Letter, John La Farge to Henry Adams, 14 Aug. 1888, La Farge Family Papers (Yale). A lengthier study of La Farge's trip to the South Seas is James L. Yarnall, "John La Farge and Henry Adams in the South Seas," *American Art Journal* 20 (1988), pp. 51-109.

2
Ten out of the eighteen chapters in La Farge's *Artist's Letters* were originally published in installments in the *Century Magazine*. They were commissioned in 1888 by Richard Watson Gilder, the editor of the magazine and a friend of La Farge's. The following titles and volume numbers pertain to the articles as published in *Century Magazine*: "An Artist's Letters from Japan," 39 (Feb. 1890), pp. 483-91; "From Tokio to Nikko," 39 (Mar. 1890), pp. 712-20; "The Shrines of Iyeyasu and Iyemitsu in the Holy Mountain of Nikko," 39 (Apr. 1890), pp. 859-69; "An Artist's Letters from Japan: Iyemitsu," 40 (Jun. 1890), pp. 195-203; "An Artist's Letters from Japan: Sketching," 40 (Aug. 1890), pp. 566-74; "An Artist's Letters from Japan: Sketching," 40 (Sept. 1890), pp. 751-59; "An Artist's Letters from Japan," 40 (Oct. 1890), pp. 866-77; "Tao: The Way," 42 (Jul. 1891), pp. 442-48; "Bric-a-Brac," 46 (Jul. 1893), pp. 419-29; "An Artist's Letters from Japan: Yokohama-Kamakura," 46 (Aug. 1893), pp. 571-76. Adams planted the seed of an idea in La Farge's head that led to the production of the journals; see Yarnall, "The Role of Landscape," p. 321.

3
Letter, Henry Adams to Elizabeth Cameron, 16 Aug. [1890], *Letters*, vol. 3, p. 260.

4
Ibid., pp. 261-62.
None of these sketches has survived.

5
Serial letter, Henry Adams to Elizabeth Cameron, 26 Aug.-8 Sept. [1890], *Letters*, vol. 3, pp. 269-70.

6
Ibid.; on Hartwell, see *Letters*, vol. 3, pp. 252-53, note 2.

7
Serial letter, Henry Adams to Elizabeth Cameron, 26 Aug.-8 Sept. [1890], *Letters*, vol. 3, p. 270.

8
Ibid.

9
John La Farge, *Reminiscences of the South Seas* (New York, 1912), pp. 29-31.

10
Ibid., p. 46.

the island of Oahu. La Farge and Adams checked into the main hotel in Honolulu, breakfasted, and had their "enormous baggage-train" brought from the ship.[5] That afternoon, they decided to abandon the hotel without so much as spending a single night to take up residence in the nearby Nuuanu valley. There, they were able to set up what they called "housekeeping" in a large and commodious house owned by Judge Alfred Stedman Hartwell (1836-1912), an old friend of Henry Adams who had houses in both Honolulu and Boston and presently was attending to business in the States.[6]

Once settled in the Nuuanu valley residence, La Farge began immediately to paint pictures of the gardens and surrounding mountains. He worked primarily in watercolor and gouache, handling the media in a fluid manner. Henry Adams described the activity with his characteristic dry wit:

La Farge has been out with his paint-box every day, and brings home, or rather brings in, wild daubs of brown and purple which faintly suggest hills and our great storm-cloud that we keep, so to speak, in our stable-yard, for it seems always to hang there.[7]

Like some of his earlier Japanese travel notes, many of La Farge's Hawaiian landscapes once again recall English and French Romantic watercolors of the mid-nineteenth century, particularly the work of artists such as Turner and Delacroix.

On Friday, September 5th, La Farge and Adams traveled by horse and carriage across the Nuuanu valley to one of the most picturesque sites on the island of Oahu, the Great Pali (a Hawaiian word for a cliff or precipice). From the peak of this lava formation dropping off suddenly into the ocean, they looked out upon what Adams called "one of the finest [views] I ever saw [that] quite smashed La Farge."[8] Several days later, on September 8th or 9th, La Farge and Adams went on another expedition to the Pali to spend a day sketching. There La Farge painted at least two watercolors of the site, only one of which is known today (Fig. 31). This surviving picture of the breathtaking vista aptly evokes the thrill of the scene. La Farge applied washes of watercolor to wet paper, blurring the contours of the mountain into a sunlit, atmospheric massing of textures and forms.[9]

On Friday, September 12th, La Farge, Adams, and Awoki left most of their baggage behind and boarded a crowded local steamer on a pilgrimage to the island of Hawaii. After a rough sea journey and several stops to let off and take on passengers, they arrived the next day on the southern tip of the island. The following morning, they set off on a journey to the volcano of Kilauea, then as today the most famous active volcano on Hawaii and a favorite tourist site. The trip over volcanic terrain was jolting, and took an entire day. As evening fell, the travelers arrived at lodgings near the crater's edge. They settled down for a three-day stay in the Kilauea Volcano House that La Farge described as "a sort of rough farmhouse, with doors opening on the veranda, and in front of the crater of the volcano."[10]

On Monday, September 15th, La Farge spent his first full day there sketching evocative views of the smoking crater and cones that stretched out for over three miles from the house. It was a fascinating and somewhat disturbing experience to grapple with the mercurial and fleeting aspects of the scene. The view of the crater painted that day (Plate 8) is a sort of case study of La Farge's technique for painting landscape at this time. He began with a quick underdrawing in graphite of the general lines of the composition. He then painted quickly in broad washes, building up areas of the watercolor before working in more details with gouache. Because of the elusiveness of the natural phenomena, which faded away even as he watched, La Farge wrote color annotations and other instructions to himself in the margins of the work to preserve his thoughts and impressions. Such notes served as aids for later retouching works in the more controlled environment of a hotel room or studio.

On the morning of Wednesday, September 17th, La Farge painted Kilauea at sunrise (The Toledo Museum of Art). He then set off on horseback with his traveling companions across the mountainous turf of Mauna Loa, heading for the coast of the Hilo district. This trip turned into a melancholy experience as the travelers witnessed the destruction of indigenous culture by modern western ways. The realization became particularly acute at a plantation in Hilo that had been described to them in glowing terms by their mutual friend, Clarence King (1842-1901), a geologist and mining engineer. In 1872, King had found the plantation teeming with innocently beautiful "old-gold girls," natives whose primary diversion involved sliding down a mountain waterfall.[11] Adams described the pathetic situation at the time of their visit:

The waterfall is still here, just behind the Severance house where we are staying. Mrs. Severance took us down there half an hour ago. She said nothing about the girls, but she did say the boys used habitually to go over the fall as their after-school amusement; but of late they have given it up, and must be paid for doing it. The last man who jumped off the neighboring high rock required fifteen dollars. Mrs. Severance told this sadly, mourning over the decline of the arts and of surf-bathing. A Bostonian named Brigham took a clever photograph of a boy, just half way down, the fall being perhaps twelve or fifteen feet. So passes the glory of Hawaii, and of the old-gold girl,—woe is me![12]

As they continued up the coast during the next five days, La Farge and Adams became increasingly aware of the encroachment of sugar-cane plantations that had stripped the land and indelibly altered the indigenous cultural life of the island. Their visit to the Island of Hawaii ended on this somber note as the party skirted the northern side of the great volcanic mountain Mauna Loa. They crossed the island and descended to the coastal bay at Kawaihae to catch the steamer *Kinau*.[13] La Farge and Adams arrived back in Honolulu on the island of Oahu on the morning of Wednesday, September 24th. They passed three days in their Nuuanu valley residence, preparing to depart on a two thousand mile sea voyage to the Samoan Islands.

On Saturday, September 27th, La Farge and Adams caught the steamer *Alameda*, a vessel regularly traversing the main trade routes to and from Samoa.[14] The ship arrived off the island of Tutuila in the Samoan Island group on Sunday, October 5th. Upon landing at the village of Nua, La Farge and Adams found themselves surrounded by Samoan men and women of striking physical beauty and the most amiable, gentle demeanor. They felt as if they had plunged into a sort of paradise rivalling the Greek Golden Age.[15] Due to inclement weather, they were unable to depart on a cutter for Upolu, some sixty miles away. Nua unexpectedly became an overnight haven for the traveling party.

After dinner that evening, some of the most beautiful girls of the village gave an animated *sivà* dance in the traditional Samoan manner. They performed naked to the waist with garlands of leaves and flowers adorning their heads and necks, glistening with perfumed oil. In the glow of kerosene lamps, the entire scene seemed eminently evocative, and the forms of the girls summoned to La Farge's mind reminiscences of antique art.

11
The most comprehensive discussion of Clarence King and the "old gold" is found in Evelyne de Chazeaux, ed., *Lettres des Mers du Sud* (Paris, 1974), p. xvii.

12
Serial letter, Henry Adams to Elizabeth Cameron, 13-24 Sept. 1890, *Letters*, vol. 3, p. 277. "Mrs. Severance" was the wife of Henry W. Severance, U.S. Consul General from 1889-1893; see *Letters*, vol. 3, p. 281, note 5.

13
Ibid., pp. 278-80.

14
Letter, Henry Adams to Lucy Baxter, 27 Sept. 1890, *Letters*, vol. 3, pp. 283-84; letter, Henry Adams to Elizabeth Cameron, 27 Sept. 1890, *Letters*, vol. 3, p. 285.

15
La Farge, *Reminiscences*, pp. 68-70, 86-87.

16
Ibid., pp. 84-85.

17
Serial letter, Henry Adams to Elizabeth Cameron, 2-23 Oct. 1890, *Letters*, vol. 3, pp. 290-91.

18
La Farge, *Reminiscences*, p. 98.

19
Ibid., pp. 98, 104.

20
Ibid., pp. 209-10.

21
Letter, Henry Adams to Anna Cabot Mills Lodge, 21 Oct. 1890, *Letters*, vol. 3, pp. 307. Cf. serial letter, Henry Adams to John Hay, 2-4 Mar. 1891, *Letters*, vol. 3, pp. 430-32.

So those lovers of form, the Greeks, must have looked, anointed and crowned with garlands, and the so-called dance that we saw might not have been misplaced far back in some classical antiquity. The girls sat in a row before us, grave and collected, their beautiful legs curled upon the lap as in East Indian sculptures; and Sifa began a curious chant. . . . I cannot describe it any better; of what use is it to say that it was beautiful, and extraordinary, and that no motion of a western dancer but would seem stiff beside such an ownership of the body?[16]

Henry Adams, less susceptible than his companion to the romantic enchantment of this first *sivà*, facetiously alluded instead to cannibalistic rites still rumored to be in practice as part of some South Sea cultures.

Naked to the waist, their rich skins glistened with oil, as though the girls had come out of the sea. . . . The mysterious depths of darkness behind, against which the skin and dresses of the dancers mingled rather than contrasted; the sense of remoteness and of genuineness in the stage management; . . . the whole scene and association gave so much freshness to our fancy that no future experience, short of being eaten, will ever make us feel so new again. La Farge's spectacles quivered with emotion and gasped for sheer inability to note everything at once.[17]

The next morning, the party departed for the island of Upolu on the cutter that had failed the day before to reach their port. This trip of only sixty miles took nearly two days because of strong head winds and rough seas. On Wednesday, October 8th, they finally reached the village of Vaiala near Apia, their home base until their departure from Samoa in late January, 1891.

In Vaiala, the natives treated La Farge and Adams with the utmost hospitality and respect. They were considered special visitors, the equivalent of visiting rulers.[18] They spent their days in a large hut that was the "guest house" of the village—"not exactly the finest, but still very well built," as La Farge put it. At night, they occupied "a little building of our own European kind, with just place for our two rooms and beds."[19] La Farge painted many pictures at Vaiala, the majority in broad washes of thin watercolor and heavy gouache. He repeated certain subjects many times, such as girls sliding down a waterfall at the Papa-seea or Sliding Rock, located about an hour from Vaiala. "The sight was charming," La Farge noted in his journal, "the pretty girls, with arms thrown out and bodies straight for balance, their wet clothes driven tightly to the hips in the rush of the water, had a look of gold against the gray that brought up Clarence King's phrase about Hawaii and the 'old-gold girls that tumbled down waterfalls.' In the plunge and the white foam, the yellow limbs did indeed look like goldfish in a blue-green pool."[20]

La Farge and Adams paid a visit on Saturday, October 16th, to the writer, Robert Louis Stevenson (1850-1894), who had come to the South Seas in 1889 for health reasons. Stevenson lived with his wife, an artist, near Vaiala, and was at work on several writings about the South Seas. Adams described with distaste this visit to "a very dirty board cabin, with a still dirtier man and woman [Stevenson and his wife] in the middle of several hundred burned tree-stumps."[21] La Farge, on the other hand, immediately developed a rapport with Stevenson, chatting with him enthusiastically for an hour about Tahiti, where Stevenson had lived for two months at Tautira. Although imparting an inflated picture of Tahitian life, Stevenson's discussions set the stage for making the necessary contacts and introductions that served the travelers well later in Tahiti.

Conforming to island customs, other excursions around the islands formed a type of *malaga* (spelled also *malanga*) which La Farge described as "a voyage where one puts up with friends, etc.; one of the fundamental social institutions of Samoa."[22] Seumanu, a primary chief of Vaiala, led them on these semi-formal expeditions, along with a retinue of native guides and servants. Throughout these travels, they went from village to village witnessing ceremonial kava-making (Fig. 32), meeting the *taupos* or village virgins, assisting at military reviews called *talolo*, joining in gift-giving rites (Plate 9), and listening to hereditary orators called *tulafales*.

At all stops along the way in Samoa, La Farge and Adams were entertained by both standing and seated versions of the *sivà* (Fig. 33). La Farge generally found the dances interesting and colorful but, even so, began to think them tedious as time went on. At a special *sivà* given in their honor at night in late October during a trip to the island of Savaii, La Farge dozed away while the natives made sure his boredom went undetected: "A gentle tap now and then, and a gentle *alofa* told me that I was all right, and could go to sleep while making believe to look on."[23]

La Farge frequently used photography to assist in his South Sea works—according to Adams, they "fired off [their] Kodaks at everything worth taking" while in Samoa.[24] Adams undertook to supply a wealth of photographic material on the chance that he might catch just the right image for La Farge to use in painting the *sivà*:

During the show, I toiled over my Kodak, and took thirty or forty views, none of which I expect to find successful, but which, even if one turns out well, may help La Farge to paint a sivà picture.[25]

A snapshot-like quality characterizes many of La Farge's Samoan figure paintings, particularly those of *sivà* dancers (Fig. 34), seeming to confirm this statement and the hypothesis that La Farge relied heavily on Adams's photographs for composing pictures. But, if La Farge did use Adams's photographs, it must have been after leaving Samoa since the photographs could not be developed there, "so I must wait indefinitely, or send home the roll for the purpose. . . . I expect to see the *sivà* figure without end, in his [La Farge's] future paintings."[26] Adams sent some of the film by steamer to Sydney, Australia, where it was developed and returned to him while he and La Farge were in Tahiti.[27]

The watercolors depicting these various native ceremonies are the best figure pieces of the South Seas trip. La Farge painted the most impressive among them long after the fact, using photographs or modest sketches done on the spot. Heavy application of watercolor and gouache lends many of these works the feeling of oil paintings, but the lustrous colors and spontaneous handling of brush strokes ultimately betray the watercolor medium. These pictures were eminently suited to exhibition, gracing the halls of the American Watercolor Society, the Boston Watercolor Club, and the New York Watercolor Club with regularity from the time of La Farge's return in 1891 until his death.

In all, La Farge and Adams regarded the four months spent in Samoa as the high point of their South Seas tour—although Adams would have gladly cut the visit a month shorter. La Farge blamed his ill health for delaying their departure, which was initially planned for early November 1890 and finally postponed until late January 1891. Adams was skeptical of La Farge's excuse, intimating that La Farge merely wanted to prolong the picturesque stay in Samoa so that he could continue to

22
La Farge, *Reminiscences*, p. 155.

23
Ibid., p. 190.

24
Serial letter, Henry Adams to Elizabeth Cameron, 2-23 Oct. 1890, *Letters*, vol. 3, p. 298.

25
Serial letter, Henry Adams to Elizabeth Cameron, 26 Oct.-3 Nov. 1890, *Letters*, vol. 3, p. 313.

26
Ibid., p. 318.

27
Ibid. See contradictory evidence concerning where the film was developed in Yarnall, "La Farge in South Seas," p. 105, note 82.

paint. They finally scheduled a departure for Tahiti aboard the cutter *Richmond* for the morning of Wednesday, January 28th, 1891.

During the week-long voyage from Samoa to Tahiti, La Farge passed the time ruminating on the history of Tahiti and its quasi-mythical place in nineteenth-century thought. Adams spent the trip "dressed in nothing but a Japanese kimono, and reading trashy novels" before eventually turning his own thoughts to Tahiti's unique place in the history of the Pacific.[28] The *Richmond* arrived off Papeete, the capital of Tahiti, on the evening of Tuesday, February 3rd, and docked in the harbor of the city the next morning.

Based largely on Robert Louis Stevenson's accounts, La Farge and Adams came to Tahiti expecting to find lost paradise. Instead, they found Papeete a dissolute, Europeanized town with poor accommodations. Compared to the truly primitive and delightfully natural islands of Samoa, Tahiti was a great letdown. La Farge and Adams lingered at Papeete for several weeks, mainly to recover from the arduous sea journey. La Farge appreciated the beauty of the surrounding landscape, and painted several charming views around their small residence on the beach near Papeete (Fig. 35). On February 24th, they sent Awoki and a cook they hired named Peraudot to the remote island village of Tautira to set up house while they themselves traveled down the coast to Papara.

At Papara, they visited with Tati Salmon (1850-1918), head of the largest native family on Tahiti and a half-hereditary high chief of the Tevas, Tahiti's most ancient royal family.[29] Tati's family made them feel more than welcome; in fact, the elders of the family formally adopted them into the clan. On Thursday, February 26th, the night before La Farge and Adams were to depart from Papara, Tati Salmon had the local natives perform a ritual song and dance called the *himene*. La Farge painted the ceremony as they watched, creating a haunting watercolor record of the event (Private Collection).[30]

The next morning, La Farge and Adams left Papara and traveled through the isthmus of Taravao to the isle of Taiarapu. La Farge stopped occasionally and painted the magnificent scenery, including the mountainous pass of Vairao along the coast (Fig. 36). This painting effectively captures the majesty of the Tahitian landscape, hinting at the masterful landscape style that La Farge exercised to its fullest during the weeks to come. At five in the evening, they reached the Tautira River Valley. Half a mile beyond the river, they found a commodious, five-room wood-frame house that Awoki and their cook Peraudot had successfully set up.[31] Adams objected vociferously to the remoteness of Tautira: "We cannot even find an interpreter to make conversation possible."[32] Within a week of their arrival, he was trying to convince La Farge that it was time to leave the South Seas altogether or, at the very least, to set off for another set of islands such as the Marquesas. He finally grudgingly resolved himself to remain while La Farge painted: "I think I can manage to hold on for some weeks, or even a month, if La Farge wants to paint; and as the natives all wear clothes of some kind, the temptation to paint is less than in Samoa."[33]

Adams was wrong about La Farge's temptation to paint. Whether or not the artist missed the native life of Samoa, he produced in Tautira some of the most ambitious and beautiful landscape watercolors of the entire South Seas tour. At Tautira, La Farge was particularly taken with the haunting beauty of the Tautira River Valley, located ten minutes away from the house where they were staying. At least eight times, he painted the entrance to the river and valley, a perspective that had been rendered famous by travel illustrations and photographs that La Farge probably had

28
Serial letter, Henry Adams to Elizabeth Cameron, 6-13 Feb. 1890, *Letters*, vol. 3, p. 402; La Farge, *Reminiscences*, p. 288.

29
Serial letter, Henry Adams to Elizabeth Cameron, 23 Feb.-8 Mar. 1891, *Letters*, vol. 3, pp. 417-23.

30
Ibid., p. 421.

31
Ibid., p. 422.

32
Serial letter, Henry Adams to John Hay, 2-4 Mar. 1891, *Letters*, vol. 3, p. 433.

33
Serial letter, Henry Adams to Elizabeth Cameron, 23 Feb.-8 Mar. 1891, *Letters*, vol. 3, p. 422.

34
Yarnall, "La Farge in the South Seas," pp. 76-78; Yarnall, "La Farge's *Portrait of the Painter*," pp. 16-18.

in mind and perhaps had at hand.[34]

The most impressive of the Tautira River Valley watercolors are among La Farge's best works in the medium, and may not have been executed in the South Seas at all. They appear to be less recordings of what La Farge observed than an attempt to elevate the Tautira River Valley to an idealized vision of South Sea existence. In one of these (Plate 10), the Tautira River Valley bathed in sunlight is the stage for a paean to South Sea existence.[35] A heroic, semi-nude native—probably modeled on an antique statue or vase painting—stands alongside a meek child. The natives seem to be passive beneficiaries of the natural order surrounding them. Another version is also set in brilliant afternoon sunlight (Plate 11).[36] The pose and physique of the spear fisherman in this case may have been intended to evoke an antique bronze or vase depiction of Poseidon or Zeus, but the design repeats exactly the figure and landscape seen in a photograph evidently taken around the time of La Farge's visit (Fig. 37). It is also similar to another watercolor of a spear fisherman identified by La Farge as a scene in Samoa that was copied directly from a photograph taken by Charles Spitz, Tahiti's only commercial photographer of the day.[37] Spitz's photographs and postcards were, presumably, among those that Henry Adams mentioned La Farge collected with a "mania" during their stay in Tautira.[38]

In late March, Tati Salmon came to Tautira and convinced La Farge and Adams to undertake an expedition to the island of Moorea, where Tati had a sort of country house. After a visit to Tati's family in Papara, La Farge and Adams traveled to Papeete to prepare for the trip. They caught up on correspondence and La Farge sent off a packet of watercolors and drawings to his son Bancel in New York, as he had done occasionally during the preceding months.[39] On the morning of Sunday, April 12th, La Farge, Adams, Awoki, and their cook Peraudot sailed on the brig *Galilee* for Moorea.

They arrived at sunset in the glorious bay of Uponohu, which inspired in Adams an outburst of great enthusiasm:

. . . the mountains, in peaks and with outlines as unreasonable as a theatre drop-scene rose around us, more like the Lake of Como than like a respectable Polynesian island. The scene was impressive; the finest we have yet struck.[40]

They moved immediately into Tati Salmon's empty house, isolated on the inner shore of the bay, far from any village. La Farge drew and painted the view from the house, a vista that was truly tropical—lush with palms and offering soaring mountains veiled in mist (Fig. 38).[41] They stayed at Moorea two weeks before being forced to make a hasty return to Papeete. In March, Adams had offered the captain of the *Richmond* a thousand dollars (equivalent to almost $29,000 today) to stop at Fiji during his next passage between Papeete and New Zealand.[42] On the evening of Thursday, April 23rd, Adams learned that the request had been denied, leaving them no choice but to go directly to Auckland, New Zealand, and probably miss Fiji altogether. Rushing back to Papeete, they were dismayed to find the *Richmond* booked solid.[43] Undaunted, Adams tried to hire a suitable sailing vessel to take them to Fiji. For $1,500 (around $43,000 today), he found a schooner willing to make the trip, but this plan fell through when the firm owning the schooner opposed it.[44] Still undaunted, Adams sought to buy a schooner outright but, once again, he failed.[45]

Ultimately, despite offers of up to $3,000 (about $87,000 today) to find passage, Adams could find no way to escape Tahiti quickly.[46] Resigned to his fate, he decided

35
Until 1985, the picture was known only from its illustration in "A Glimpse of John La Farge's Work, as shown at the Montross Gallery," *New York Mail and Express Illustrated Saturday Magazine*, 9 Feb. 1901, p. 4. Mary A. La Farge has documented that this was purchased in 1901 from La Farge's exhibition held at Montross Gallery, New York, by or for Julia Ward Howe (1819-1910), American suffragist and reformer.

36
Mary A. La Farge has documented the descent of this work in the family of Mrs. Charles Boyden (d. 1927), who purchased it in 1898 at Doll and Richards according to a typescript maintained by La Farge's primary dealers between 1874 and 1910, "List of Pictures by Mr. John La Farge sold by Doll & Richards, Inc., Boston," p. 4, Henry A. La Farge Papers (hereafter "List of Pictures, Doll and Richards").

37
Discussed and illustrated in Yarnall, "La Farge's *Portrait of the Painter*," pp. 17-19 and p. 20, note 29; cf. Yarnall, "Nature and Art in the Painting of John La Farge," pp. 112-13; E. John Bullard, "John La Farge at Tautira, Tahiti," *National Gallery of Art Reports and Studies in the History of Art* 2 (1968), p. 151, proposed that some correlation with photography might exist long before the actual photograph illustrated here was known.

38
Serial letter, Henry Adams to Elizabeth Cameron, 6-13 Feb. 1891, *Letters*, vol. 3, p. 408, noting "La Farge has settled down to painting, varied by his usual mania for collecting photographs."

39
Serial letter, Henry Adams to Elizabeth Cameron, 13-25 Apr. 1891, *Letters*, vol. 3, p. 457. La Farge undoubtedly enclosed or sent separately letters to Bancel, his own wife in Newport, and other members of his family throughout the South Seas trip, but such letters back home have either been destroyed or else have not yet come to light. In the preface to La Farge, *Reminiscences*, Grace Edith Barnes notes that she drew upon these letters when preparing the text, saying they contained the artist's most valuable impressions.

40
Ibid., p. 458.

41
Ibid.

42
Ibid., p. 459.

43
Ibid.

44
Serial letter, Henry Adams to Elizabeth Cameron, 3-14 May 1891, *Letters*, vol. 3, pp. 472-74.

45
Ibid., p. 474.

46
Ibid., p. 473.

to record a history of Tahiti as remembered by members of Tati Salmon's family, a project not completed and published until 1901.[47] La Farge meanwhile painted assiduously, and he also contributed to Adams's project by interviewing members of Tati Salmon's family, filling his journals with folk poems and stories that he heard each day.[48]

The *Richmond* returned, arriving outside the reef of Papeete harbor on Monday, June 1st. Adams was surprised to discover that for $2,500 ($72,000 today), the captain would at last agree to go out of his way to take the travelers to Fiji.[49] Adams immediately closed a deal to depart on June 5th. By late that afternoon, the ship was passing Moorea and heading off toward Fiji as, from the boat, La Farge painted his last watercolors of Tahiti.[50]

Fiji lay two thousand miles away, over ten days by steamer. At roughly the halfway point between Tahiti and Fiji, the *Richmond* stopped overnight on July 9th at Rarotonga, a Tongan Island lying due south of Samoa.[51] La Farge painted only one picture during this stop, a colorful study of a seated Tongan girl (Fig. 39). This is arguably the best watercolor portrait that he painted in the South Seas, executed with thick washes of vivid color laid down boldly and expressively.

On Tuesday, June 16th, the *Richmond* entered the harbor of Suva on the southeastern tip of Viti Levu island, Fiji. La Farge and Adams were conducted ashore by a man they identified as "Spence," the private secretary of the British colonial Governor, Sir John Thurston (1836-1897).[52] During their visit to Fiji, they stayed with the governor in his residence called the Government house and were never out of his protective custody as a precaution against inhospitable native elements. Adams, with colorful phrasing, credited the situation in Fiji to Thurston's attitude: "he has sound views on savages, and insists on their retaining all the savagery possible, consistent with a cuisine which excludes man-steaks from the *menu*."[53]

Their first trip into the Fijian countryside took place on Thursday, July 18th. La Farge and Adams accompanied Thurston on a comfortable steam launch up the Rewa River as he attended to business with a local chief. There, they observed a ceremony of kava-making similar to the ones they had seen in Samoa, witnessed an address by a *tulafales* or orator, and saw war dances or *mekke-mekke*.[54] La Farge's most impressive Fijian watercolor represents the war dance witnessed that day (Fig. 40). The picture is painted with an elaborate mixture of media, including gouache, ink, and watercolor. Like most of the figure studies pertaining to Fiji, it evidently was executed using photographs, probably around ten years after the actual visit.[55]

La Farge and Adams were introduced to the rigors of Fiji during a more extended trip that took them into mountainous reaches of Viti Levu, where few white men had ever penetrated. Thurston led them on this three-week expedition that had the ostensible purpose of scouting for the site of a proposed sanitarium. This official excuse thinly disguised Thurston's real intention of treating his guests to the Fijian equivalent of a safari. "The journey is very amusing," quipped Adams, "Sir John travels like Stanley in Africa."[56]

On Saturday, June 27th, the traveling party assembled up the Rewa River from Suva at Vunidawa in the house of a British magistrate, Adolph Brewster Joske (1855-1937). The core participants for the expedition into what the locals termed the "Devil Country" were La Farge, Adams, Joske, Carew (another magistrate), Thurston, a Mr. Berry (Thurston's brother-in-law), and Spence, Thurston's secretary. They were accompanied by an armed constabulary, the Governor's herald and servants, Awoki, and "a hundred and fifty native carriers and attendants" to transport them over

47
Ibid. Eventually published as Henry Adams, *Tahiti: Memoirs of Araii Tamai e Marama of Eimeo, Teriinere of Tooarai, Terrenui of Tahiti, Taurraatua i Amo* (Washington, D.C., 1901).

48
La Farge published a portion of these accounts as "Tahitian Literature" in Charles D. Warner, ed., *Library of the World's Best Literature*, (New York, 1902), vol. 24, pp. 14389-398. Portions of the folk tales were published in La Farge, *Reminiscences*, pp. 331-35, 345-48, and 353-78.

49
Serial letter, Henry Adams to Elizabeth Cameron, 17 May-3 June 1891, *Letters*, vol. 3, pp. 481-82; cf. letter, Henry Adams to Theodore F. Dwight, 2 Jun. 1891, *Letters*, vol. 3, p. 484.

50
La Farge, *Reminiscences*, pp. 385-86. One watercolor of "The Last Sight of Tahiti" is in the Worcester Art Museum. The other has been lost since the 1930s.

51
Serial letter, Henry Adams to Elizabeth Cameron, 4-23 Jun. 1891, *Letters*, vol. 3, pp. 486-87.

52
Ibid., p. 488; La Farge, *Reminiscences*, pp. 397-98.

53
Ibid., pp. 489.

54
La Farge, *Reminiscences*, pp. 403-04.

55
The subject of this painting has been confused in the past. Recently discovered inscriptions under the mat indicate that it was painted on the Rewa River. Yarnall, "La Farge in South Seas," p. 91, postulated the wrong site.

56
Serial letter, Henry Adams to Elizabeth Cameron, 28 June-1 Aug. 1891, *Letters*, vol. 3, p. 498. Cf. letter, Henry Adams to William Hallett Phillips, 8 Oct. 1891, *Letters*, vol. 3, p. 553, comparing expedition to "Stanley in Africa."

difficult or watery terrain on litters.[57] Their caravan departed on Monday, June 29th and crossed mountain villages for several days. Neither La Farge nor Adams recorded detailed descriptions of the rugged trip through the mountains. Their progress seemed a blur of activities: witnessing native ceremonies and dances; bathingdaily in cold mountain streams; staying in bee-shaped huts typical of the mountain villages; collapsing in exhaustion and being carried on litters up mountains or over rivers; encountering wild animals and wilder natives; and viewing exotic mountain scenery.[58]

The party arrived at the mountain village of Nasogo (also spelled Nasongo) on the evening of Friday, July 3rd. The next day, which was rainy, provided a chance for La Farge to paint a number of views of the quaint and colorful huts while Thurston and Berry photographed the natives and the village.[59] At Nasogo or at Matakula, another village they reached on July 6th, La Farge and Adams posed for a picture in front of a bee-hive hut, the only known photograph of either traveler taken during the South Sea tour (Fig. 41).[60]

They descended from the mountains for the next several days in order to reach the coast where Thurston's steamer, the *Clyde*, was waiting in the harbor to transport them back to Suva. The *Clyde* slipped out of port at seven on the morning of Friday, July 10th, steaming along the coast. For the next several days, they visited various towns along the way, staying overnight on sugar plantations. On July 13th, La Farge sketched the picturesque contours of the coast near Thambone with its purple, rolling mountains swept by clouds (Plate 12). Late that afternoon, the steamer ran aground in the low tide and they were put up overnight at Tongavere by the local magistrate, Jonii Mandraiwiwi.[61] The next morning, the high tide released the *Clyde* from the sands. They boarded and proceeded along the coast to Naiserlangai where Jonii Mandraiwiwi had a frame house in the European style and they would stay the night. La Farge painted the view down to the coast as they relaxed at this residence during the afternoon (The Huntington Museum of Art, Huntington, West Virginia).

On the morning of Wednesday, July 15th, the party steamed around Viti Levu Bay, arriving at Suva as evening fell. "So we have fairly done Fiji," Adams noted, "and know about as much about it as anyone wants to know."[62] La Farge and Adams remained for another week at the Governor's House, but this last leg of their Fijian stay appears to have been completely uneventful.

On Thursday, July 23rd, La Farge, Adams, and Awoki departed from Fiji aboard the steamer *Rockton*. For the next eight days, they traveled toward Australia, suffering greatly from seasickness as the ship bucked the heavy trade winds. Australia was little more than a stopover on the way to sight-seeing in Ceylon (today called Sri Lanka). They left Sydney on August 6th, and started a trip to Singapore aboard the steamer *Jumna*. The journey was a long one but pleasant because the trade winds were behind them. On Friday, August 21st, the *Jumna* stopped at Bali, near Java, and La Farge went ashore to send telegrams to Batavia (today called Jakarta). Upon returning, he brought back a peck of mangosteens, the first time La Farge and Adams had come across this tropical fruit during their travels.[63] Back on board the *Jumna*, La Farge painted two mangosteens, one of the few still lifes that he had executed since leaving San Francisco (Private Collection).[64]

For the next two weeks, they traveled through the Java Sea, docking at various ports in Sumatra and Malaysia, until arriving at Singapore on Monday, August 31st. The next day, they boarded the steamer *Melbourne*, a ship bound for Marseilles that would drop them at Ceylon on the way. On the morning of Sunday, September 6th,

57
Ibid., p. 498; La Farge, *Reminiscences*, pp. 421-22.

58
Ibid., pp. 498-504; La Farge, *Reminiscences*, pp. 422-40.

59
Ibid., p. 501.

60
Henry Adams inscribed the photograph: "J.L.F. and H.A. sitting at the door of their palace." See caption in *Letters*, vol. 3, opp. p. 498.

61
Ibid., p. 507.

62
Ibid., p. 509.

63
Serial letter, Henry Adams to Elizabeth Cameron, 12-22 Aug. 1891, *Letters*, vol. 3, p. 524.

64
Adams had in fact claimed in Java that "I have not seen [La Farge] touch a brush since we left Tahiti three months ago" (serial letter, Henry Adams to Elizabeth Cameron, 26 Aug.-6 Sept. 1891, *Letters*, vol. 3, p. 534). This is an erroneous statement given Adam's own written references to La Farge's painting activity in Fiji, as well as the evidence of numerous pictures that clearly were done on-the-spot there.

Ceylon loomed on the horizon and, by eight that evening, the party had debarked at the capital, Colombo.

After a night in a hotel, La Farge and Adams boarded a train in the afternoon to travel to Kandy, renowned for its great Buddhist Temple of the Sacred Tooth.[65] The temple was less interesting than Adams had hoped, comparing poorly to Japanese temples they had visited, but the countryside struck him as among the loveliest he had seen in his travels. La Farge seems to have painted only one watercolor at Kandy, a sketch of the reservoir or "Tank at Kandy" (The Toledo Museum of Art, Toledo).

While at Kandy, Adams purchased photographs of the ruins of the ancient capital of Ceylon, Anuradhapura, and convinced La Farge that they should undertake a pilgrimage to the site. Evidently leaving Awoki behind in Kandy with their luggage, La Farge and Adams set out on September 11th on a rugged two-day journey through the jungle in ox-carts. They were disappointed at what they found upon their arrival at Anuradhapura. The ruins were far less impressive than they had imagined. They left Anuradhapura by ox-cart at about eight in the evening on the same day they had arrived.

On the return trip to Kandy, La Farge and Adams went out of their way to visit Dambulla (also spelled Dambula) where they explored some of the famous rock-cut caves filled with Buddhist statues.[66] They then went through Polonnaruwa, where La Farge painted a watercolor of a colossal statue still standing today in a group of sculpture at the Gal Vihara (Fig. 42).[67] They arrived back in Kandy the next day, then headed back to Colombo to catch a steamer scheduled to depart for Marseilles on Thursday, September 17th.

After an unexpected delay, the party finally steamed out of Colombo on the *Messageries Djemnah* on Monday, September 21st. They skirted Asia and on October 3rd, La Farge painted the last recorded work of the trip, a simple sketch of the Red Sea made as the *Djemnah* prepared to enter the Suez Canal (Private Collection).[68] Six days later, the *Djemnah* had crossed the Mediterranean and La Farge, Adams, and Awoki debarked at Marseilles. From here, it was a day-trip by train to Paris where the travelers split up. Adams went off to England and La Farge traveled to Brittany to visit his French relatives.[69]

On November 11th, La Farge and Awoki crossed the English Channel and, unable to rendezvous with Adams in London to bid farewell, made their way to Liverpool. They departed Thursday, November 12th, on a steamer that crossed the Atlantic and arrived in New York a week later. La Farge had thus circumnavigated the globe in just under a year and three months.[70]

65
Ibid., pp. 538-39; serial letter, Henry Adams to Elizabeth Cameron, 8 Sept.-8 Oct. 1891, *Letters*, vol. 3, pp. 540-41.

66
Serial letter, Henry Adams to Elizabeth Cameron, 8 Sept.-8 Oct. 1891, *Letters*, vol. 3, pp. 544-45.

67
The statue is illustrated and discussed in Benjamin Rowland, *The Art and Architecture of India, Hindu, Jain* (New York, 1967), pp. 372-73.

68
Serial letter, Henry Adams to Elizabeth Cameron, 8 Sept.-8 Oct. 1891, *Letters*, vol. 3, pp. 548-49.

69
Letter, Henry Adams to Lucy Baxter, 16 Nov. 1891, *Letters*, vol. 3, p. 571.

70
Serial letter, Henry Adams to Elizabeth Cameron, 5-12 Nov. 1891, *Letters*, vol. 3, p. 560.

VI

Late decorative period 1886–1910

La Farge had become a decorative artist almost by chance, the result of being catapulted into fame by his first major opportunity as a decorator. For ten years beginning in 1875, ecclesiastical and secular commissions demanded his constant attention. After his return from Japan in 1886, the artist realigned his priorities. While decoration remained his primary occupation until his death in 1910, he found time to engage in writing, lecturing, traveling, painting pictures for exhibition, and promoting his oils and watercolors.

Echoes of La Farge's voyages to Japan and the South Seas continued to reverberate throughout the last twenty-five years of his life. After his return from Japan in late 1886, La Farge worked for two years to compile and expand the material he had produced or collected there into an elaborate illustrated travelogue. The *Century Magazine* serialized ten articles in 1890 and 1893. La Farge later reworked the articles and added eight additional chapters in 1897 for publication as a book by The Century Company.[1] This work has suffered the fate of much nineteenth-century travel writing. While of little use today as a guide to Japan, it also lacks substantial value as a revealing historical document. In La Farge's day, however, these writings were highly successful and critically acclaimed. Contemporary reviewers felt that the text and the illustrations provided profound new insights into the country, its religion, its architecture, and its people.[2]

Of the over forty illustrations that La Farge reproduced in his writings, he executed fewer than a dozen in Japan. He created the rest around 1888 in his New York studio, working from photographs, book illustrations, his own on-the-spot sketches, and memory.[3] In order to expedite the translation of the illustrations into black and white, he employed monochromatic media such as charcoal or sepia washes (Fig. 25). The transfer of most of the images to the printed page was accomplished by the photogravure process that had become popular during the 1880s. This circumvented the hand of the engraver, employing mechanical reduction to transform the design to black and white. Even so, La Farge evidently appreciated the aesthetic effects of conventional wood engraving, and had several plates specially rendered by his favorite engravers. At this time, La Farge did not work directly on uncut woodblocks, as he had in the 1860s. He prepared his design in ink wash or watercolor on paper. Photographic processes then trans-

1
John La Farge, *An Artist's Letters from Japan* (New York,1897).

2
Yarnall, "Role of Landscape," pp. 325-27, citing "[Review of] An Artist's Letters from Japan," *Art Interchange* 27 (Nov. 1897), p. 320. Cf. Lefor, La Farge and Japan, p. 320; Waern, *John La Farge*, p. 80; and Adams, "Mind of John La Farge," p. 69.

3
A sepia drawing of the temple of Iyemitsu in the Metropolitan Museum of Art is the only one of these designs to bear any evidence of dating. On the backing paper formerly attached to the picture, La Farge had written the date 1888 and the words "Jap. series," suggesting that similar works were undertaken at this time.

ferred the design to a woodblock for cutting by the engraver.[4]

This use of photographic methods left La Farge's original designs for illustrations intact. As a result, the artist found himself with a multitude of pictures for exhibition and sale. Since the early 1880s, he had commanded good prices for his watercolors, particularly floral subjects. His travel sketches quickly evolved into a second genre that brought the kind of money from picture sales that had eluded him during the 1860s. In 1887, La Farge began including large numbers of Japanese sketches when he sent his decorative studies to exhibitions at the Architectural League of New York. By 1890, he had built a solid critical reputation for these works and began holding one-man shows in different cities, seeking to broaden his market.[5] Each show featured between thirty and fifty Japanese travel pictures listed separately in the catalogues under the heading "Japanese Studies and Sketches."

When La Farge set off for the South Seas in August 1890, he departed in the midst of this burgeoning sale activity. He left matters in the hands of his son Bancel, then his primary assistant. Bancel was particularly astute at advancing the reputation of the travel sketches. During La Farge's absence in the South Seas, Bancel exhibited the artist's pictures in many forums, as far afield as Paris.[6] Augmenting this exposure was the wide circulation of La Farge's articles on Japan published in *Century Magazine* beginning in 1890. When the artist arrived back in New York in late 1891, he found the stage set for what became a virtual rage for his travel pictures.

Three months after his return from the South Seas, La Farge mounted a show that included over sixty of his Japanese works at the gallery of his Boston dealers, Doll and Richards. Half of the pictures sold within several days of the exhibition's opening, netting $5,000 (over $140,000 today).[7] La Farge still held in reserve the works that he had sent from the South Seas to Bancel, who had unpacked and stored them safely in the artist's New York studio. By late 1892, La Farge had reviewed, touched up, and framed these pictures in preparation for sale. In March 1893, he mounted at Doll and Richards a large exhibition composed of an even mixture of Japanese and South Sea subjects. The artist made $2,800 in sales for Japanese subjects and over $4,000 for South Seas pictures, for a total of almost $7,000 (nearly $196,000 today).[8]

The overwhelming success of these sales proved the great commercial appeal of La Farge's travel sketches. Their success can be attributed to various factors, among them the current fascination with exotic subject matter and a kinship in color and spontaneity to French Impressionism, then at the height of popularity in this country. In 1894, on one of several trips to Europe that he made late in his career, La Farge passed through Paris on his way to Italy. He mingled there in the artistic circles of the Société Nationale des Beaux-Arts, the controlling authority of the annual French Salons. A contemporary newspaper recounted the outcome:

> *It appears that Mr. La Farge was some time ago the guest of Puvis de Chavannes, Carolus-Duran and other Frenchmen at a dinner in Paris. He was invited by them to make a special display of his work at the next Salon of the Champs de Mars. Two rooms of the exhibition which opens in the spring have been assigned to him, and he has been gathering together his Samoan and Japanese sketches to show with his designs in glass . . .* [9]

Such an invitation to show two rooms of pictures at the Salon was a special honor accorded to few artists during the nineteenth century.[10] In response to the invitation, La Farge organized what he entitled his *Records of Travel* exhibition. This

4
La Farge's notes to the engraver appear on a proof of one wood engraving now in the La Farge Family Papers (Yale). The notes include his complaints about contrast, handling of line, and use of shadow by the engraver.

5
Doll and Richards, Boston, *Catalogue of Drawings, Watercolors, and Paintings by Mr. John La Farge on Exhibition and Sale*, 25 Jan.-6 Feb. 1890; Reichard and Co., New York, *Catalogue of Drawings, Water Colors, and Paintings by Mr. John La Farge*, 15 Apr.-1 May 1890; Saint Louis Exposition, Saint Louis, Missouri, *Catalogue of the Art Collection of the St. Louis Exposition and Musical Hall Association. Seventh Annual Exhibition*, [Sept.] 1890.

6
In June 1891, Durand-Ruel had included seven watercolors by La Farge in his Paris gallery's *Exposition des Peintures et Sculptures d'Artistes Américains*, cat. nos. 90-96. Among the pictures shown were four Japanese travel pictures and one Hawaiian landscape. Bancel also showed the Japanese and South Sea sketches to selected visitors who came to the studio at the suggestion of La Farge and Adams as a result of correspondence from the South Seas.

7
Doll and Richards, Boston, *Catalogue of Drawings, Watercolors, and Paintings by Mr. John La Farge on Exhibition and Sale*, 25 Mar.-6 Apr. 1892. Prices contained in "List of Pictures, Doll and Richards" p. 4.

8
Doll and Richards, Boston, *Catalogue of Water Color and Oil Paintings by Mr. John La Farge on Exhibition and Sale*, 10-22 Mar. 1893. Prices contained in "List of Pictures, Doll and Richards," pp. 2-3.

9
"The Chronicle of Arts," *New York Tribune*, 24 Feb. 1895, p. 24.

10
Phone conversation with Lois Marie Fink, Curator of Research, National Museum of American Art, Smithsonian Institution, 19 Oct. 1987.

11
"Our Artistic Library," *Boston Sunday Herald*, 17 Feb. 1895, p. 13. Doll and Richards, Boston, *Exhibition and Private Sale of Paintings in Water Color and Oil from the South Sea Islands and Japan*, 14-20 Feb. 1895. Durand-Ruel Galleries, New York, *Paintings, Studies, Sketches and Drawings, Mostly Records of Travel 1886 and 1890-91 by John La Farge*, 25 Feb.-5 Mar. 1895. Salon of 1895, Champ de Mars, Paris, France, *Etudes, esquisses, dessins: Souvenirs et notes de voyage (1886 and 1890-91) par John La Farge, traduction du catalogue américain*, Mar.-Apr. 1895.

12
"List of Pictures, Doll and Richards," p. 3.

assemblage of over two hundred travel sketches of Japan and the South Seas was shown first in February 1895 at Durand-Ruel Galleries in New York. In March, a slightly smaller version of the exhibition traveled to Paris for showing at the Salon. La Farge also held what the press called a "send-off" of the pictures at the gallery of Doll and Richards in Boston in January 1895.[11] This smaller grouping consisted of sixty-five South Sea works that still belonged to La Farge and were to be included in the *Records of Travel* exhibition. Just under half of the works sold during the preview, many at prices higher than previously realized for La Farge's watercolors. The artist's revenues from this sale totaled over $16,500 ($566,000 today).[12]

The promise of a Paris exhibition evidently proved a great boon to La Farge's sales, but it also created a serious problem in terms of organizing a well-rounded show. Many of the pictures he wanted to include had already been sold into private collections and it was not always easy to borrow them back for the exhibition. One anecdote epitomizing this dilemma recounts difficult dealings that La Farge encountered with Isabella Stewart Gardner. She had purchased a choice *sivà* picture from him only several months after his return from the South Seas (Isabella Stewart Gardner Museum, Boston).[13] La Farge had sold it on the condition that she would lend it back to him either to replicate in oil or to include in important exhibitions later on. His request for the loan came to her on October 19, 1894:

Would you rather let me have it now, that I may use it for my other work, or would it suit you better to send it to me for the Champ de Mars Salon this spring of 1895 or both . . . [14]

Forgetful of the conditions of sale, Mrs. Gardner refused to let the picture out of her hands again. She gave La Farge access long enough to make a careful replica in watercolor (The Carnegie Museum of Art, Pittsburgh).[15] This appeared at the Paris Salon in place of the original and it later served as the basis for an enlarged oil version destroyed by fire in 1914.[16]

Fortunately, many of the artist's friends or business associates were more than willing to lend back to La Farge the pictures they had purchased. The most generous collector in this regard was Henry Lee Higginson (1834-1919), the founder of the Boston Symphony Orchestra. Higginson had purchased at least thirty-five South Sea pictures directly from La Farge by 1893, when he began paying installments to the artist on a balance of just under $25,000 (roughly $693,000 today).[17] Another willing lender was Edward William Hooper (1839-1901), the brother of Henry Adams's late wife and the father of Mabel Hooper, who married La Farge's son Bancel in 1898. In conjunction with William Sturgis Bigelow, Hooper had purchased many South Sea studies between 1893 and 1895 from Henry Lee Higginson, their mutual friend.[18] Bigelow also acted independently, spending lavishly at Doll and Richards on La Farge's travel sketches.[19]

La Farge also painted many new works specifically for the exhibition, producing some of the best watercolor travel sketches of his career. Among the most beautiful is *Fayaway* (Fig. 43), a picture that represented for La Farge the essence of his South Sea experience. The subject derives directly from an episode of Herman Melville's romantic novel of life in the Marquesas Islands, *Typee* (1846), to which La Farge alluded repeatedly in his South Sea writings. In Melville's story, Fayaway ingeniously propels a canoe by removing her garment for use as a sail:

In a moment, the tappa was distended by the breeze—the long brown tresses of Fayaway

13
Philip Hendy, *Isabella Stewart Gardner Museum Catalogue of Exhibited Paintings and Drawings* (Boston, 1931), p. 197, recording purchase on 20 Jan. 1892.

14
Letter, John La Farge to Isabella Stewart Gardner, 19 Oct. 1894, Isabella Stewart Gardner Museum Archives, Boston.

15
The identification of the work as the replica owned by La Farge is confirmed by a typescript of lenders created at the time of the New York showing of the 1895 exhibition, La Farge Family Papers (Yale). No lender appears on the list for this picture, indicating that it belonged to the artist. Cf. Henry Adams *et al.*, *American Drawings and Watercolors in the Museum of Art*, Carnegie Institute (Pittsburgh, 1985), pp. 67-69.

16
Although only the underpainting of the oil was completed before La Farge's death, Grace Edith Barnes put the picture on the market in 1912 (letter to Robert C. Vose, Jan. 12, 1912, Vose Galleries Papers). In 1914, Vose exhibited the work in a show without a published catalogue (see "Works by John La Farge," *Boston Evening Transcript*, 25 Mar. 1914, p. 9). The painting's destruction by fire in July 1914 is recorded on a gallery inventory card (Vose Card 3251, Vose Galleries Papers).

17
Mr. and Mrs. Henry Lee Higginson are discussed in Pamela S. Taaba, "The Great Boston Collectors: The Copley Square Years," *The Great Boston Collectors* (Boston, 1984), p. 16. No complete inventory of Higginson's works has been located, but a partial list indicating the approximate number of works and history of payments is in the Letterpress Book of Bancel La Farge, p. 77, La Farge Family Papers (Yale). This listing is dated 16 Feb. 1896 and is entitled: "Statement regarding picture account with Henry L. Higginson." Higginson purchased three additional South Sea pictures through Doll and Richards in 1895 for a total of $1925 (over $64,000 today), as recorded in "List of Pictures, Doll and Richards," p. 3.

streaming in the air—and the canoe shot towards the shore . . . a prettier mast than Fayaway was never shipped aboard any craft.[20]

Fayaway symbolized uncorrupted natural beauty and innocent goodness, what the nineteenth century considered the "natural man." Writing in his journal as he left Hawaii, La Farge noted his yearning to see a "Fayaway sail her boat in some other Typee" before the close of their South Sea tour.[21] The year after he returned from the South Seas, La Farge conceived his first image of *Fayaway* when commissioned for a frontispiece to illustrate an edition of Melville's *Typee.*[22] Over the next several years, La Farge evolved the final idealized watercolor representation of Fayaway, at first setting the scene before the Tautira River Valley in Tahiti, and later employing a simple azure expanse of water.[23] *Fayaway* ultimately served as the centerpiece of an article on Hawaii published in *Scribner's Magazine* in 1901 that formed part of a serialization of La Farge's South Sea writings.[24]

The *Records of Travel* exhibition was a great success in New York, but in Paris it failed miserably. Reviewers ignored the works, a snub that seems to have been deliberately planned. Royal Cortissoz, the art critic for the New York *Herald-Tribune* who later became La Farge's second major biographer, went to Paris specifically to meet with Ary Renan, who was in charge of the official notices of the salon. Cortissoz hoped to submit a review of La Farge's works that could be translated into French and published alongside the regular reviews distributed by the salon critics. Renan told him:

Our critic will, as he always does, enjoy in full freedom the works of Mr. La Farge, but they do not seem to us to merit a separate study. Their success among artists does not match your expectations.[25]

It is difficult to comprehend such an aloof response to his work, given the previous warm welcome that La Farge had received in France. Perhaps it can be traced to professional jealousy or the nationalistic and political undercurrents of the time, or it may have reflected a genuine deficiency in terms of works sent to Paris.[26] In any case, La Farge's contribution to the Paris Salon of 1895 went almost unnoticed in France.

The failure of the *Records of Travel* exhibition in Paris had little impact on sales of La Farge's travel pictures in this country. He continued to offer Japanese and South Sea sketches in scaled-back versions of the show that traveled to Cleveland in 1896-1897, to Chicago in early 1897, and to Saint Louis in mid-1897.[27] In fact, until the end of his career, La Farge continued to derive income from sales of his travel pictures in shows of all kinds. Indeed, his success in selling these pictures was so great that La Farge found himself in the dilemma of having too few good examples to either exhibit or sell. This seems to be the primary reason that he frequently made replicas or variations on works as he sold them, creating a mind-boggling situation for scholars seeking to date pictures and understand the artist's development.

La Farge had never hesitated to copy or recycle his works, at times by using photography to transfer a design for use as a sort of underdrawing to paint over.[28] Commercial gain motivated this activity on occasion, but more often than not La Farge seems to have simply enjoyed rendering a successful design in another medium or repeating a favorite motif with variations. His skill as a copyist, formed at a young age under the tutelage of his grandfather, has led to great confusion over the years in studying his work and charting the development of his style. The best example of the

18
Both individuals are notable for collecting the works of other artists as well. Hooper had impressive holdings of pictures by Whistler and Homer, as well as old master paintings. Although it is as yet unclear just how the works were shared or transferred, Higginson alluded to this relationship in a letter recently discovered by Mary A. La Farge (Higginson to Mabel Hooper La Farge, 11 Feb. 1911, Private Archives, New Canaan, Connecticut): "[La Farge] & I always had friendly & agreeable relations-& he gave me the first chance at his Samoan sketches, which your father [Edward Hooper], [William] Sturgis [Bigelow] & I divided." Another allusion to the sharing of works was made by Hooper, who annotated a copy of La Farge's *Records of Travel* exhibition catalogue, La Farge Family Papers (Yale), with the numbers from Higginson's listing of works, terming them "our works".

19
In 1892, he put down $1,400 ($40,000 today) for two of the finest Japanese sketches. In 1895, he purchased six South Sea pictures for a total of $2,750 ($92,000 today). See "List of Pictures, Doll and Richards," pp. 2-3.

20
Herman Melville, *Typee* (New York: Dodd, Mead and Co., 1951), p. 144.

21
"Passages from a Diary in the Pacific: Hawaii," *Scribner's Magazine* 29 (May 1901), pp. 545-46.

22
Arthur Stedman, notes and introduction to Herman Melville, *Typee: A Real Romance of the South Seas* (New York, 1892), ill. p. xxxviii. Cf. La Farge to Arthur Stedman, 9 Mar. 1892, Gratz Manuscripts, Archives of American Art, Smithsonian Institution (Reel P22, frame 279); and letter, La Farge to Stedman, attached to verso of drawing when sold at Sotheby's Arcade Auctions, New York, *American 19th and 20th Century Paintings, Drawings and Sculpture*, 20 Jan. 1987, lot 109.

23
The watercolor of Fayaway before the Tautira River Valley is privately owned. It follows the pose of the figure in the final version closely, although it is rendered with less idealization.

pitfalls that this practice continues to impose on La Farge scholarship is the case of two watercolors related to the artist's early drawing of his wife and young son Bancel in the pose of a Madonna and Child (Fig. 4).

Due to the subject depicted, for years scholars supposed that these watercolors dated from the mid-1860s, considering them as attempts to color the composition in preparation for transferring the design into oils. Since one watercolor depicts the main figure in pink against a green background (Fig. 44) and the other employs a light blue figure on a pink background (Fig. 45), scholars suspected that optical theories of color perception also might be involved. Both watercolors display subtle handling, combining gouache and watercolor in vibrant, translucent layers over graphite underdrawing. This mastery of effects seemed to suggest that La Farge had attained great proficiency in watercolor early in his career.

Several years ago, however, documentation discovered in a scrapbook kept by the original owner of one of the watercolors (Fig. 44), Dr. Charles Carroll Lee (1839-1893), shattered these theories. Lee had attended Mount Saint Mary's College with La Farge during the early 1850s and they became fast friends.[29] During the 1860s, Lee frequently took his family to Paradise, where the children of both families recalled playing together. In later years, Lee and La Farge attended auctions together in New York and belonged to the same men's clubs. In 1884, Lee purchased the drawing of a mother and child at one of La Farge's auctions, evidently attracted to it as a memento of the days he had spent with La Farge's family.[30] In his scrapbook, Lee noted that he asked La Farge to copy the design into watercolor in May 1888. Obligingly, the artist then "retraced and carefully colored" the drawing for Lee.[31] La Farge made two watercolor versions of the drawing, the one given to Lee and the other kept for later sale. The two watercolors and the drawing are of nearly identical size, buttressing Lee's statement that the copying involved some sort of tracing process. The dating of both watercolors to 1888 today seems logical. Nothing in La Farge's early watercolor work of the 1860s suggests that he could have handled the medium with such proficiency then.

The most original foray into watercolor painting during La Farge's late career occurred around 1897 when he turned out roughly twenty-five pictures inspired by oriental subjects. Exhibited together in 1898 at Doll and Richards as "Fantasies on Oriental Themes," the works portray incidents from Japanese and Chinese history, folklore, literature, and mythology.[32] La Farge seems to have become interested in these subjects as an offshoot of lectures on Japanese painters that he prepared in 1893 and 1896.[33] These pictures may have been intended for display during the lectures, or perhaps La Farge planned to publish the lectures with illustrations based on the watercolors.

Today, the majority of these so-called "oriental fantasies" are lost, but those that have turned up are among La Farge's best late works in any media. Some of the pictures are quasi-historical, such as the startling *The Strange Thing Little Kiosai Saw in the River* (The Metropolitan Museum of Art, New York), a factual account of an episode in the life of the painter, Kiosai. Others are delightfully perplexing, such as the vividly colored and vigorously painted *The Aesthete* (Plate 13) that La Farge captioned in French:

La Paix descend sur tout chose,
Mon esprit calme se repose
Dans l'équilibre du milieu.[34]

24
"Passages from a Diary in the Pacific: Hawaii," pp. 537-46; "Passages from a Diary in the Pacific: A First Day in the South Seas," *Scribner's Magazine* 29 (Jun. 1901), pp. 670-84; "Passages from a Diary in the Pacific: Tahiti," *Scribner's Magazine* 30 (Jul. 1901), pp. 69-83. A fourth article on Fiji that was not related to this early series of articles and reproduces a folk tale, not a travelogue, is "A Fiji Festival," *Century Magazine* 67 (Feb. 1904), pp. 518-26. Although the ultimate product that La Farge envisioned from his journals and sketches was a book, the book that was published by Grace Edith Barnes after his death, *Reminiscences of the South Seas*, was not what he had in mind.

25
Letter, Ary Renan to Royal Cortissoz, 23 Apr. 1895, Royal Cortissoz Correspondence, Beinicke Rare Book and Manuscript Library, Yale University, New Haven, Connecticut. The translation from the original French is my own. Cortissoz discussed his visit to Paris in *John La Farge*, p. 183.

26
Only about half of the works shown in New York were shown in Paris. In the catalogue of the Paris exhibition, works not actually shown were listed but bracketed. Edith Wharton, writing to Royal Cortissoz in 1926, noted that she would "never forget the sharp drop I felt when I saw his [La Farge's] collection of water colours years ago in some French exhibition," evidently a reference to this show. See letter, Edith Wharton to Royal Cortissoz in R.W.B. Lewis and Nancy Lewis, eds., *The Letters of Edith Wharton* (New York, 1988), p. 488.

27
Gallery of the Picture Exhibition Society, Cleveland, *Catalogue. Paintings, Studies, Sketches and Drawings, Mostly Records of Travel 1886 and 1890-91, by John La Farge*, 23 Dec. 1896-5 Jan. 1897. Art Institute of Chicago, Chicago, *Catalogue. Paintings, Studies, Sketches and Drawings, Mostly Records of Travel 1886 and 1890-91, by John La Farge*, 26 Jan.-21 Feb. 1897. Saint Louis Museum of Fine Arts, Saint Louis, Missouri, *A Group of Paintings, Studies, and Sketches, Records of Travel 1886, 1890, and 1891, by John La Farge*, 5-20 Mar. 1897.

28
Yarnall, "New Insights on John La Farge and Photography," pp. 61-77.

29
Two years of their education at the school overlapped. Lee graduated in 1856.

30
Lee purchased the drawing at the Ortgies and Company auction held in New York, lot 75, as "Madonna and Child. Crayon on India paper."

31
"Catalogue of Charles Carroll Lee," [not paginated], Archives, Mount Saint Mary's College, Emmitsburg, Maryland. This typescript was provided by Kelly Fitzpatrick, Director of the Archives.

32
Doll and Richards, Boston, *Exhibition and Private Sale of Paintings in Water Color Chiefly from South Sea Islands and Japan by Mr. John La Farge*, 18-30 Mar. 1898, cat. nos. 17-38.

33
John La Farge, "An Artist of Japan: Lecture Delivered Before the Architectural League of New York (With Illustrations), June 1893" (unpublished manuscript, La Farge Family Papers [Yale]); John La Farge, *Hokusai: A Talk About Hokusai, The Japanese Painter at The Century Club, March 28, 1896* (New York, 1897).

34
[Peace descends on all things, /My calm spirit reposes/ In the equilibrium of the scene]. Doll 1898, cat. no. 24. A plaque on the frame of the picture repeats this brief poem, and includes the date 1898 for the picture.

35
Letter, D. Dodge Thompson to author, 29 Sept. 1987, Henry A. La Farge Papers. Thompson suggested a hanging scroll by Huang Shen (1687-after 1768) of a *Man Gazing at Magnolias* in the Freer Gallery of Art, Washington, D.C. (acc. no. 62.14) as a suitable prototype.

36
Doll 1898, cat. no. 17.

37
Doll 1898, cat. no. 17, *A RISHI CALLING UP A STORM*; cat. no. 18, *SAME SUBJECT. A RISHI AND ATTENDANT*; cat. no. 19, *SAME SUBJECT. A GROUP OF RISHIS.* The first picture in the group is the one known today. The second picture was last known in 1941 when it appeared on the New York art market. Henry A. La Farge viewed it at that time and noted in his unpublished catalogue raisonné: "In immediate foreground, a robed figure, standing on cliff, facing left, followed by a smaller figure who raises one arm. The main figure in red mantle over green robes fluttering in the wind, silhouetted against rich blue background (water or sky?). Whitish clouds, horizontal, move across top (of picture). The smaller figure clad in violet dress." The last picture in the group has not resurfaced since the 1898 exhibition. It was described only once in "The Fine Arts: Exhibition of South Sea Islands and Japan. Pictures by John La Farge," *Boston Weekly Transcript*, 25 Mar. 1898, p. 5: "we see a lofty green promontory from the top of which no less than five Rishis overlook a vast expanse of splendid blue ocean. These Rishis wear costumes of yellow, red, purple and green; and they are busily beckoning up the spirit of the storm from the vasty [sic] deep, which is beginning to stir uneasily from its sleep in response to their invocation."

Imagery similar to that seen in *The Aesthete* appears in Chinese Zen scroll paintings of the Ch'ing dynasty, where philosophers and priests meditate on nature.[35] La Farge has introduced several layers of ambiguity into this basic premise. The aesthete reclines before a landscape vista that is actually a large screen painting. He is absorbed in this scene, but whether his pleasure derives from the beauty of the work of art or the beauty of the landscape shown in the work is left for the viewer to ponder. A strange instance of life imitating art is provided by a vase of flowers nearly lost in front of the screen, while from an incense burner, a vaporous trail rises into the air. The picture is a clever conceit that baffles without disappointing. The handling of watercolor is virtuosic but extremely subtle, drawing the viewer into the work without drawing attention to itself.

More legendary and less elusive in content is La Farge's animated watercolor of a creature called a Rishi (Plate 14). According to the artist, "Rishis in Chinese and Japanese myth are human beings who have attained practical immortality, and who, retired in wild places, enjoy control over nature."[36] Although La Farge painted three watercolors of Rishis in the act of summoning up storms, this is the only one that can be presently located.[37] It shows the imaginary being standing resolutely on a rocky protrusion against a backdrop of wetly painted waves that break with a fury reminiscent of the most tempestuous seascapes of Winslow Homer. The Rishi's garments, whipped by the winds of the storm he summons, echo the calligraphic swirls of the nearby sea.

The *Spirit of the Storm* (Fig. 46) complements this depiction of a Rishi, in essence portraying the answer to his summons. La Farge swirled heavy washes of watercolor into a vortex to represent the spirit of the gathering storm. The spirit is not entirely incorporeal, but has two small hands delineated with wide strokes that appear to have been made by a Japanese brush. The hands evidently serve the useful purpose of allowing the spirit to grasp a tree in order to build up the tension that will propel it forth like a rock fired from a slingshot.[38]

For many artists, such a diverse and imaginative body of material as this might suffice for a late career but, for La Farge, it was simply the product of spare time in a life dedicated to decorative work. During his last twenty-five years, he executed five major mural schemes and hundreds of stained-glass windows. During this period, he maintained a large studio at the Tenth Street Studio Building in New York. He surrounded himself with a retinue of helpers and personal assistants, including his son Bancel, his personal valet Awoki, and his secretary and later executrix, Grace Edith Barnes.

The most pressing decorative project facing La Farge after his return from Japan was the commission for a mural in the Church of the Ascension, New York (Fig. 29). The vestry of the church had approved the artist's proposal for a mural on June 4, 1886, the day he departed for Japan.[39] By then, La Farge had already decided on the general grouping of apostles around the figure of the risen Christ, a composition derived from hybrid Renaissance sources.[40] In Japan, he found an appropriate "stage" for this tableaux, the contours of Mount Fuji viewed from the plain below (Fig. 30). In early 1887, La Farge began drawings and color studies for specific parts of the mural. Most of the surviving studies are for angels surrounding the figure of the protagonist like "a halo of spiritual meaning around the Christ."[41] The artist painted these pictures in heavy, wetly applied watercolor and gouache. They convey succinctly the painterly feeling and iridescent tone captured by La Farge's assistants in rendering the mural.[42]

La Farge's murals and stained glass of the late 1880s and 1890s display features different from his earlier work. His figures attain a new breadth of handling, dignity of presentation, majesty of form, and solemnity of gesture. His settings are more atmospheric and illusionistic, a feature particularly well suited to distant viewing of the decorations. The interaction of figure and setting is more integrated and natural, lending the entire composition great conviction. In glass, an early emphasis on jewel-like ornamentation gives way to broader, flatter planes of plated and juxtaposed glass used to form palpable ambiances for the figures. The contrasts are most evident when La Farge returned to decorative motifs from his earlier works. In 1889, the artist adapted his altarpiece in the Church of St. Thomas to a two-lancet memorial window for the Church of the Ascension. In the right lancet of the window, he placed the three Marys in a slightly altered pose from that adopted for the mural. In the left lancet, he represented the angels of the Resurrection, gesturing to the women that Christ had arisen. The landscape setting, which the mural had treated in realistic terms, appears in the window as a shimmering curtain of streaming light and color. La Farge's primary color study for the angelic figures in the window shows this feature (Fig. 47). With a series of bands of cloud, land, and sky that evoke the mysterious, ethereal realm appropriate to the subject, the artist created a moody and atmospheric setting for the scene.

La Farge's last major ecclesiastical decorative project was carried out for the Church of St. Paul the Apostle in New York. This commission came as a result of the artist's long and close relationship with Father Isaac Thomas Hecker, founder of the Paulist order. Hecker had conceived the idea of building a monumental church during the late 1860s. He consulted La Farge on the church as early as 1875, initially for advice on architectural matters.[43] La Farge's deeper involvement began nearly a decade later, after the completion of the exterior of the Church. In 1884, the La Farge Decorative Art Company received a contract to paint an illusionistic ceiling representing the "starry firmament on the 25th of January, 1885, the festival of the conversion of St. Paul, the patron of the church."[44] The company also may have been responsible for coloring the upper nave walls at this time. After an interlude due to the dissolution of the company, La Farge resumed work in 1887 and for the next several years designed windows for the facade and nave.

Hecker died in 1888 and, as a memorial to him, the decoration of the chancel was undertaken in 1895 under the direction of his niece, Mrs. Jesse Albert Locke (née Caroline Hecker).[45] By this time, La Farge was working in close association with his son Bancel, who had begun serving as his father's primary assistant around 1886. During the late 1890s, La Farge and Bancel made numerous proposals for murals and stained glass for the chancel. Many of these designs seem to have been joint products of both hands, if not solely Bancel's. A group of highly finished color studies executed around 1896 (Cooper-Hewitt Museum of Design, Smithsonian Institution, New York) are clearly a product of La Farge's overall vision, but the watercolor is applied with a meticulousness and lack of verve that suggests the hand of Bancel overlaying La Farge's design.

The identification of different studio hands in La Farge's late works is an issue that remains as problematic today as it was in his own time. La Farge was an adamant proponent of the *bottega* concept of the Italian Renaissance, whereby the master conducted work through his assistants.[46] To execute his late murals and large easel paintings, he employed any help he could get, in at least one instance putting his secretary, Grace Edith Barnes, to work on a backdrop with a brush.[47] At other times, he person-

38
Only three additional "oriental fantasies" can be located today, and all are privately owned. They include a representation of a human-like *Uncanny Badger* before a waterfall, beating his hands against his stomach; a quasi-historical portrait of the Chinese poet Li-Tai-Pe, garbed in a robe swirling with color and standing before a wondrous opalescent waterfall pouring over the side of a cliff; and *Kwannon, Bearer of the Lily, Protectress of the Sea*, depicting the Japanese goddess Kannon or Kwannon floating above a dark ocean. These pictures are rendered sensuously with painterly abandon. Among the works in this series that have remained unknown since 1897, there are some worth listing if only to suggest delightful pictures that may yet turn up: *The Tiger-Cat Butterfly, A Japanese Fantasy*; *Em Ma, a King of Hell*; *The Snow Ghost*; *The Bad Buddha*; *Kiomori Arresting the Sun*; *Choshi (Chuang Tseu) and the Butterfly*; and *The Chinese Princess*. Finally, there are several lost watercolors with decidedly non-oriental subject matter that La Farge inexplicably listed among his oriental fantasies: *The Pig-God. Hawaii*; *Ceylonese Girl Posing as Lakshmi, Goddess of Love and Fortune*; and *A Snake Spirit (Mexican)*.

39
Weinberg, *Decorative Work*, p. 177, citing *Minutes of the Meetings of the Vestry* 3 (1870-1904), 4 Jun. 1886, p. 232, Church of the Ascension Archives.

40
Weinberg, *Decorative Work*, p. 179.

41
John La Farge, "The Making of the Ascension," *New York Herald*, 5 Apr. 1903, second literary section, p. 2; cf. Weinberg, *Decorative Work*, p. 180. In 1909, La Farge claimed that he had not made "heaps of cartoons and studies" for the Ascension mural, and in fact stated that the landscape sketch of Mount Fuji was the only study necessary before the painting began (Notes on a conversation with La Farge, 18 May 1909, Royal Cortissoz Correspondence, Beinicke Rare Book and Manuscript Library, Yale University). This statement is contradicted by the many studies of angels for the mural that have survived.

42
The mural was executed in a special tempera mixture consisting of different oils, wax, and varnishes that Weinberg described as an "opalescent effect which gives an illusion of vaporous mystery consistent with the spiritual theme of the painting" in *Decorative Work*, p. 186.

43
Weinberg, *Decorative Work*, pp. 215-17.

44
Ibid., p. 221, citing *Journal of the Paulist Fair of 1884* 2 (6 Dec. 1884), p. 1, Paulist Fathers Archives, New York.

45
Ibid., p. 227.

ally executed a work up to a certain point and then turned it over to someone else. For example, La Farge annotated an 1898 color study for a window with a message to George Rose, an assistant at the time: "George, will you find time to finish this for me . . ."[48] La Farge even discussed the hypothetical situation whereby a future scholar of his work might seek to apply the so-called Morellian method of analyzing particular areas of his murals for various hands involved. Although such a critic might allege that he could attribute each part of a large tableaux to a different studio assistant, La Farge noted that "it would be a La Farge, all the same."[49] In his own day, La Farge was the target of criticism and legal action for his failure to distinguish between works from his own hand and pictures carried out for projects under his general direction. Today, the issue remains a potent one. Attempts to distinguish works by the artist himself from those executed by or with his assistants remains of paramount concern to collectors and scholars.

A large unfinished color study for an Angel of the Annunciation (Fig. 48) typifies the compositions of La Farge's late windows in which a single figure, often standing, fills the entire vaguely defined, atmospheric space of the window. There is minimal narrative other than the suggestiveness of the gesture, which in this case is that of the Archangel Gabriel announcing the coming of Christ to the Virgin in an adjoining window. The majestic serenity of the figure contrasts with the animated setting for the scene. At the top, the sun forms a halo of flames that cut across the upper lancet. At the bottom, cottony clouds billow into a support for the figure. The design is at once agitated and pensive, creating a tension of passive and active elements often found in La Farge's late decorative works.

The figures in La Farge's late windows tend to be emphatically realistic, to the extent that the features accurately identify the original model. In particular, he used one female model for angelic figures throughout the 1890s. She appears as the protagonist in mural ensembles in the Church of St. Paul the Apostle (the *Angel of the Sun* and the *Angel of the Moon*), as well as in two large cartoons for figures of *Adoration* (The Brooklyn Museum) never executed into a more finished media. A photograph from the artist's studio shows the model (Fig. 49) in a pose like that seen in the decorations of the Church of St. Paul the Apostle. This actually served as the basis for an unrelated window in a church in Sewickley, Pennsylvania.[50] La Farge translated the photograph faithfully into glass, evidently finding the photographic realism fully in keeping with the effects he desired.

The same photographic realism is apparent in two monumental windows designed around 1900 for the Long Island residence of financier William C. Whitney (1841-1904). Often said to be La Farge's "masterpieces in stained glass," these represent allegories of the seasons of *Autumn* and *Spring*.[51] Each window consists of a single monumental figure engulfed by a landscape swirling with leaves and flowers of the particular season. La Farge rendered dozens of drawings and several alternate color studies for each window. For *Autumn*, La Farge executed two elaborately painted color studies of identical size specifically to help Whitney decide the disposition of the figure in the window, as well as select the degree of nudity that would be employed.[52] One of these (Plate 15) shows the figure from the side, largely naked, dropping leaves into a pool below that contains her own clear reflection. The second (Fig. 50) depicts the figure frontally, fully clothed, with greater emphasis on the graceful pose and a less insistent reflection. Whitney chose the second study as the basis for the window. The companion window depicting *Spring* presents a half-naked female figure at close range, and all known color studies suggest that the artist never

46
Cortissoz, *John La Farge*, p. 239; cf. Frank Jewett Mather, "John La Farge—An Appreciation," *World's Work* 23 (Mar. 1911), pp. 14085-100.

47
Mather, "John La Farge," p. 14087. This allegedly took place around 1895 during the execution of the *Athens* mural for Bowdoin College. Ruth Berenson Katz, "John La Farge as Painter and Critic (unpublished Ph.D. dissertation, Radcliffe College, 1951), p. 136, proposed the hands of different assistants in La Farge's last major easel painting, *The Wolf Charmer* (now lost).

48
Minerva Decorating a Memorial Stele; Study for C.C. Felton Memorial Window, Harvard University, Cambridge, Massachusetts, The Brooklyn Museum, Brooklyn, acc. no. 26.433.

49
Cortissoz, *La Farge*, p. 239; cf. Mather, "John La Farge," p. 14087.

50
The window is the Emma Knox Cain and Amanda Knox Jennings Memorial Window in the east wall of the nave, The Presbyterian Church of Sewickley, Pennsylvania.

51
D. Dodge Thompson, "John La Farge's masterpieces in stained glass," *The Magazine Antiques* (Mar. 1989), pp. 708-17.

52
La Farge, "Catalogue Raisonné," entry G1902.1.

considered clothing the figure. The choice of composition and the question of whether or not to clothe the figures seem to have depended solely on coordinating the two windows in the confined space of a small hall.[53]

La Farge baffles many critics because he so consistently avoided consistency. At any given stage of his career, he would diverge from a tendency prevalent in his work and revert to a previous style. This is precisely the case for two windows executed for Wellesley College around 1900 that are reminiscent of his work of the early 1880s.[54] A thickly painted color study for *Semita Certe* calls to mind the works of Titian or Giorgione (Plate 16). The soft, fuzzy handling of landscape and idealized form of the figure stand in sharp contrast to La Farge's other late works. In both style and technique, the watercolor recalls the *Angel of Help* (Plate 5), executed in 1884.

La Farge's late activities took place against the backdrop of an often sad personal life. Although La Farge was in love with his work and evidently felt that he had made the right choice in deciding to all but abandon his family for it, his guilt never subsided. His faltering attempts to reconcile his need to stay in New York with his family residing in Newport never succeeded. La Farge's youngest son, John La Farge, S.J., gave a poignant summary of this situation.

In 1891, when I was a boy of eleven, Father returned from his trip to the South Seas with Henry Adams. . . . I was charmed to see that Father was a real person, who wore an impressive black beard. I was glad to know that I really had a father in fact, since my picture of him before that time had been quite indefinite. . . . The reason for father's absence from home was simple enough. He was so hampered by the enormous amount of decorative work he was doing, in murals and stained glass, that it seemed impossible for him to transfer his activities away from the city. He had tried living in Newport several times in earlier years, and each time he found it "impossible," . . . [55]

As the years advanced, La Farge compensated in part for this familial schism by employing his children in the studio. His eldest son Christopher Grant (known as Grant) became a primary aid to his father during the years of the La Farge Decorative Art Company. After its collapse, Grant formed an architectural firm with George Heins, the husband of La Farge's youngest sister Aimée, and provided his father with several opportunities for decorative work. La Farge's second eldest son, Bancel, eventually came to enjoy the closest affiliation with his father. Sometime around 1887, Bancel became both an assistant in executing work for La Farge and the artist's studio manager. This cooperative relationship continued until around 1900, when financial disputes led to a falling out. This resulted when, to help out his father in a time of need, Bancel agreed to work without wages, and even loaned him some of his personal savings. When it became evident that La Farge could not possibly repay the money, Bancel filed a lawsuit seeking restitution. Predictably, the legal action caused a rupture of major proportions, leading Bancel to move to Switzerland to live. The wound never really healed although, just before La Farge's death, he wrote to Bancel asking forgiveness and made him a beneficiary of his will.[56]

La Farge had made the equivalent of millions on sales of his watercolors during the early 1890s, but, as the decade closed, cost overruns for decorative commissions, legal problems, and a lush lifestyle of men's clubs, travel, and fine food left him bereft of funds. After Bancel left him, Grace Edith Barnes, La Farge's personal secretary, assumed the role of studio manager. During the artist's last decade, she literally ran his life, overseeing his speaking tours, writing career, exhibitions, sales, and even his

53
The windows were in place for only two years before Whitney died. Not long after their installation, Whitney expressed his dissatisfaction with them, claiming that they darkened the hall they were intended to illuminate. After Whitney's death, the *Spring* window was placed in a pool pavilion on another Whitney estate at Manhasset, Long Island, where it remained until 1977 when donated to the Philadelphia Museum of Art. The *Autumn* window was placed in the Payne Whitney house at 972 Fifth Avenue, New York, now the French Cultural Consulate, where it remains today.

54
The Wellesley commission dated back to 1897 and initially involved a five-lancet scheme with figures in each lancet. After several years of internal disputes among the different representatives of the college, La Farge carried out two individual windows in 1900-1901.

55
La Farge, *Manner is Ordinary*, pp. 3-4.

56
Ibid. Cf. La Farge, *Manner is Ordinary*, pp. 4-7.

daily personal needs. Much to her credit, she also persuaded the artist to review the vast contents of his studio, which had become filled with tens of thousands of drawings, photographs, and other paraphernalia. "I don't know if I have ever told you that my studies go by the thousands," he wrote just a year before his death to the editor Gustav Kobbe. "I have numbered and stamped 8000 for glass, and a little more, say for general subjects, and there must be 50,000 or 60,000 more."[57] La Farge ultimately kept but a small number of these works, often marking them in red ink with a seal that contained a cipher of his name in Japanese and annotating them to indicate subject matter and dating as best he could remember. Unfortunately, his memory frequently failed him.

Like Bancel, Grace Barnes unwittingly assisted La Farge's decline into increasingly greater debt, staving off bankruptcy by foregoing a salary and lending the artist her own savings. During the artist's last year, she briefly quit her employ with La Farge after fighting bitterly with him over money. When La Farge invited her back, she returned with the promise of inheriting whatever remained of his studio and personal effects.[58] She became the executrix of La Farge's estate, claiming the property, manuscripts, and pictures necessary to reimburse for her losses over the years.[59]

During these years, Margaret La Farge remained primarily on the sidelines. Although increasingly bitter at La Farge's inability to provide financially for the family, she stood by him at the end. In the spring of 1910, La Farge became gravely ill and entered a hospital in New York for several weeks. Margaret La Farge believed he would not survive this brush with death, but he rallied and left the hospital by July. Later that month, Margaret brought him to Newport, stoically determined to take care of him until the end. By September, La Farge had deteriorated mentally to such an extent that Margaret felt the need to place him in Butler Hospital, an insane asylum in Providence. He remained there until dying quietly in his sleep around six o'clock in the evening on November 14, 1910. "It is indeed a blessed relief to know that all is over," Margaret wrote to her son Bancel a couple of weeks later, "and to know that the terrible perplexities have come to an end so peacefully. I suppose there never was a more complicated nature in one person than your father or one more difficult to manage."[60]

At the time of his death, La Farge was more than $35,000 in debt, the equivalent of $575,000 today.[61] His estate sale in early 1911 made a great deal of news but did not bring in great prices. The proceeds did not even pay off the most pressing debts, forcing Margaret La Farge to contribute some of her personal financial resources to appease the most voracious creditors. Grace Barnes faced years of work selling leftover pictures, seeing unfinished manuscripts through publication, and generally seeking to recover her lost savings and wages. The family received almost nothing, although Grace Barnes allowed family members to look through La Farge's studio for any pictures or personal items that might have sentimental value. Margaret La Farge had to override La Farge's last wish to be buried at the fashionable Woodlawn Cemetery, just outside New York. To save several thousand dollars, she moved his body from a temporary crypt at Woodlawn, where it had been taken at the time of La Farge's funeral, to a vacant niche in the La Farge family mausoleum at Greenwood Cemetery in Brooklyn.[62] She aptly summed up this final financial defeat as "a shipwreck and tragic end to his most varied and remarkable career."[63]

57
Letter, John La Farge to Gustav Kobbe, 21 Nov. 1909, Private Archives, Princeton, New Jersey.

58
Letter, Margaret La Farge to Bancel La Farge, 30 Sept. 1910, La Farge Family Papers (Yale). Cf. La Farge, *Manner is Ordinary*, pp. 144-45.

59
Yarnall, "Role of Landscape," pp. 416-17.

60
Letter, Margaret La Farge to Bancel La Farge, 6 Dec. 1910, La Farge Family Papers (Yale).

61
"Debts May Eat Up La Farge's Estate," *New York Times*, 28 Dec. 1910, p. 3; "La Farge Left $599 Here," *New York Times*, 14 Jun. 1914, p. 1; letter, Margaret La Farge to Bancel La Farge, 18 Jul. 1911, La Farge Family Papers (Yale).

62
Letter, Margaret La Farge to Bancel La Farge, 29 May 1911, La Farge Family Papers (Yale). Cf. La Farge, *Manner is Ordinary*, p. 146.

63
Ibid.

La Farge's career and life had been nothing if not varied and remarkable. So too is the legacy of his work, which has provided students and connoisseurs with ample material for study and appreciation since his death eighty years ago. From the vicissitudes of fashion and reputation, La Farge has emerged as a leading artistic figure of his day, a virtual "Renaissance man" who was at once innovative and a guardian of tradition. His watercolors and drawings are an essential part of this legacy, providing a microcosmic view of his varied and complex work and a rich resource for future generations.

Illustrations

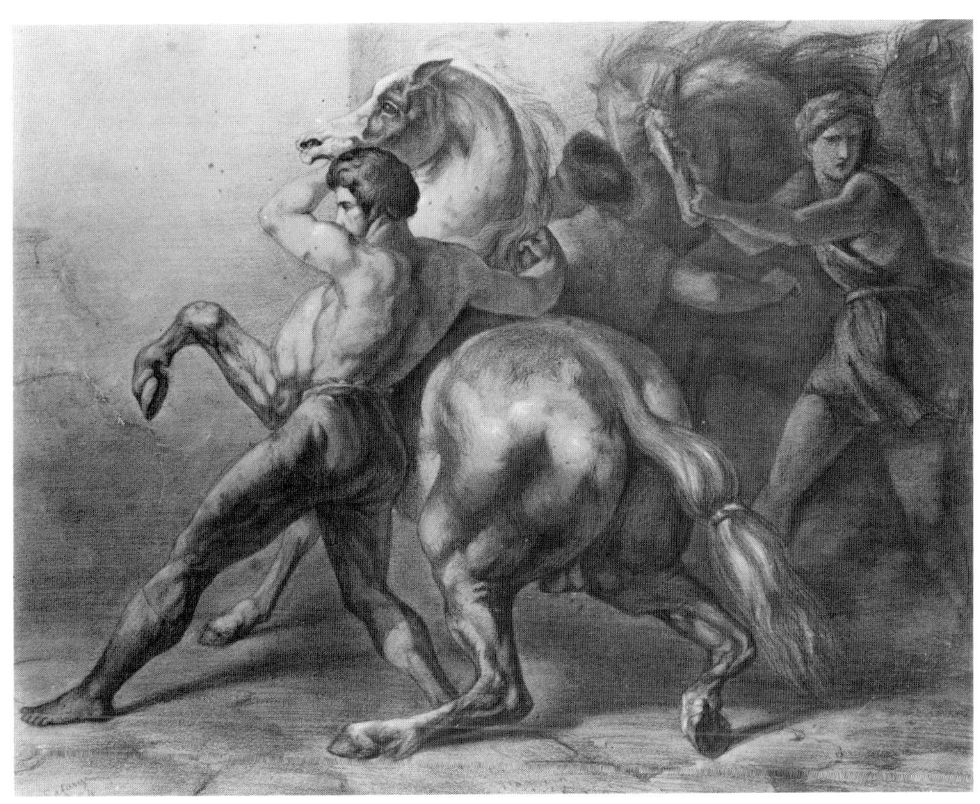

1

The Start of the Barbieri Horses,
after Gericault, 1854.

Carbon pencil and white chalk on paper.
Sight: 12 1/2 x 16 5/8 in. (31.0 x 56.4 cm.).
Private Collection.

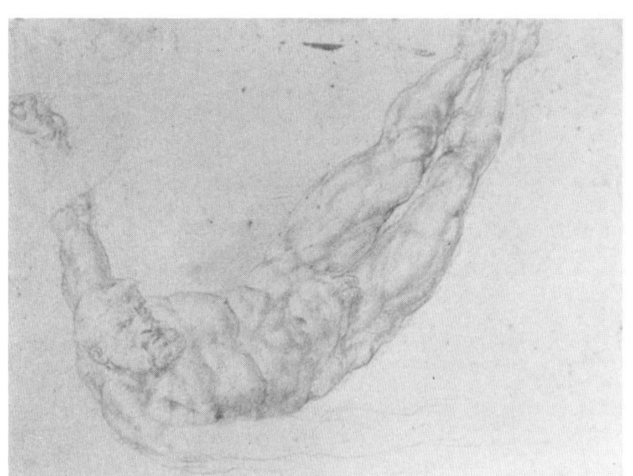

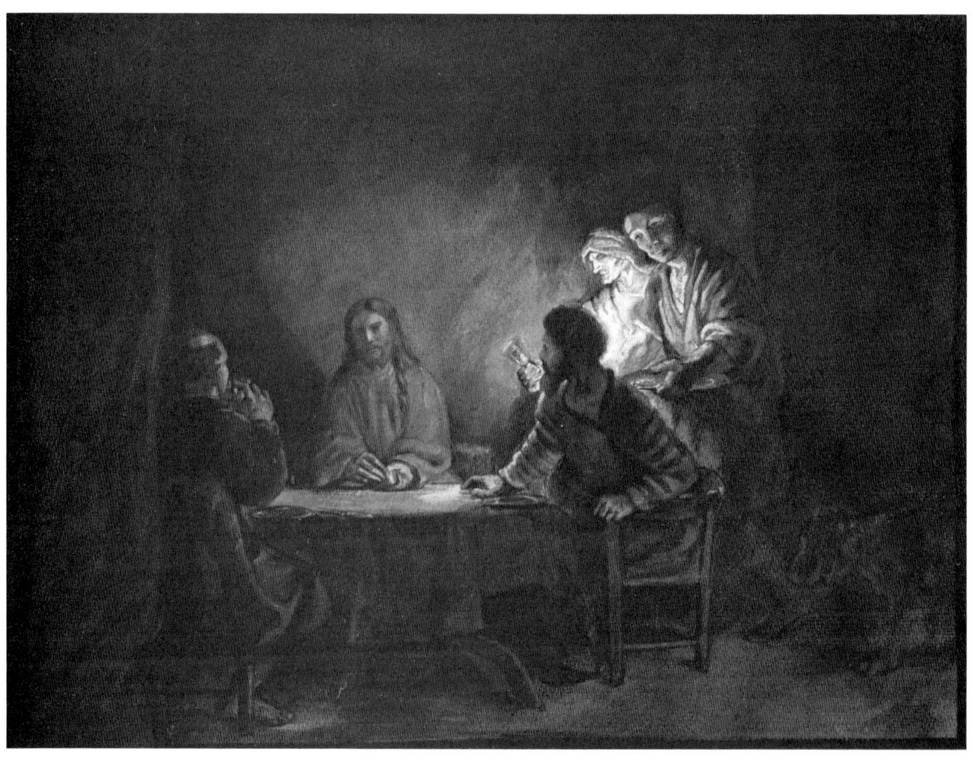

2

The Crucifixion of Saint Peter; Study after a drawing by Michelangelo for a mural in the Pauline Chapel of the Vatican, Rome, 1856.

Red chalk on grainy brown paper.
7 1/4 x 10 in. (18.0 x 25.4 cm.).
Bowdoin College Museum of Art, Brunswick, Maine.

3

Christ and the Disciples at Emmaus. Copy of Rembrandt. July 1856, 1856.

Watercolor and gouache or ink wash over graphite and possibly red chalk on paper.
13 x 17 1/2 in. (33.0 x 43.7 cm.).
Hood Art Museum, Dartmouth College, Gift of George Breed Zug, Class of 1920H.

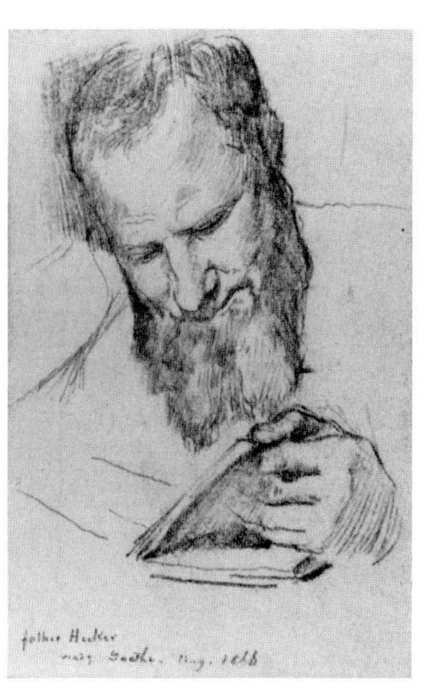

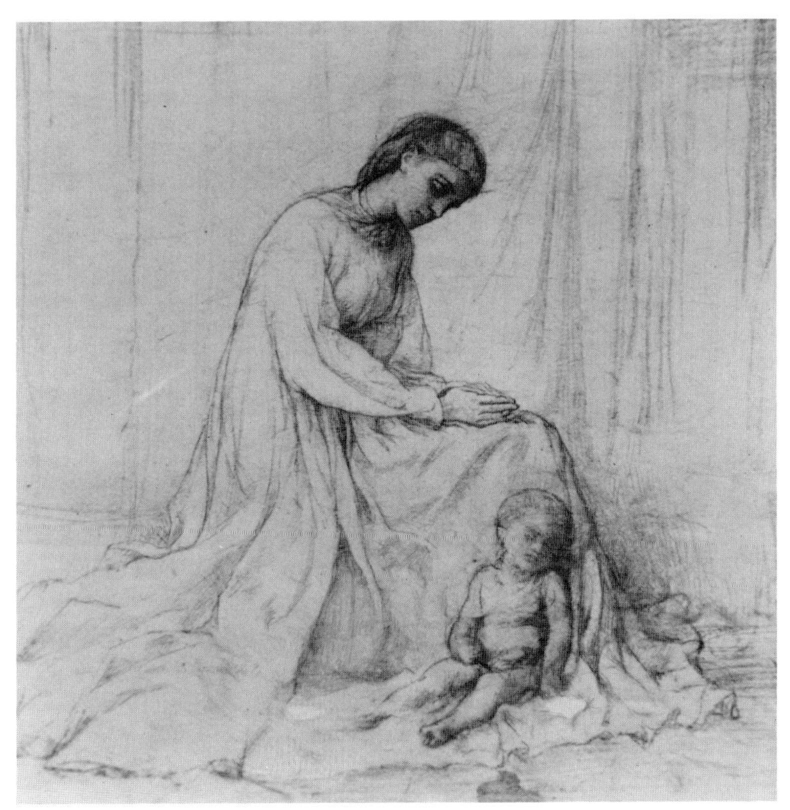

4

Mother and Child, c. 1866.

Graphite on Japanese mulberry vellum. Sight: 7 1/4 x 7 1/2 in. (18.3 x 18.9 cm.). Lee-La Farge Collection, Mount Saint Mary's College, Emmitsburg, Maryland.

5

Father Isaac Thomas Hecker Reading Goethe, 1866.

Charcoal on rice paper, mounted. 6 11/16 x 4 1/4 in. (16.2 x 10.8 cm.). The Metropolitan Museum of Art, New York, Gift of Mrs. Samuel M. Hamill, 1990.

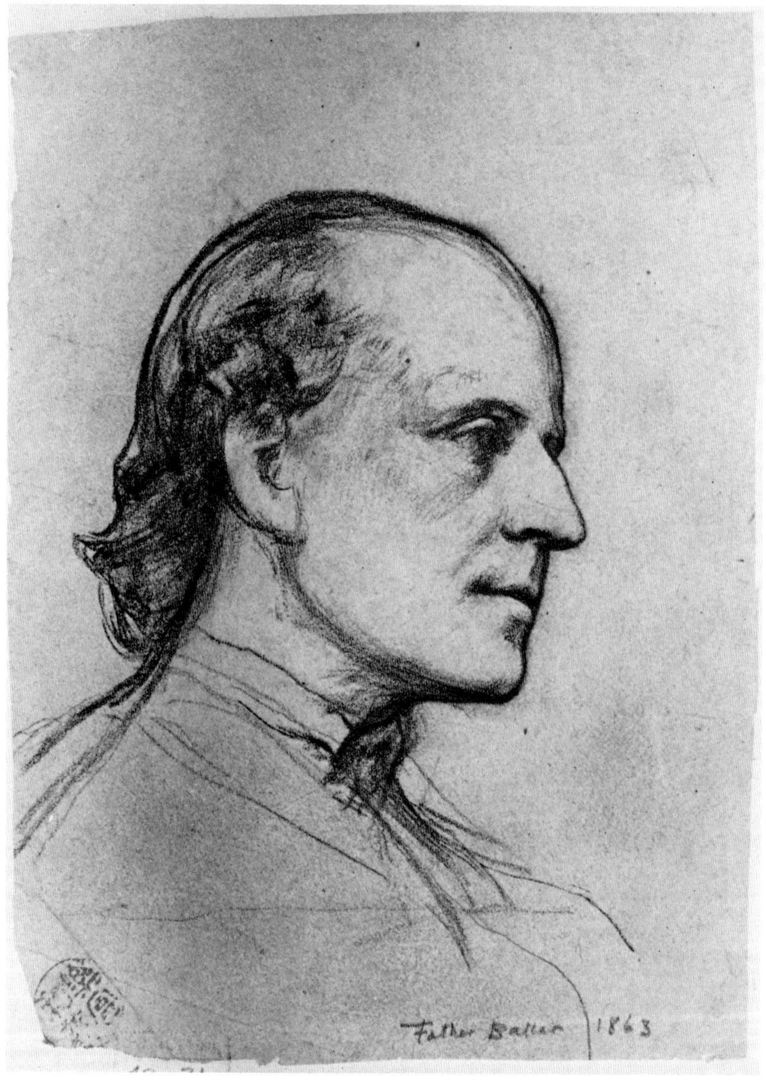

6

Father Francis Aloysius Baker, 1863.

Soft graphite or black crayon on thin paper.
5 7/8 x 4 in. (13.8 x 10.2 cm.).
The Art Museum, Princeton University,
Princeton, New Jersey. Gift of
Frank Jewett Mather, Jr.

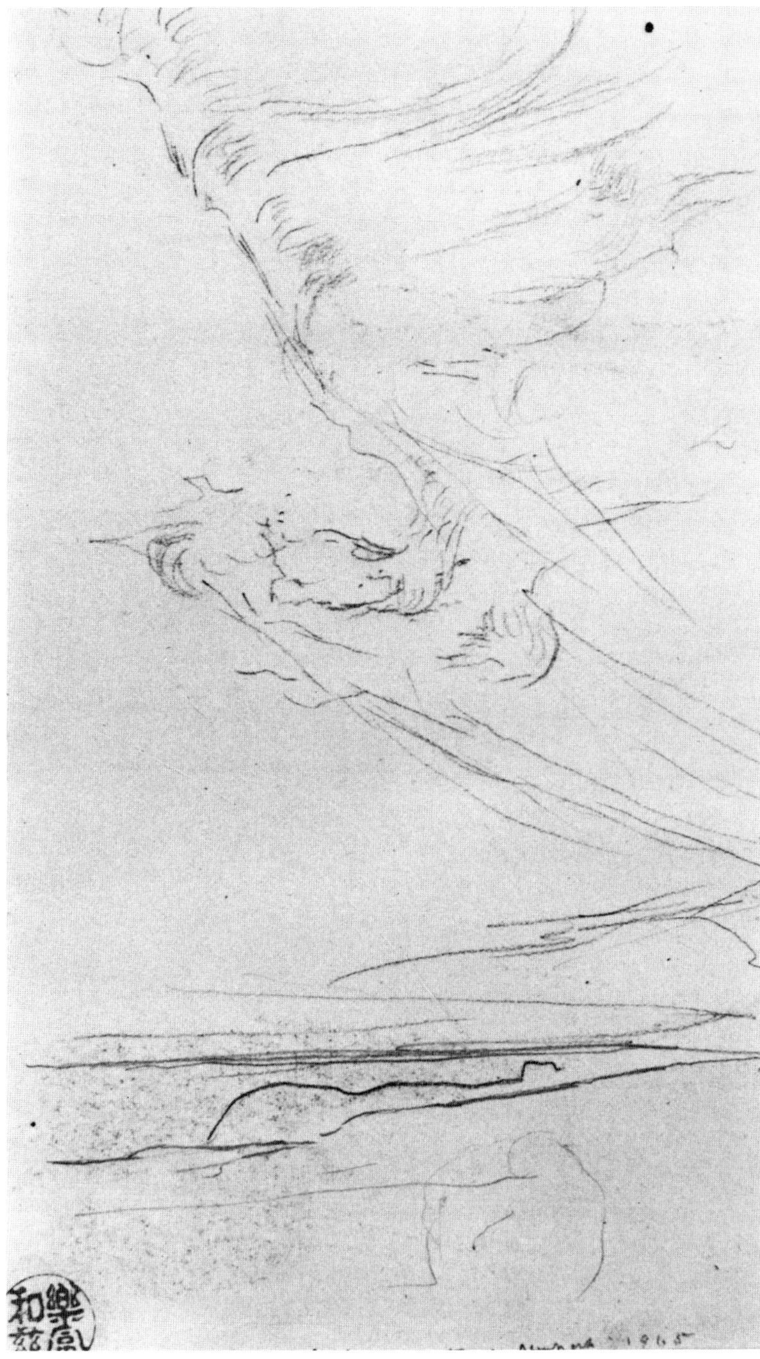

7

Study of Cloud Movement, Newport, 1865.

Graphite on paper.
Sight: 6 3/4 x 3 15/16 in. (17.2 x 10 cm.).
Museum of Fine Arts, Boston, Gift of Major H.L. Higginson

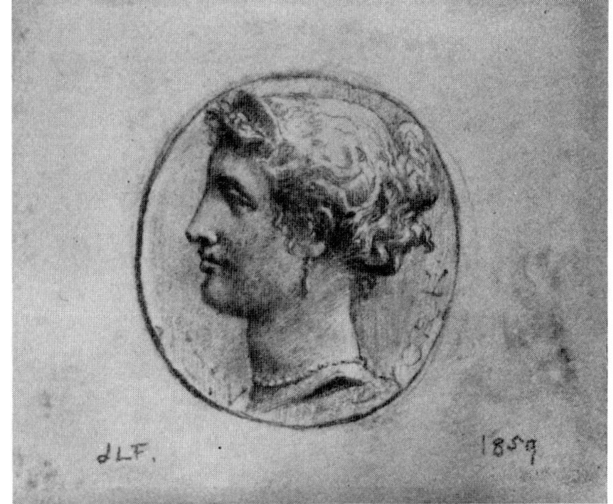

8

Design for a Coin (Allegory of New York), 1859.

Graphite on vellum.
2 5/16 x 2 7/8 in. (5.4 x 6.0 cm.).
Sterling and Francine Clark Art Institute, Williamstown, Massachusetts. Gift of L. Bancel La Farge.

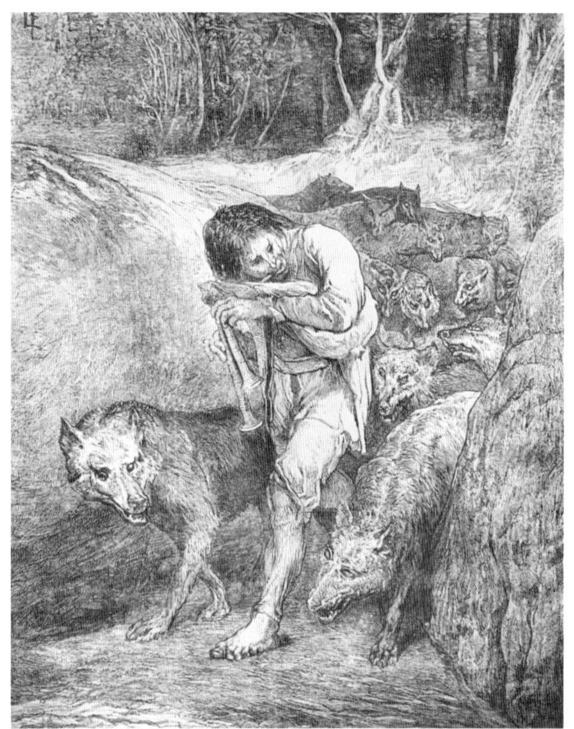

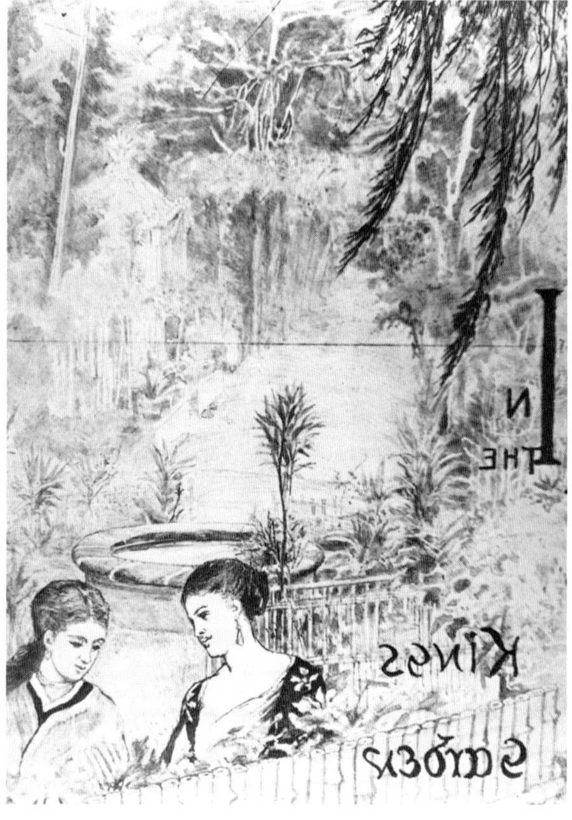

9

The Wolf-Charmer, 1867; published in *The Riverside Magazine for Young People*, December 1867.

Wood-engraving on paper.
6 5/8 x 5 5/16 in. (16.8 x 13.5 cm.).
Private Collection.

10

In the King's Garden, 1868.

India ink and Chinese white on uncut woodblock.
5 3/4 x 4 3/16 in. (13.5 x 10.3 cm.).
Private Collection.

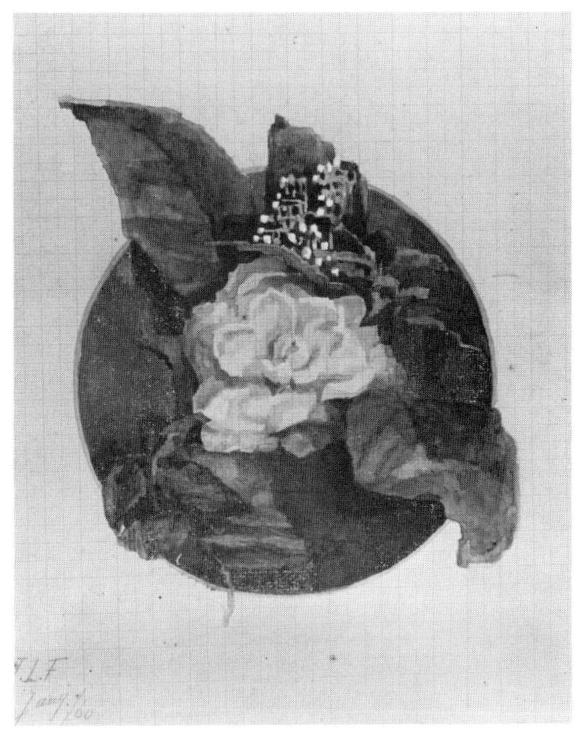

11

Study of Flowers for Embroidery, 1860.

Watercolor, gouache, and gold leaf over graphite on graph paper.
8 1/4 x 6 3/4 in. (21.0 x 17.0 cm.).
The Preservation Society of Newport County.

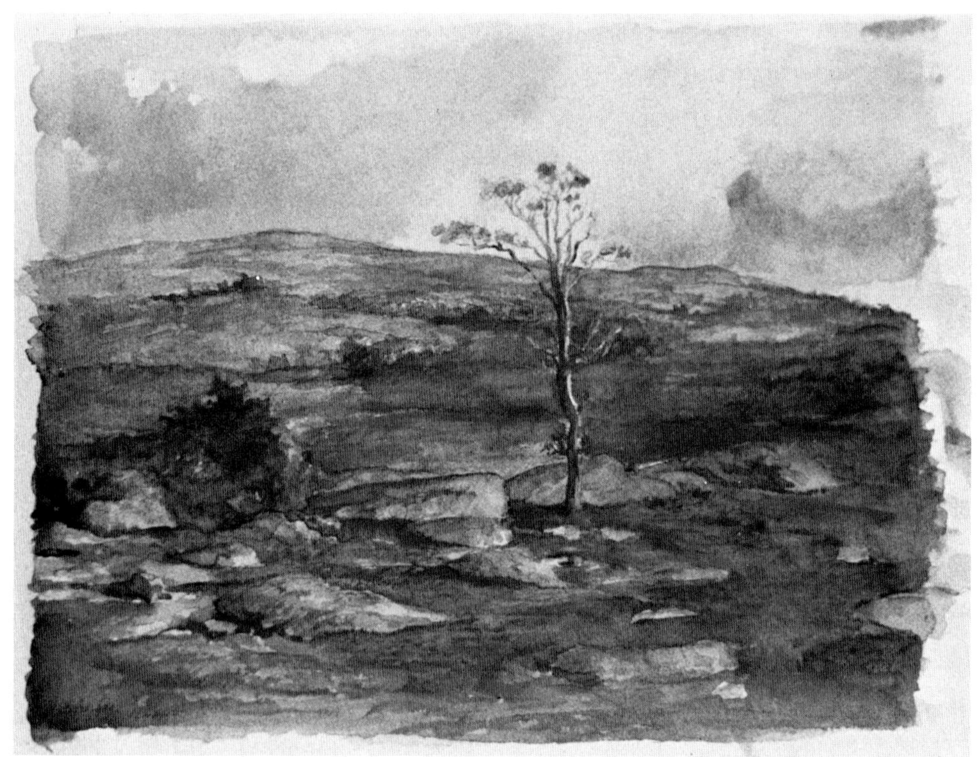

12

Pastoral Study.—Paradise, Newport, R.I., c. 1864-1865.

Watercolor on paper.
Sight: 7 x 9 in. (17.2 x 23.2 cm.).
Yale University Art Gallery, Bequest of John I.H. Downes, B.A.1889.

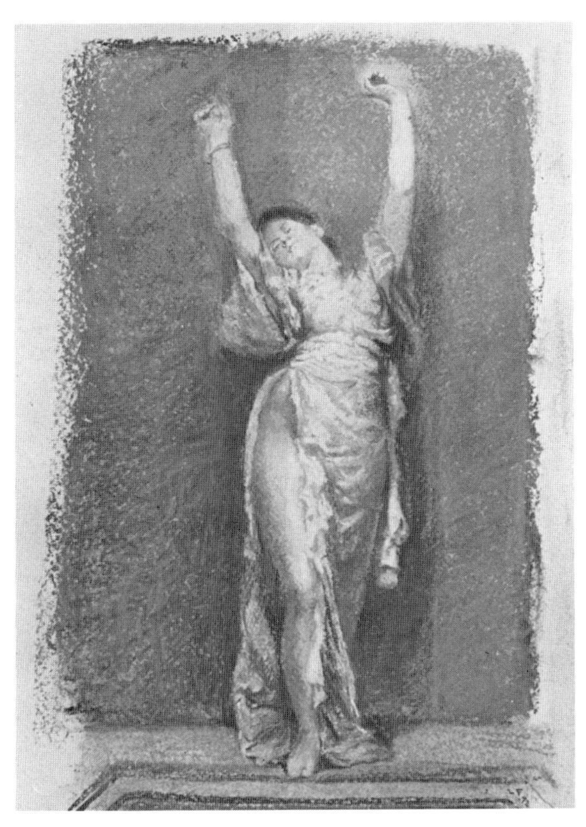

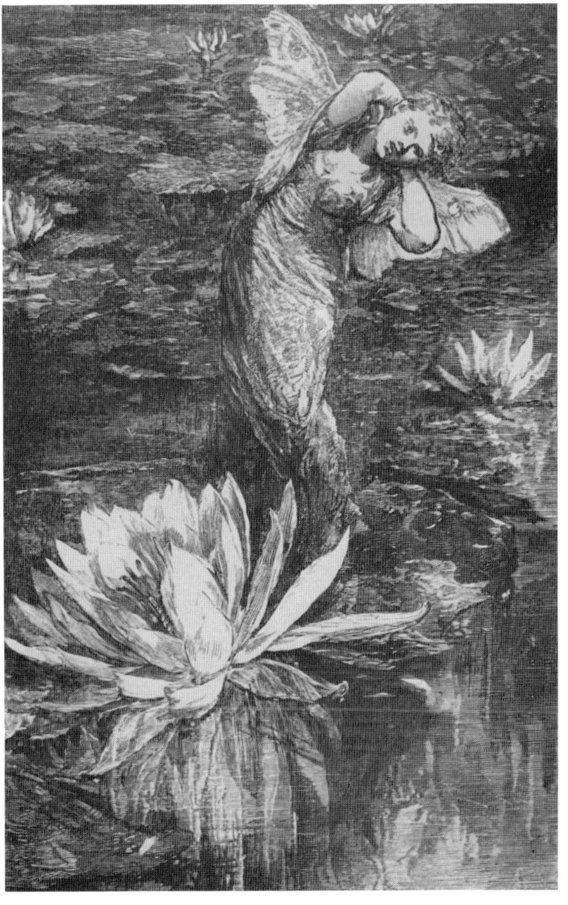

13

Salome's Dance, 1872.

Pastel on paper.
15 1/2 x 11 3/8 in. (38.1 x 28.3 cm.).
Private Collection.

14

The Spirit of the Water-Lily, 1872; published in Abby Sage Richardson, *Songs from the Old Dramatists* (New York, 1873).

Wood-engraving on paper.
5 1/4 x 3 1/2 in. (13.3 x 8.9 cm.).
Private Collection.

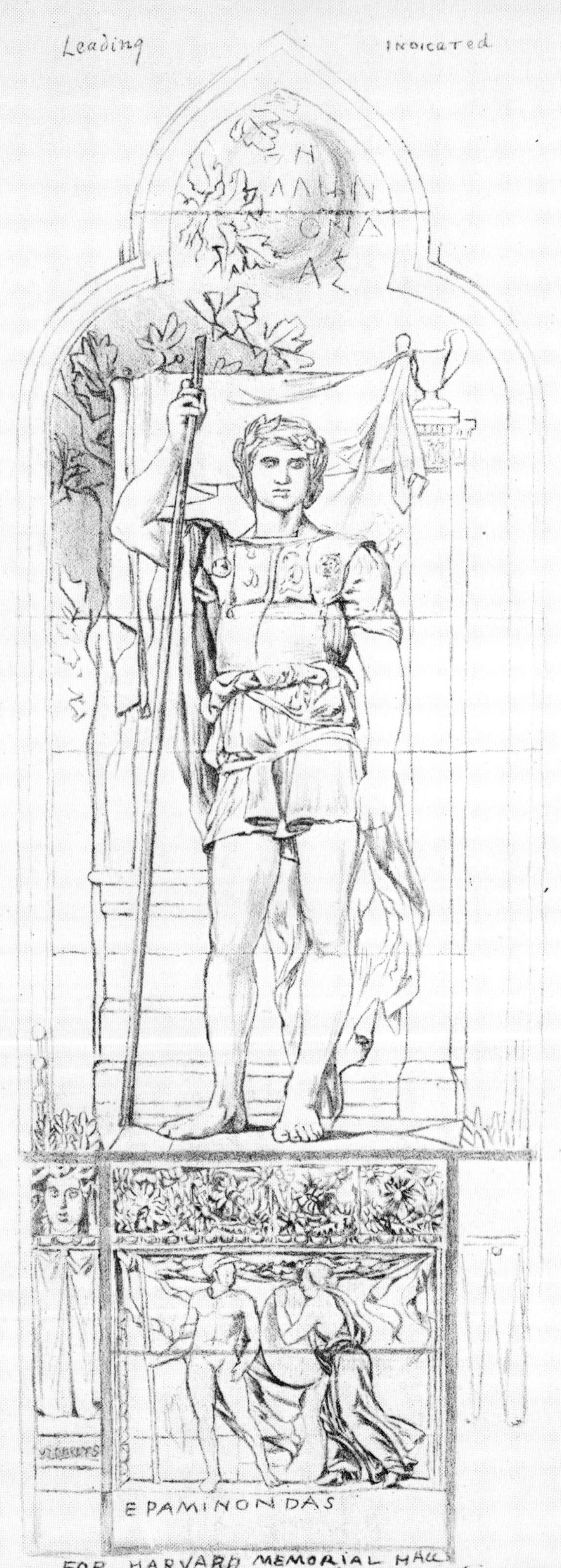

15

Epaminondas; Study for Window, Memorial Hall, Harvard University, Cambridge, Massachusetts, 1874.

Lithograph.
12 1/8 x 5 1/16 in. (30.6 x 12.8 cm.).
The Art Institute of Chicago, Chicago, Print Department Purchase.

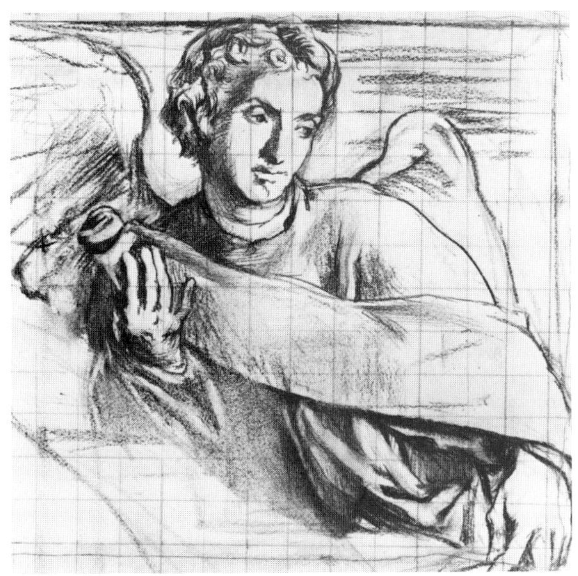

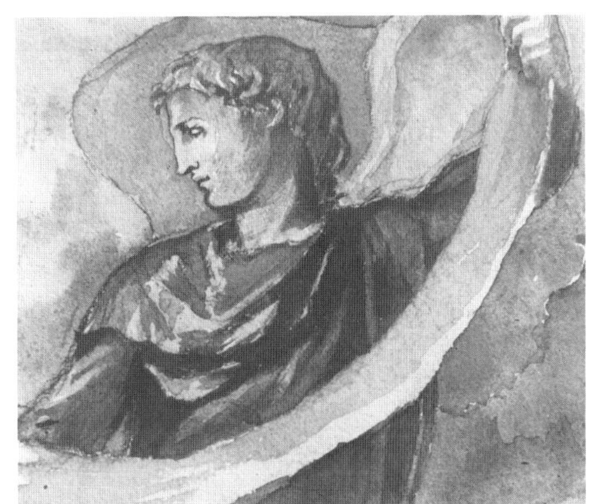

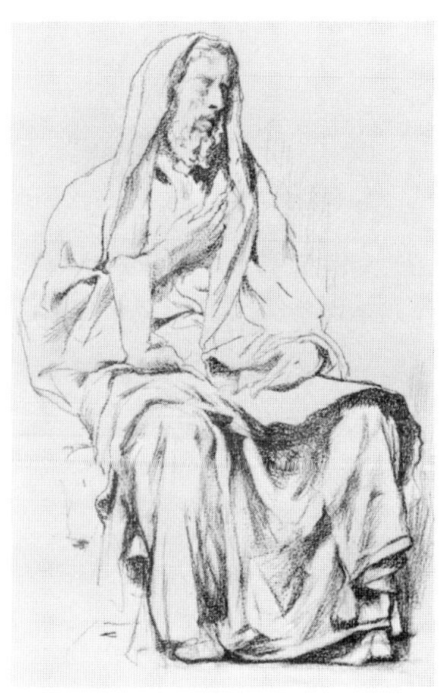

16

Angel with Scroll; Working Drawing for Mural, Trinity Church, Boston, 1876.

Charcoal on squared paper.
Sheet: 14 13/16 x 18 1/8 in. (11.0 x 45.8 cm.).
Sterling and Francine Clark Art Institute, Williamstown, Massachusetts. Gift of L. Bancel La Farge.

17

Angel; Study for Trinity Church, Boston, 1876.

Watercolor and gouache over graphite on coarse buff paper.
Sight: 5 x 6 in. (12.7 x 14.9 cm.).
Yale University Art Gallery, Gift of Neva Bicknell Hecker.

18

Nicodemus, c. 1877.

Graphite on heavy Whatman paper.
14 x 10 in. (35.6 x 25.4 cm.).
Private Collection.

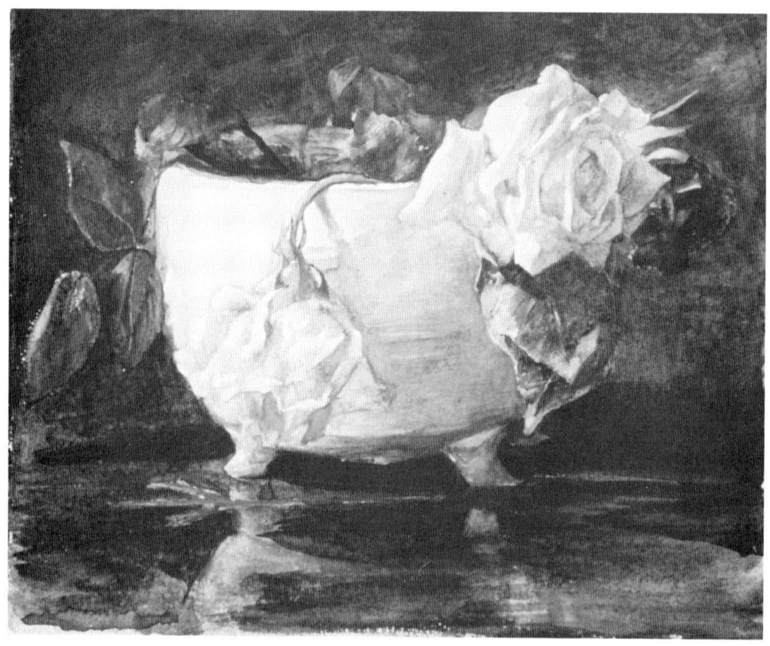

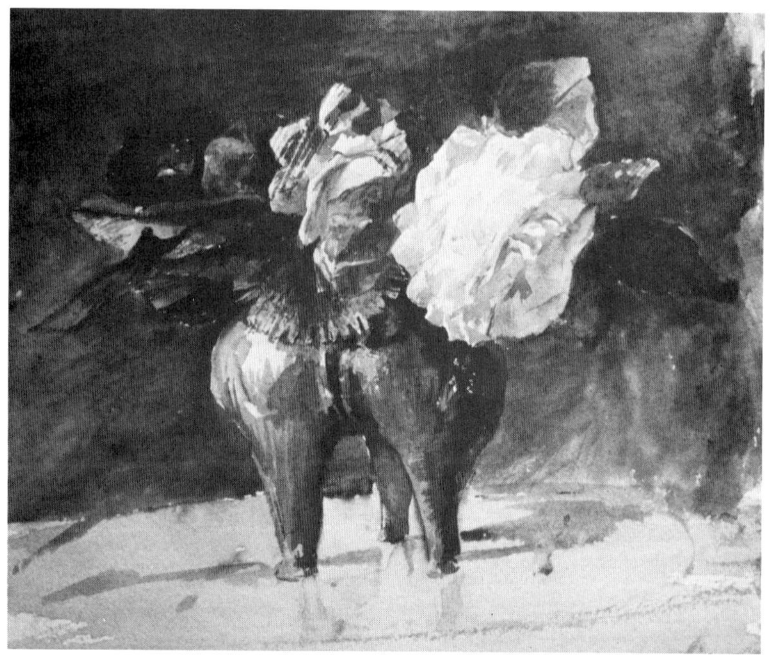

19

Roses, c. 1880.

Watercolor and gouache over graphite on off-white paper.
8 1/2 x 10 3/4 in. (21.6 x 27.3 cm.).
Private Collection.

20

Flowers. In a Blue Chinese Vase, of Antique Shape, c. 1879-1884.

Watercolor and gouache on paper.
6 3/4 x 8 1/8 in. (16.0 x 20.4 cm.).
Private Collection.

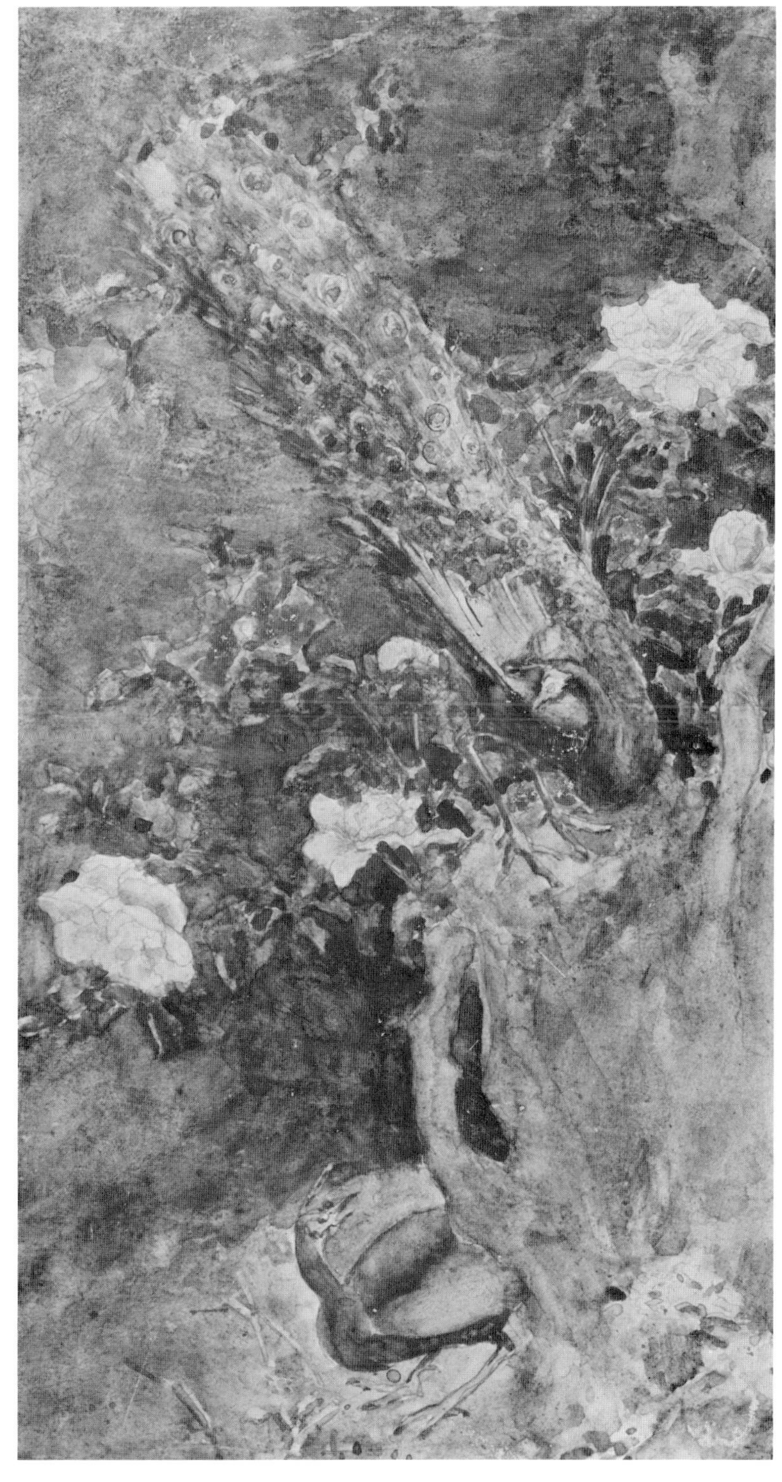

21

Peacocks and Peonies;
Color Study for Window in
Frederick Lothrop Ames House,
Boston, c. 1882.

Watercolor over graphite on paper.
7 5/8 x 4 1/4 in. (18.4 x 10.4 cm.).
Private Collection.

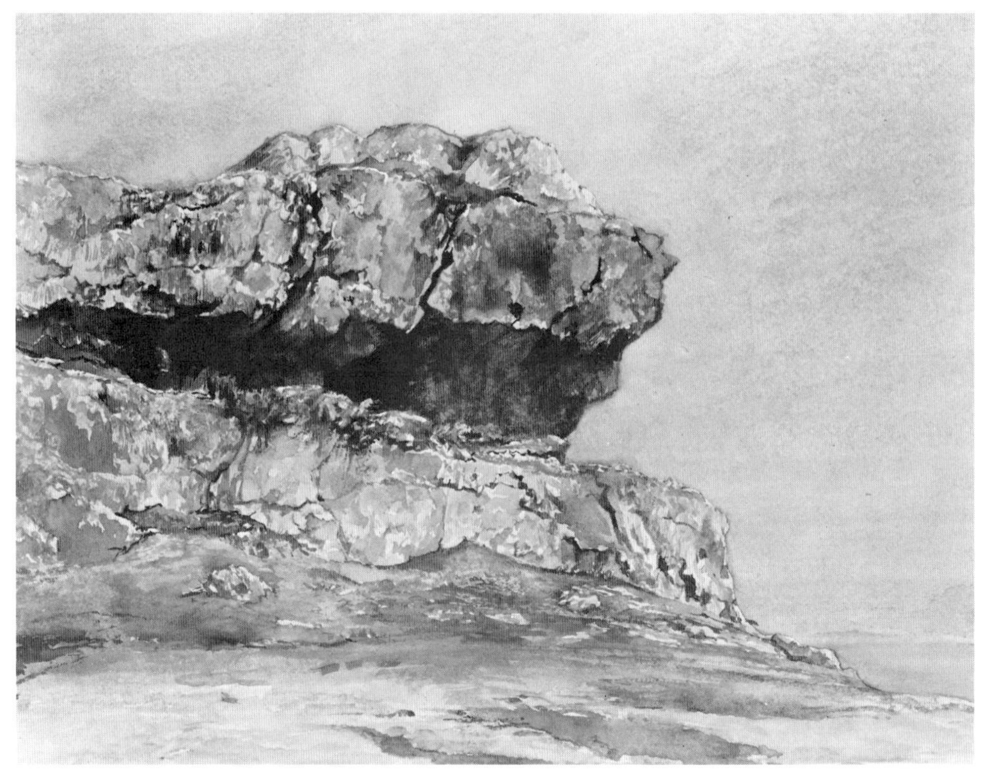

22

Study at Berkeley Ridge or Hanging Rock, c. 1883-1884.

Watercolor and gouache on paper.
10 1/2 x 13 in. (26.7 x 33.0 cm.).
Museum of Fine Arts, Boston,
Bequest of Mrs. Henry Lee Higginson.

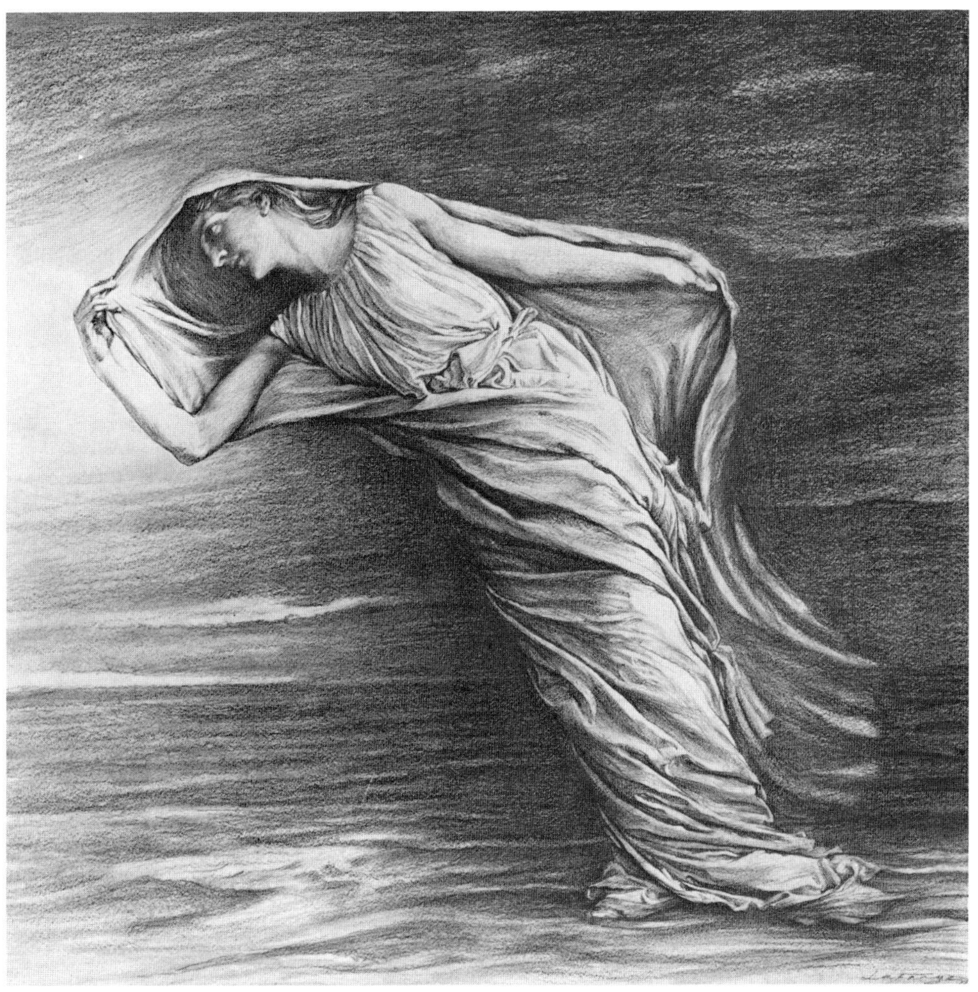

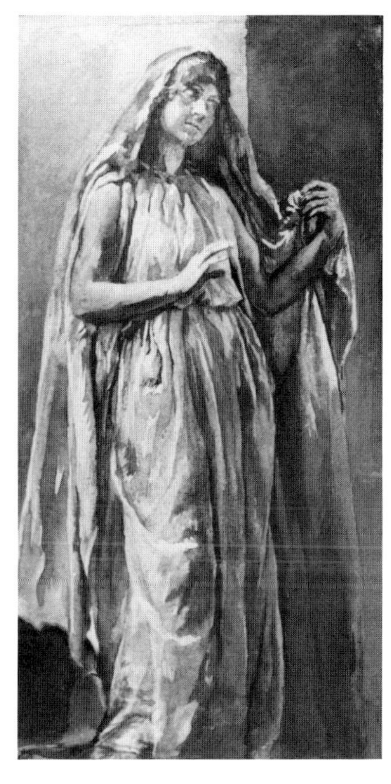

23

The Dawn; Design for Cornelius Vanderbilt II House, New York, 1880.

Crayon on faded tan paper.
13 x 13 in. (33.0 x 33.0 cm.).
Harvard University Art Museums, Fogg Art Museum, Cambridge, Massachusetts, Gift of the Family of the late Frederick A. Dwight.

24

*Female Figure in a Pink Dress with Blue Cloak, with Hand Extended.—Study for a Figure of Andromach*e, c. 1883-1884.

Watercolor and gouache on paper.
8 1/4 x 4 1/8 in. (21.0 x 10.5 cm.).
Private Collection.

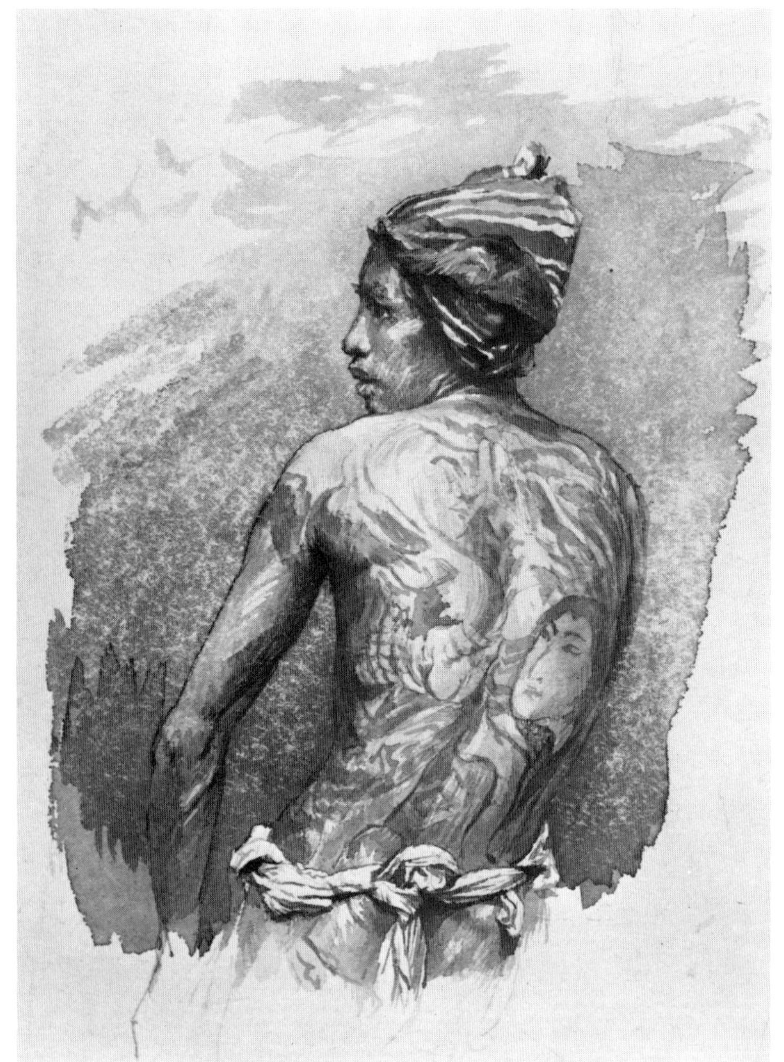

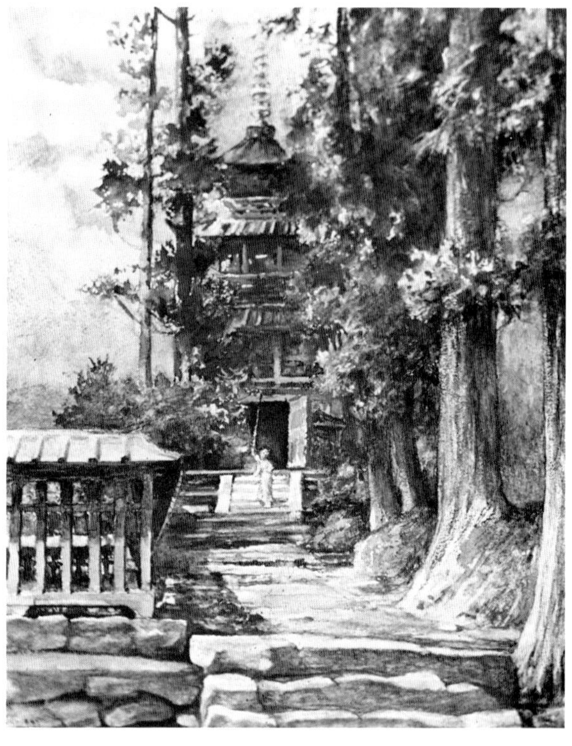

25

Tattooed Jinrikisha Boy, c. 1888.

India ink on paper.
13 7/16 x 10 7/16 in. (33.5 x 25.8 cm.).
Bowdoin College Museum of Art, Brunswick, Maine.

26

Red Pagoda, Nikko, 1886.

Watercolor on paper.
11 7/8 x 9 1/2 in. (30.1 x 24.2 cm.).
Albright-Knox Art Gallery, Buffalo, New York; bequest of Edmund Hayes, 1924.

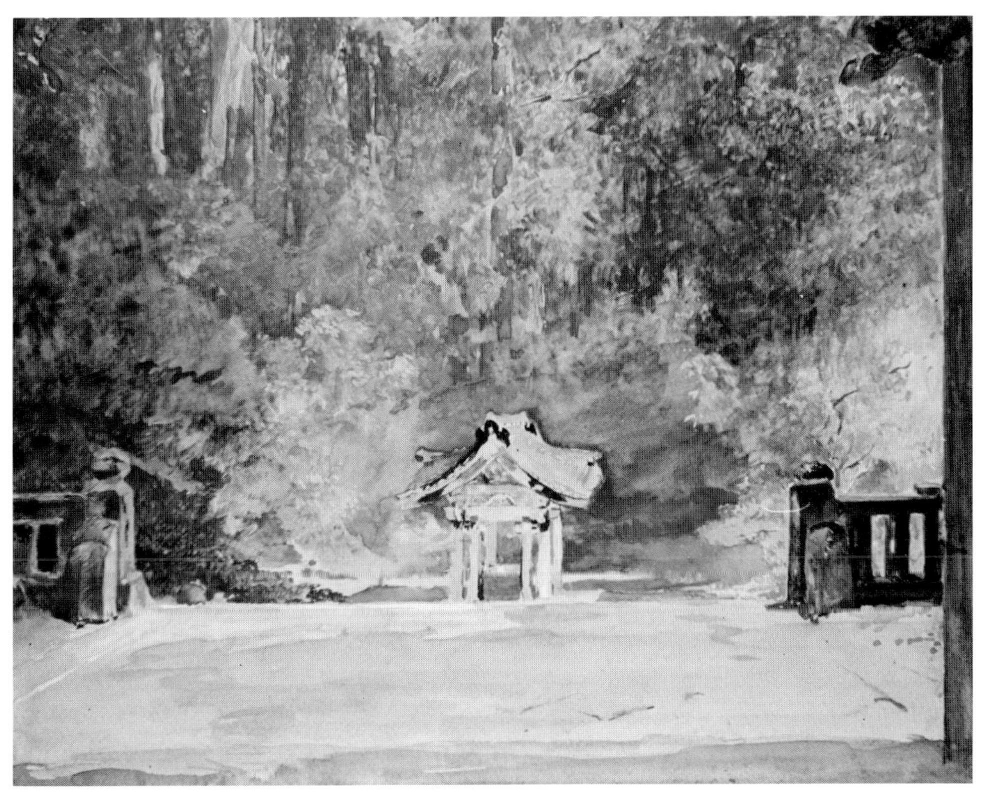

27

Sacred Font in the Temple of Iyemitsu, Nikko. From the Platform of the Second Gate, 1886.

Watercolor and gouache over graphite on paper, mounted.
9 1/2 x 11 3/4 in. (24.1 x 29.8 cm.).
Collection of Mr. and Mrs. Richard N. Carrell.

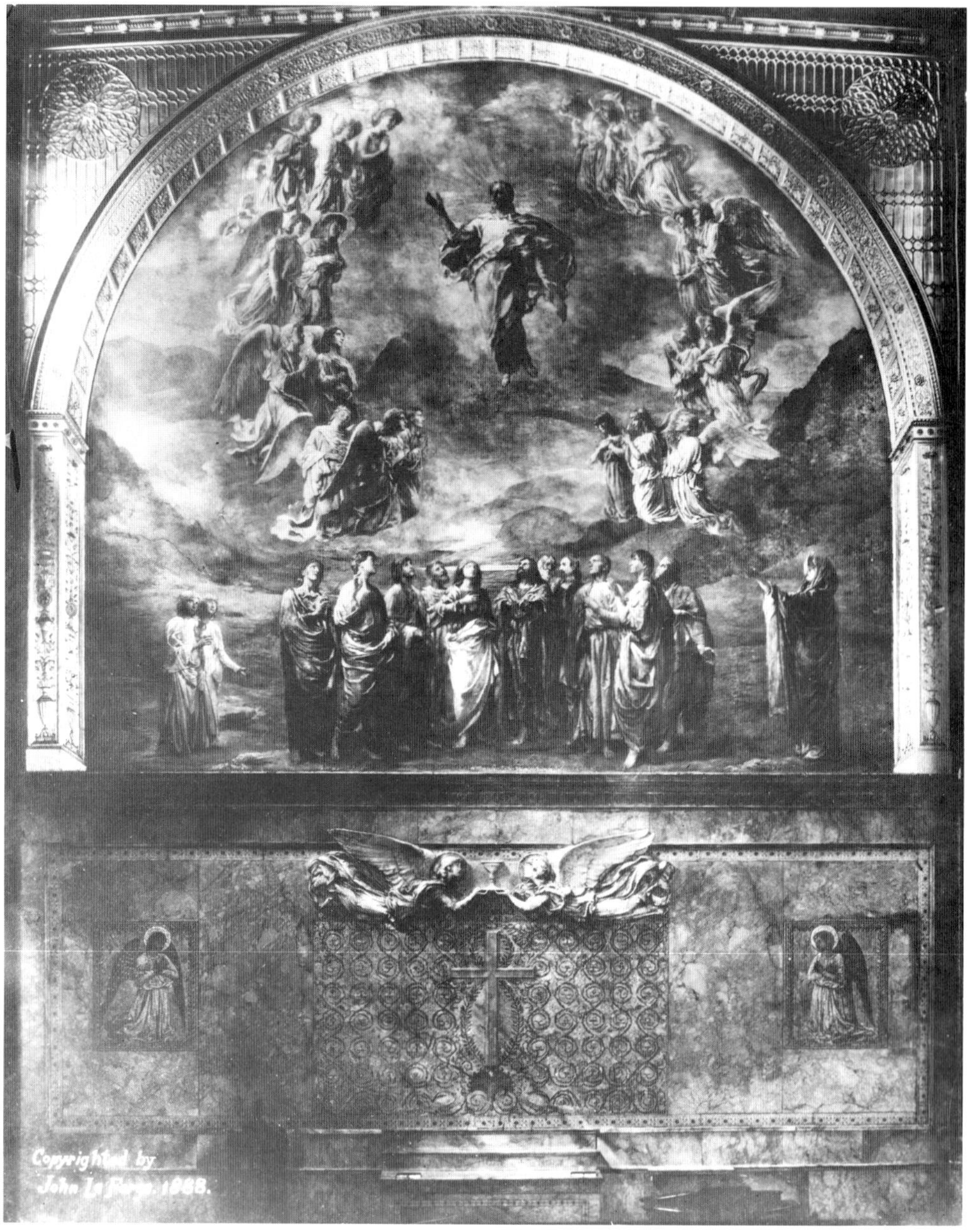

28

Sunset in Fog Over Kiyoto, 1886.
Watercolor on paper.
6 7/8 x 11 3/4 in. (18.1 x 29.8 cm.).
Private Collection.

29

Ascension; Mural in the Church of the Ascension, New York, c. 1888.
Church of the Ascension, New York.

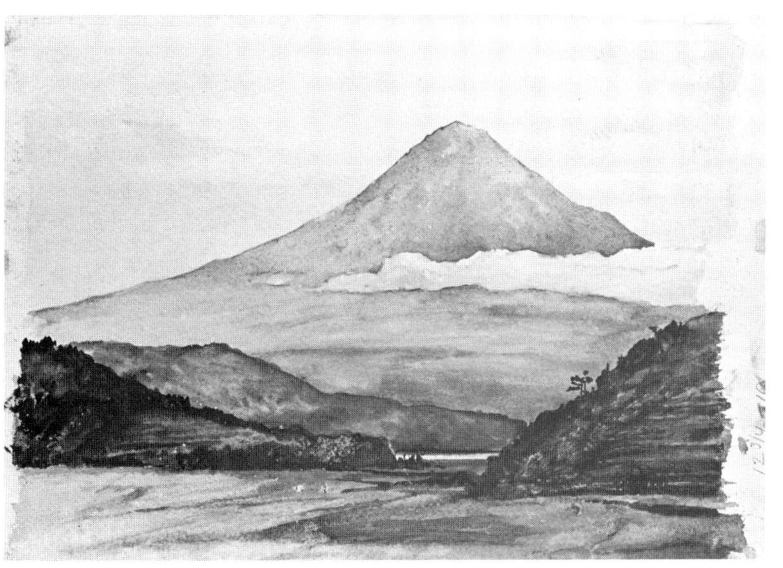

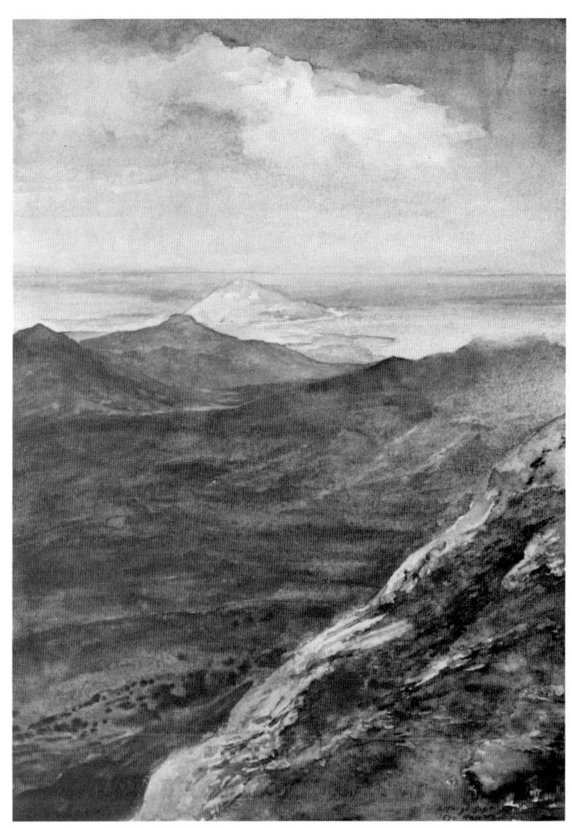

30

Mountain of Fuji-San from Fuji-Kawa, 1886.

Watercolor on paper.
Sheet: 10 3/4 x 14 15/16 in. (26.2 x 36.5 cm.).
Georgia Museum of Art, University of Georgia, Athens, Georgia, Eva Underhill Holbrook Memorial Collection of American Art, Gift of Alfred H. Holbrook.

31

The Great Pali, 1890.

Watercolor and gouache on paper.
16 1/8 x 11 5/8 in. (42.9 cm. x 29.5 cm.).
Private Collection.

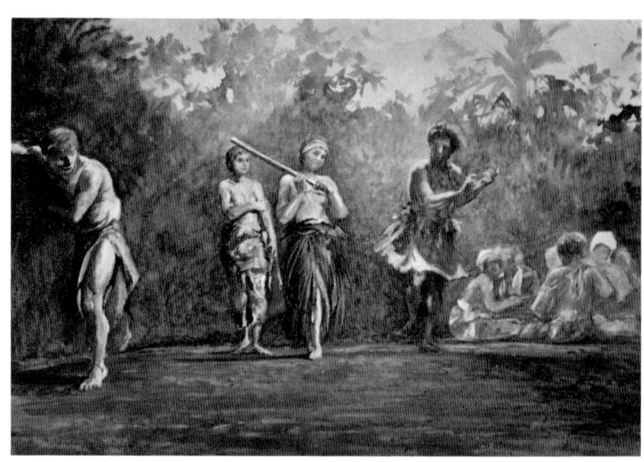

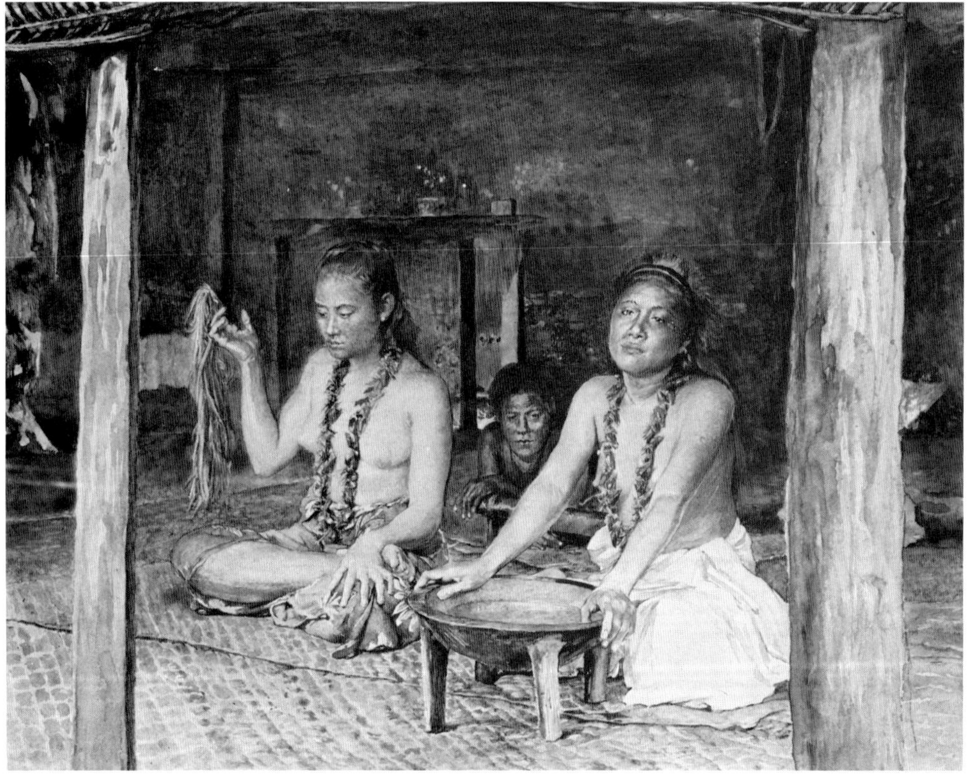

32

Sivà with Siakumu Making Kava in Tofae's House, c. 1891-1895.

Watercolor on Japanese mulberry vellum. Sheet: 18 9/16 x 23 3/4 in. (46.3 x 59.2 cm.). Sterling and Francine Clark Art Institute, Williamstown, Massachusetts. Gift of L. Bancel La Farge.

33

Another Standing Dance, 1890.

Watercolor and gouache on paper. Sight: 8 1/2 x 11 in. (21.6 x 27.9 cm.). Collection of Mr. and Mrs. Willard G. Clark.

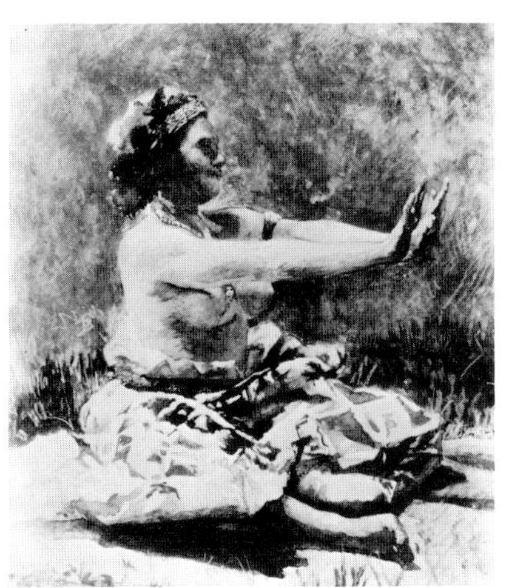

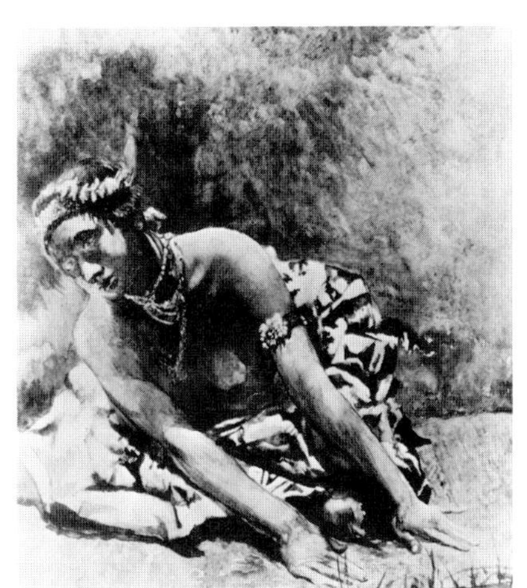

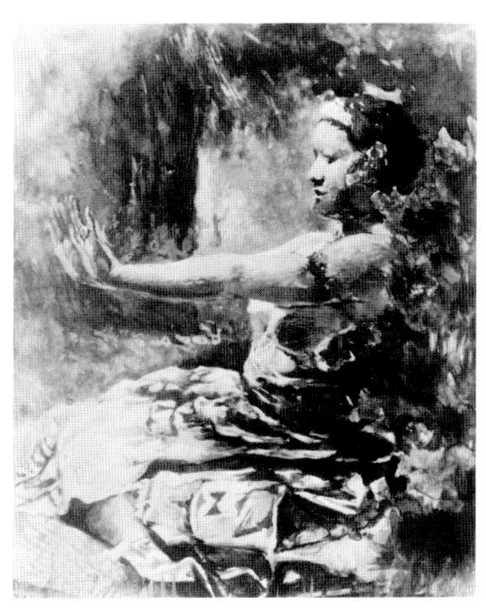

34

Sivà Dance (Triptych of Seated Single Figures), 1890.

Watercolor on paper.
Each: 11 1/8 x 9 1/4 in. (28.2 x 23.1 cm.).
Private Collection courtesy of
Jordan-Volpe Gallery, Inc.

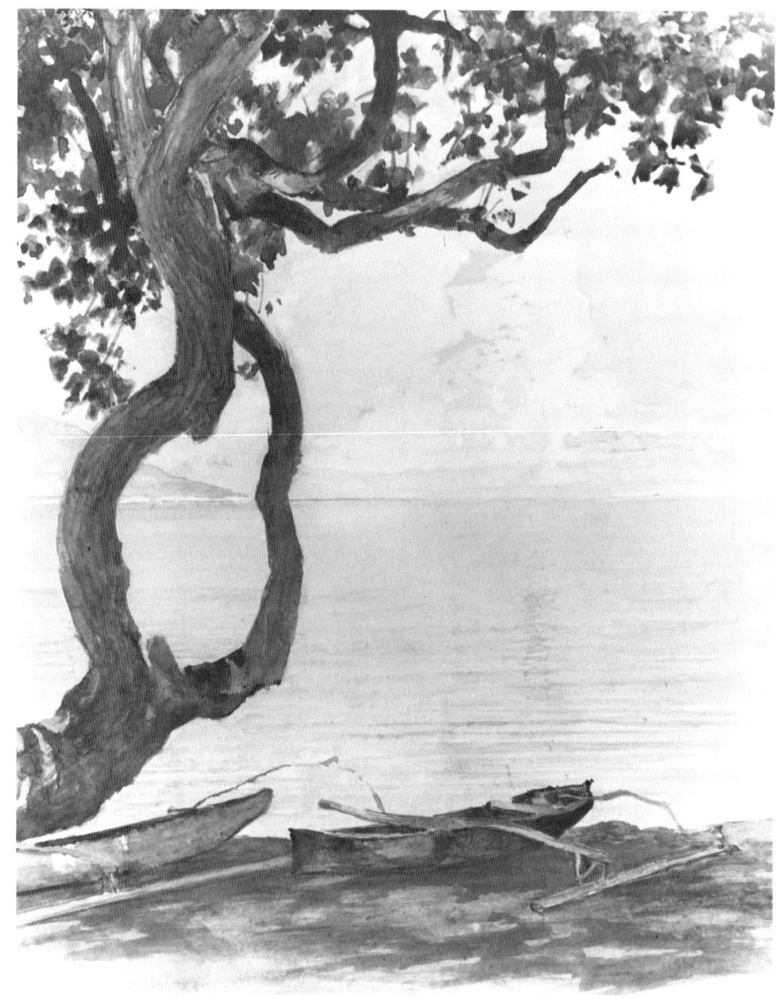

35

In Front of Our Gate, Papeete, Tahiti, 1891. Morning, 1891.

Watercolor and gouache over graphite on paper.
10 1/4 x 8 7/8 in. (21.3 x 21.2 cm.).
Private Collection.

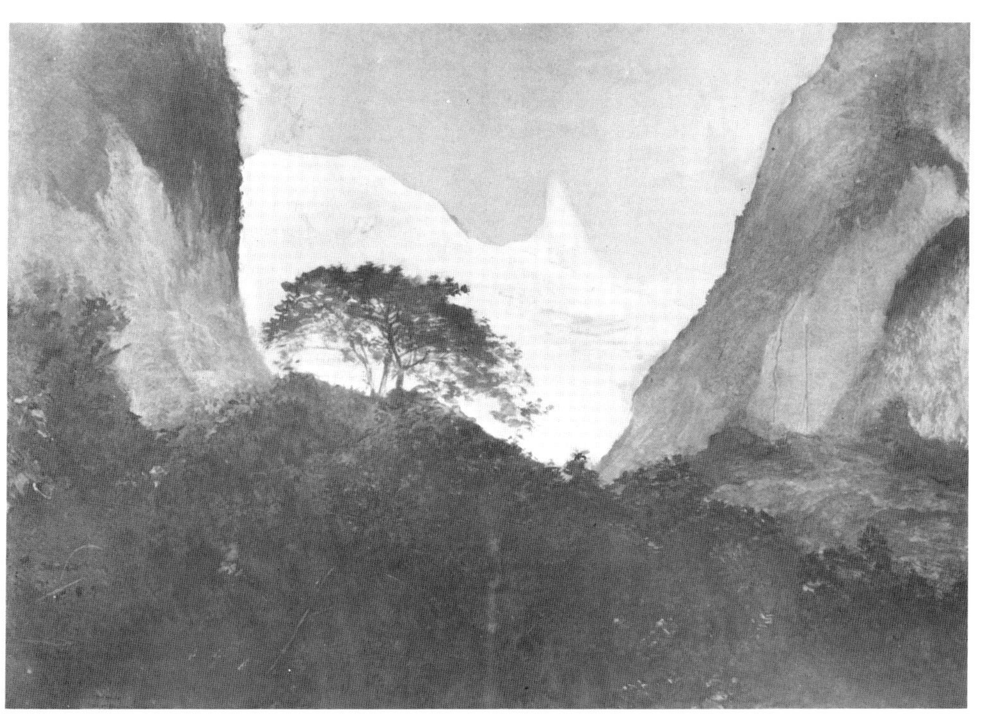

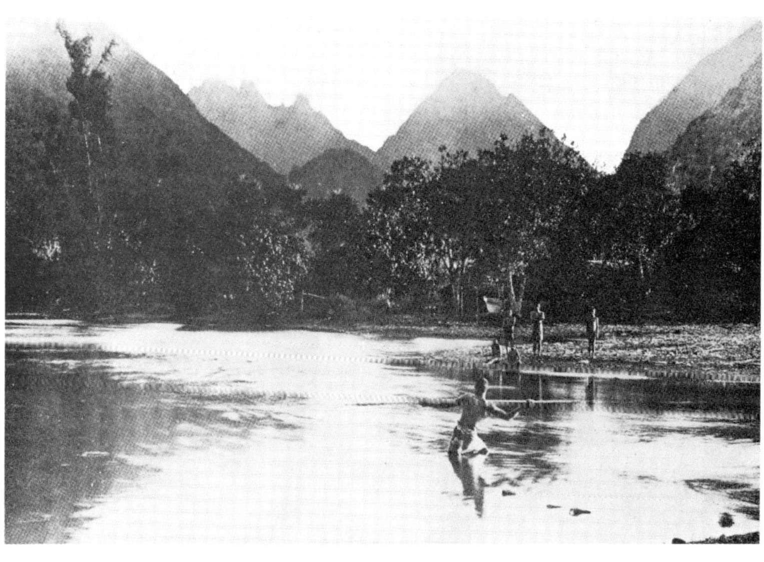

36

*Landscape. Evening.
Tahiti. Pass and Peak of Vaiaroa,
Taiarapu*, 1891.

Watercolor and gouache on rice paper.
Sight: 14 1/2 x 21 3/8 in. (36.1 x 53.7 cm.).
Private Collection.

37

Brown Brothers, *Spear Fishing*,
c. 1885-1890; published in Frederick
O'Brien, *Atolls of the Sun* (New
York, 1922).

Photograph

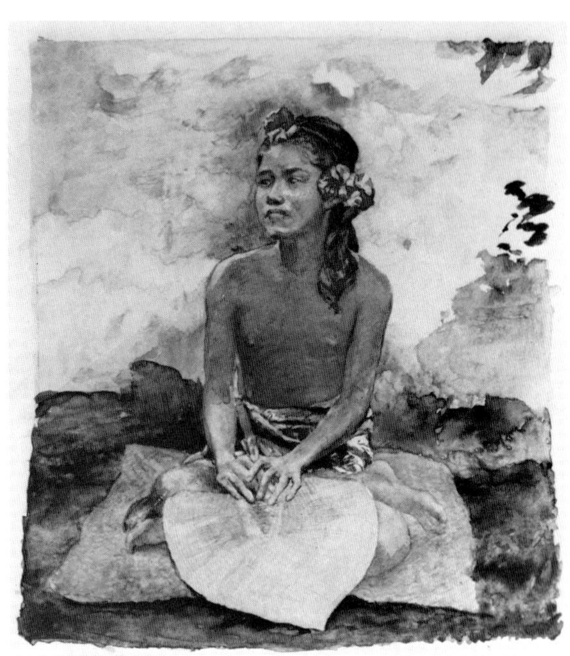

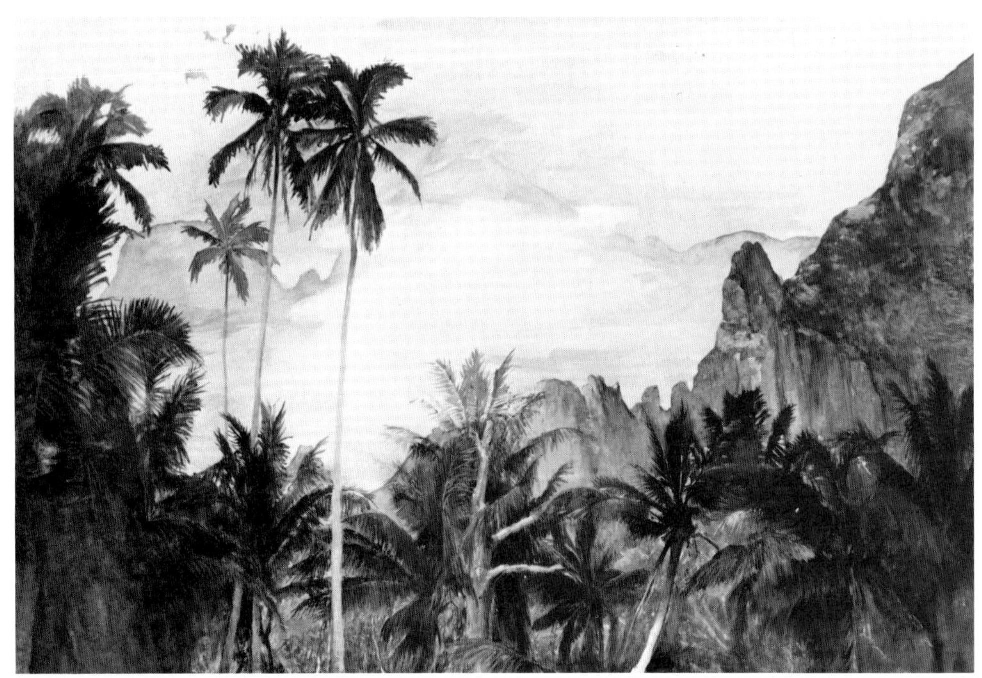

38

The End of Cook's Bay. Island of Moorea. Society Islands. 1891. Dawn, 1891.

Watercolor and gouache on paper.
14 1/2 x 22 in. (36.1 x 55.9 cm.).
New Britain Museum of American Art,
Helen Russell Stanley Fund.

39

Study of Tongan Girl. With a Fan, 1891.

Watercolor and gouache on paper.
Sight: 9 x 7 3/8 in. (23.2 x 18.2 cm.).
Eleanor S. Lunde

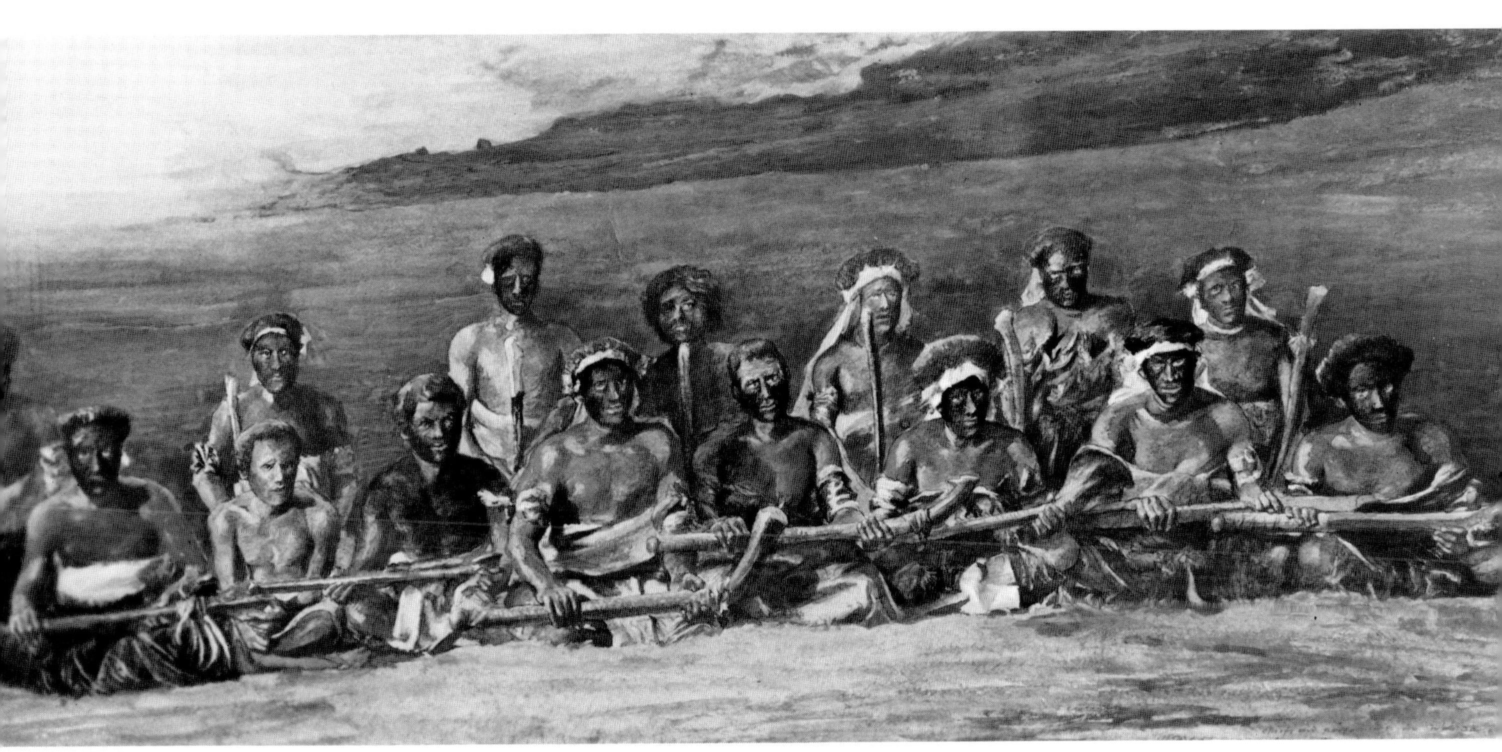

40

Chiefs in War Dress Seated After a Dance. Islands of Fiji, c. 1899-1901.

Watercolor, gouache, and tempera on paper mounted on illustration board. 9 1/2 x 21 in. (24.1 x 53.3 cm.). The Phillips Collection, Washington, D.C.

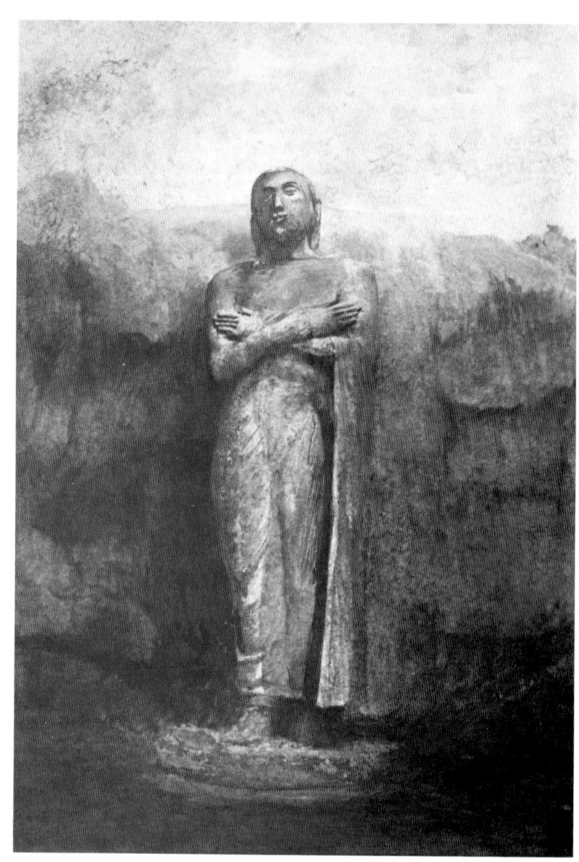

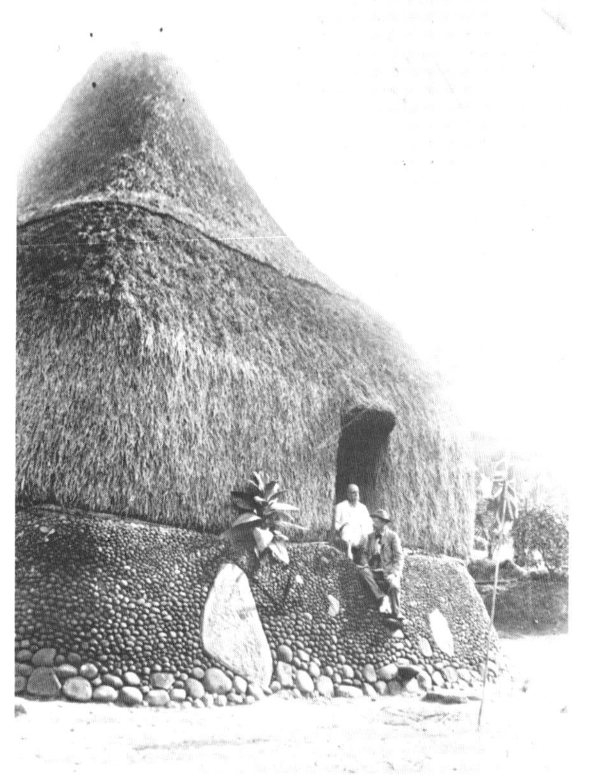

41

Unknown Photographer,
John La Farge and Henry Adams at the Door to Their Fiji Hut, 1891.
Photograph.
Massachusetts Historical Society, Boston.

42

Colossal Statue of Ananda, near the Ruined City of Pollanarua. Ceylon, 1891, 1891.
Watercolor and gouache on paper, mounted on board.
9 7/8 x 7 in. (25.1 x 17.8 cm.).
Mr. and Mrs. Fred D. Bentley, Sr.

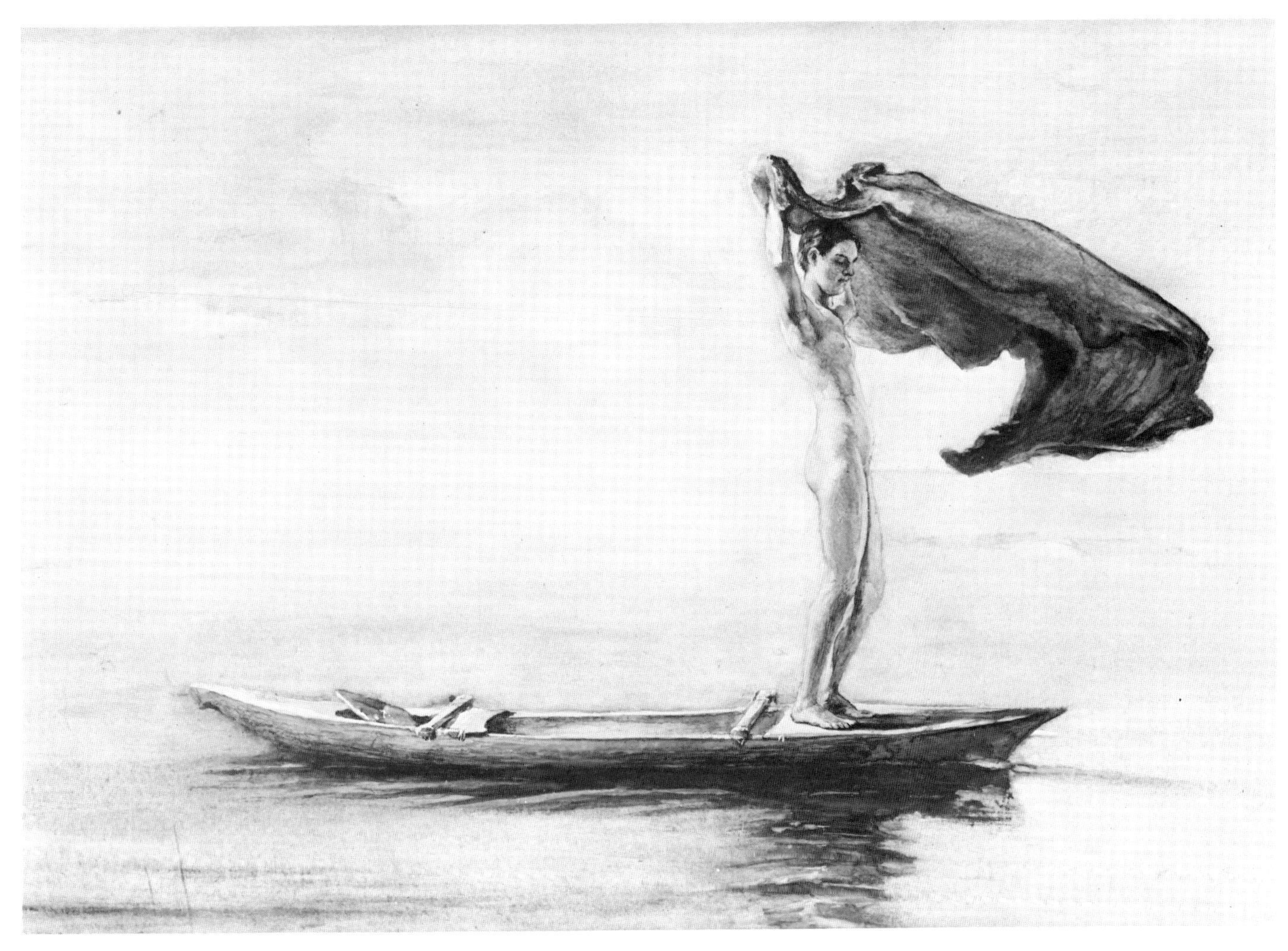

43

Fayaway (Girl in Bow of Canoe Spreading Out Her Loin-Cloth for a Sail), c. 1895-1896.

Watercolor and gouache over graphite on thin Japanese paper laid down on thick, cream-surfaced artist's board. 15 3/16 x 21 3/16 in. (38.6 x 55.4 cm.). The Corcoran Gallery of Art, Museum Purchase.

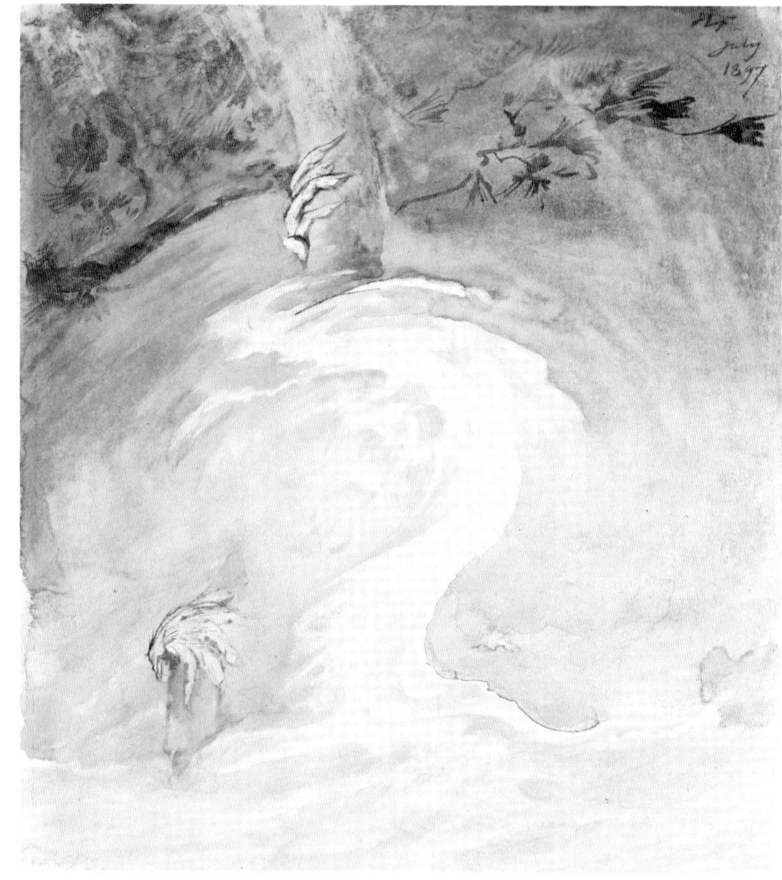

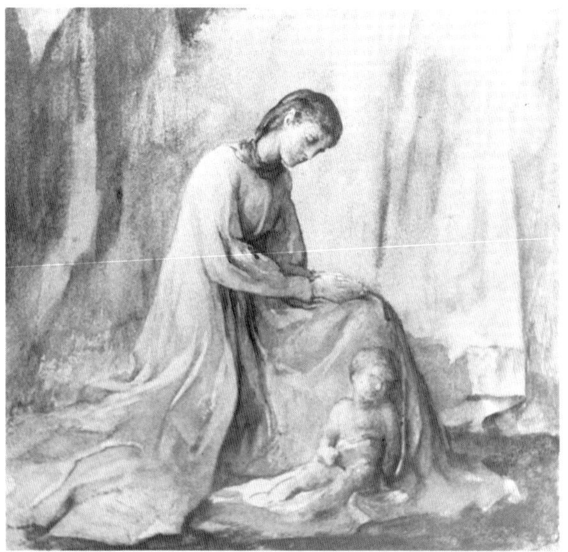

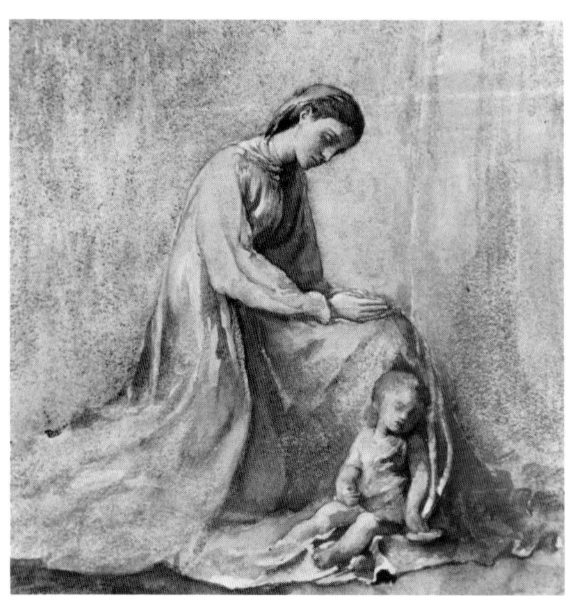

44

Mother and Child, 1888.

Watercolor and gouache on paper.
7 5/8 x 7 1/4 in. (17.8 x 18.5 cm.).
Lee-La Farge Collection, Mount Saint Mary's College, Emmitsburg, Maryland.

45

Mother and Child, c. 1888.

Watercolor and gouache over graphite on off-white paper.
7 3/8 x 7 3/8 in. (19.5 x 19.5 cm.).
Private Collection.

46

Spirit of the Storm. Japanese Folk Lore, 1897.

Watercolor and ink wash on Japanese paper.
15 3/8 x 10 3/4 in. (39.0 x 27.3 cm.).
The Toledo Museum of Art; Gift of Edward Drummond Libbey.

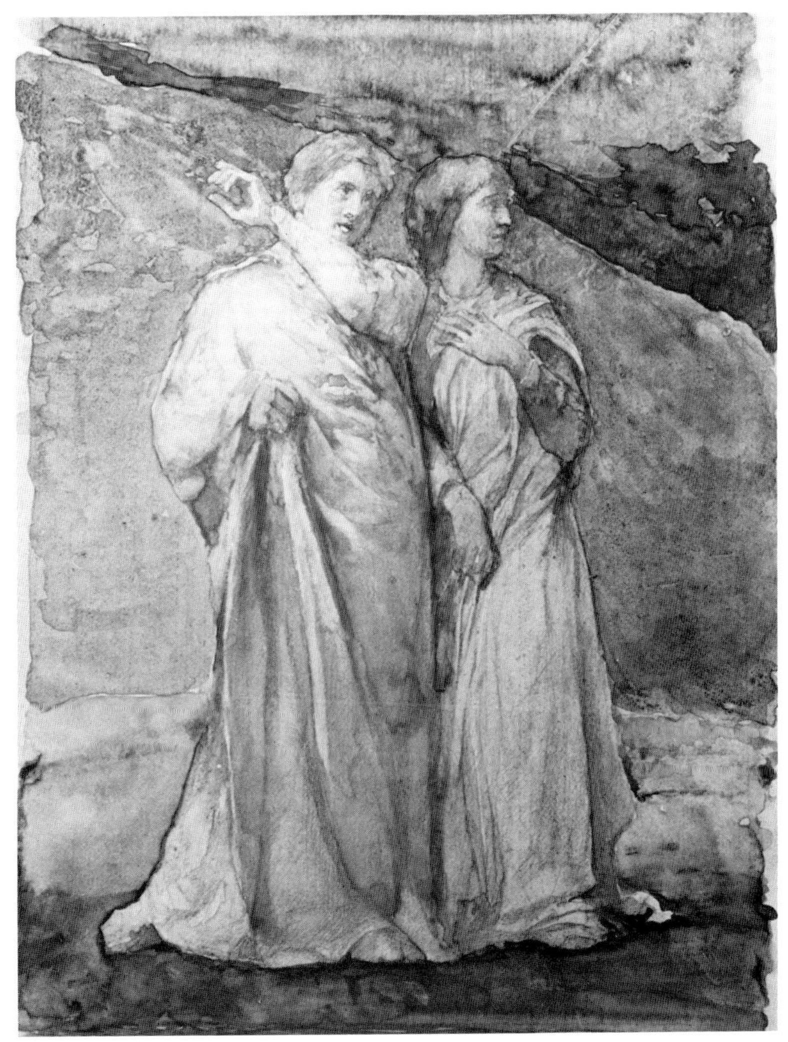

47

Angels of the Resurrection;
Color Study for Emily Martin
Southworth Memorial Window,
Church of the Ascension,
New York, c. 1889.

Watercolor and gouache on paperboard.
Sheet: 11 1/4 x 9 7/8 in. (28.2 x 23.7 cm.).
Harriet B. Lidgerwood.

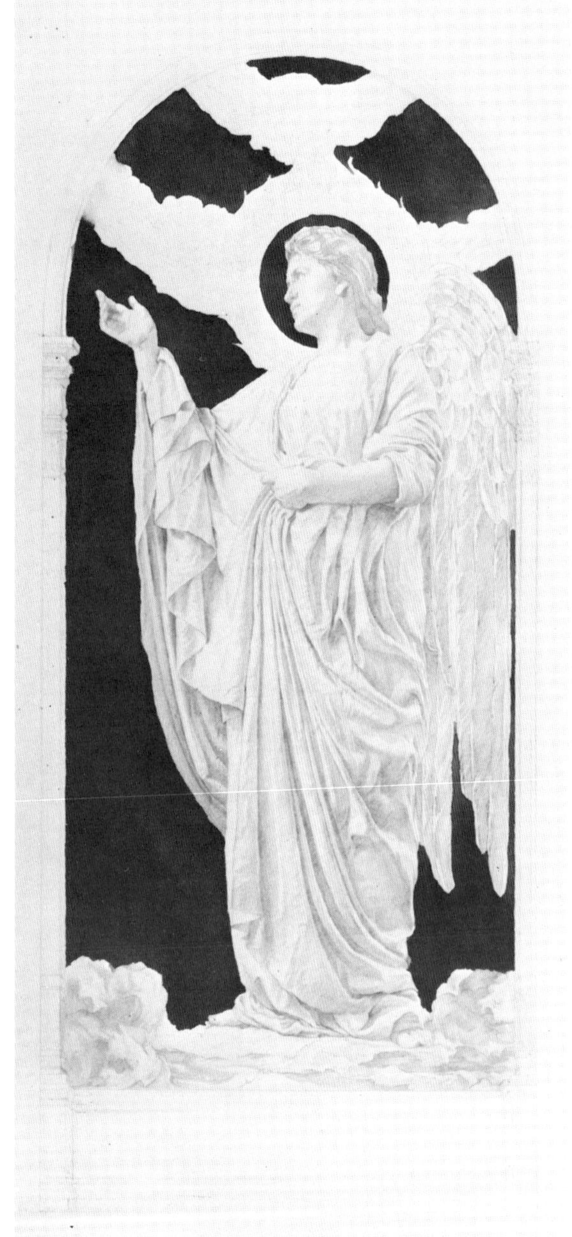

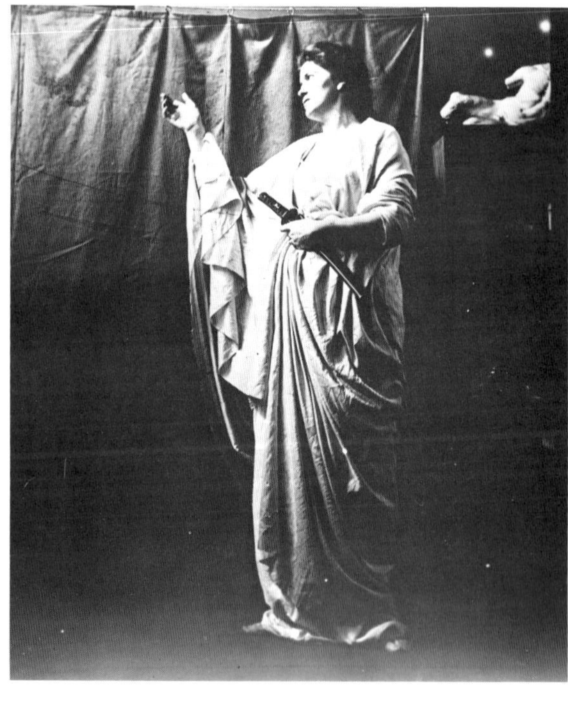

48

Angel of the Annunciation;
Color Study for Emma Knox Cain and Amanda Knox Jennings Memorial Window, The Presbyterian Church of Sewickley, Sewickley, Pennsylvania, c. 1896-1899.

Watercolor and graphite on paper.
Sheet: 25 1/4 x 15 3/4 in. (63.8 x 38.9 cm.).
Collection of Stuart Pivar.

49

Unknown Photographer,
Standing Model, c. 1896-1900.

Photograph.
La Farge Family Papers, Division of Manuscripts and Archives, Sterling Memorial Library, Yale University.

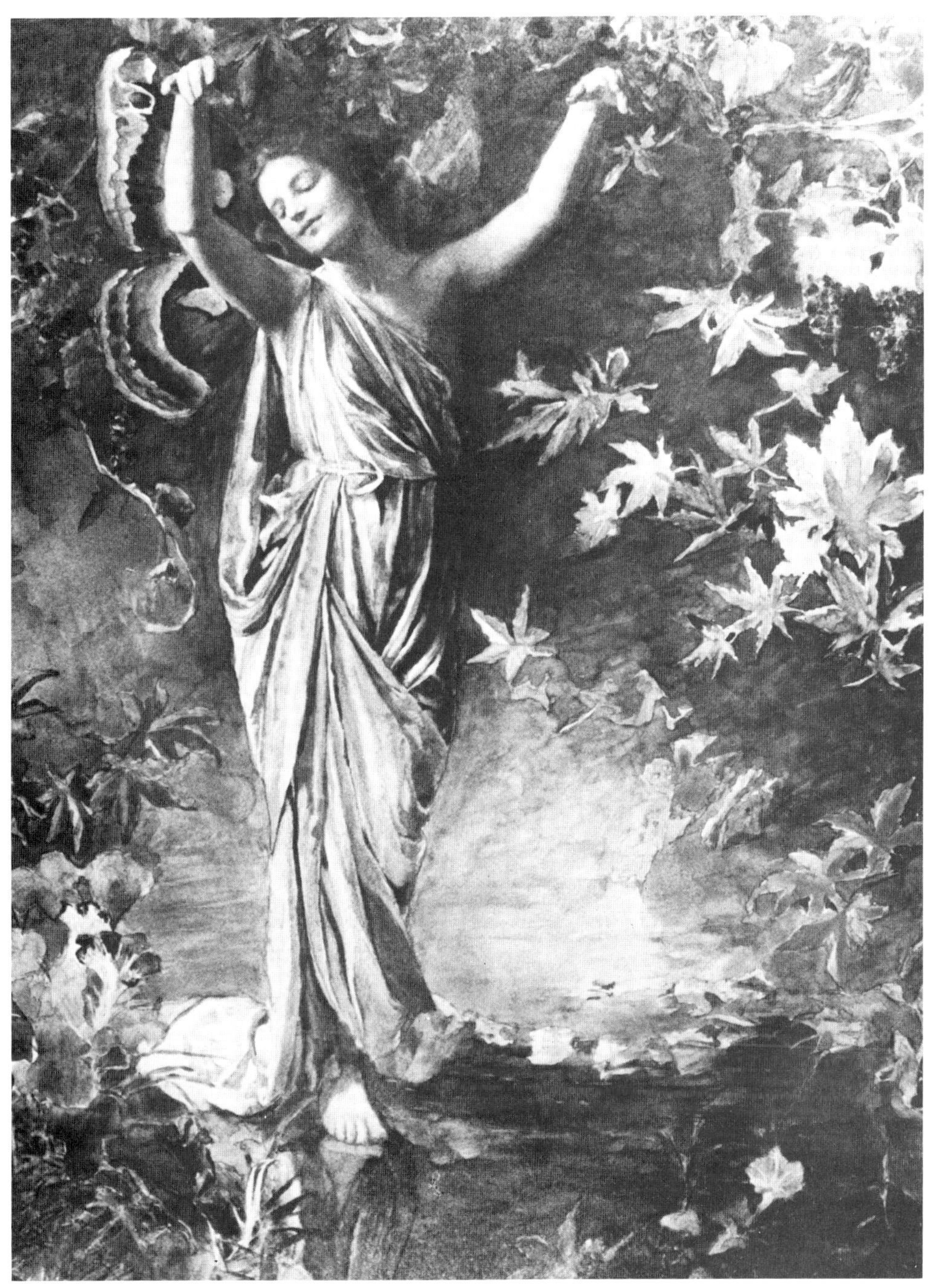

50

Autumn Scattering Leaves;
Color Study for Window Intended for William C. Whitney House, Old Westbury, Long Island, New York, c. 1900.
Watercolor and gouache on paper.
18 1/2 x 13 1/2 in. (47.0 x 32.4 cm.).
Private Collection.

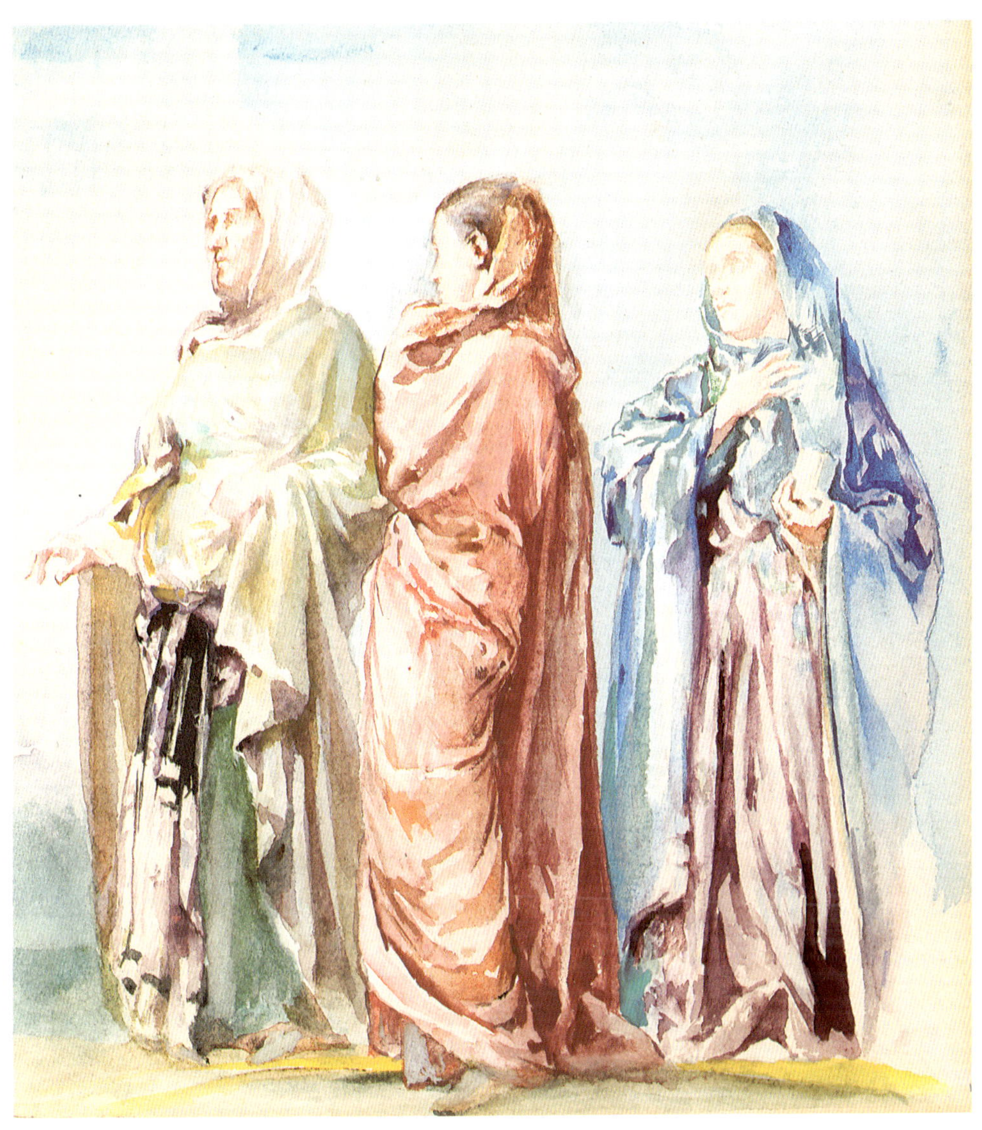

1

The Three Marys; Color Study for Altarpiece, St. Thomas's Church New York, 1877.

Watercolor on paper.
9 3/16 x 8 5/16 in. (23.0 x 20.6 cm.).
Private Collection.

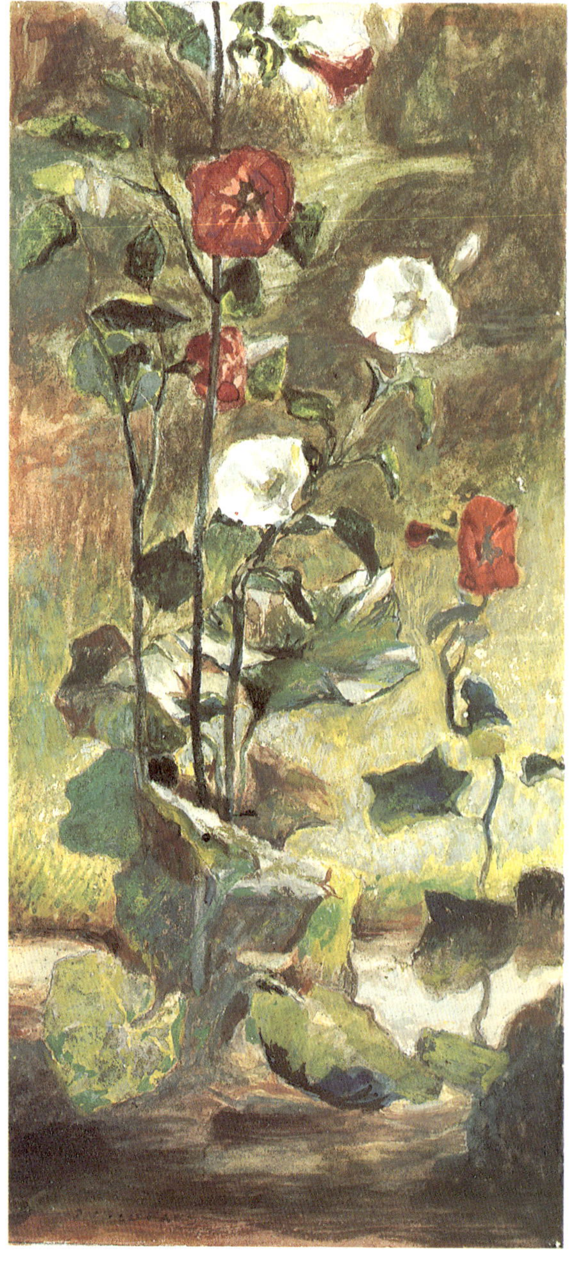

2

Hollyhocks, c. 1879-1882.
Watercolor on paper.
7 1/4 x 3 1/2 in. (18.0 x 8.1 cm.).
Private Collection, courtesy of Thomas Colville Fine Art, Inc.

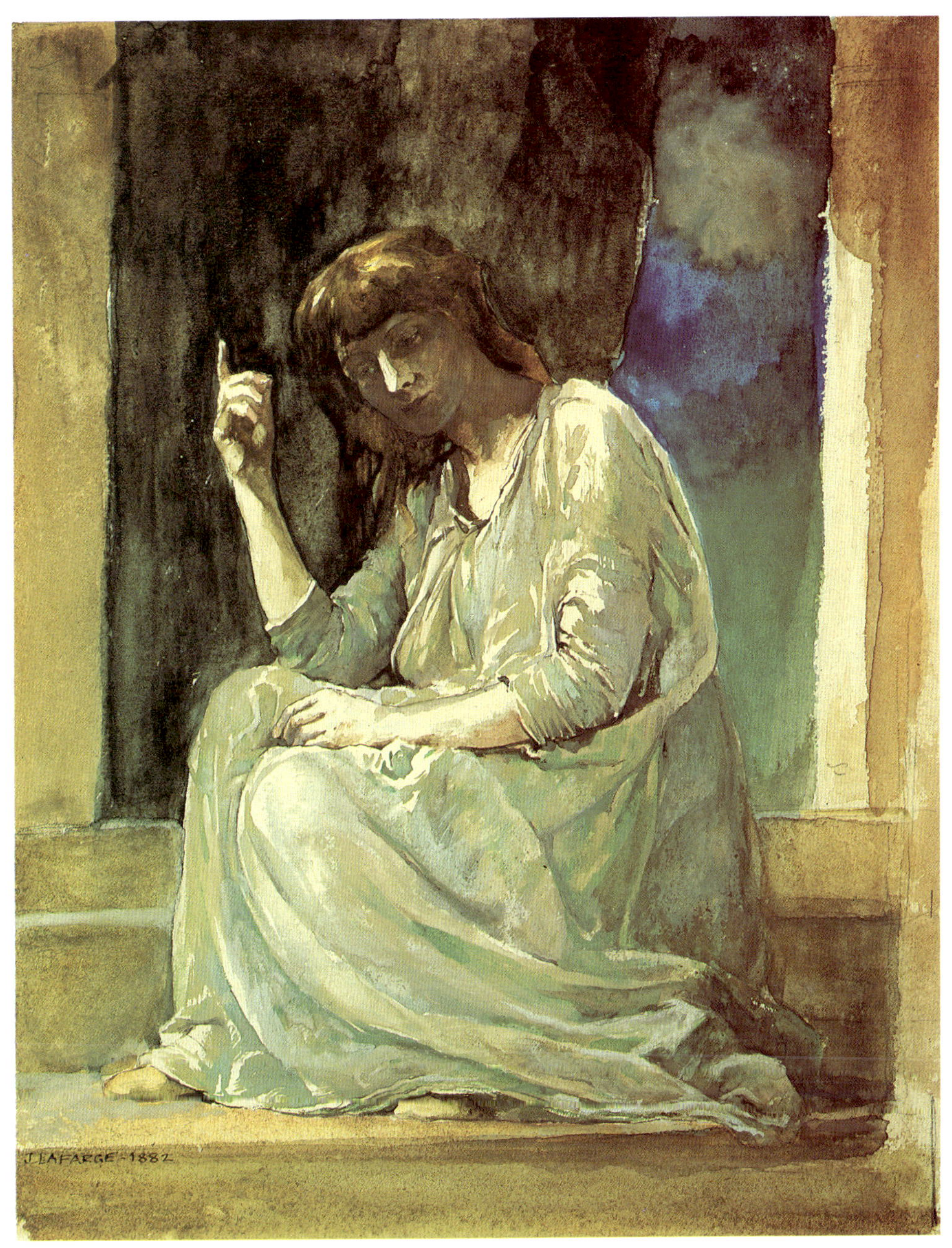

3

Study of Female Figure. Intended to Illustrate a Verse of Isaiah, 1882.

Watercolor and gouache over graphite on coarse buff paper.
13 x 9 3/4 in. (33.0 x 24.8 cm.)
Private Collection.

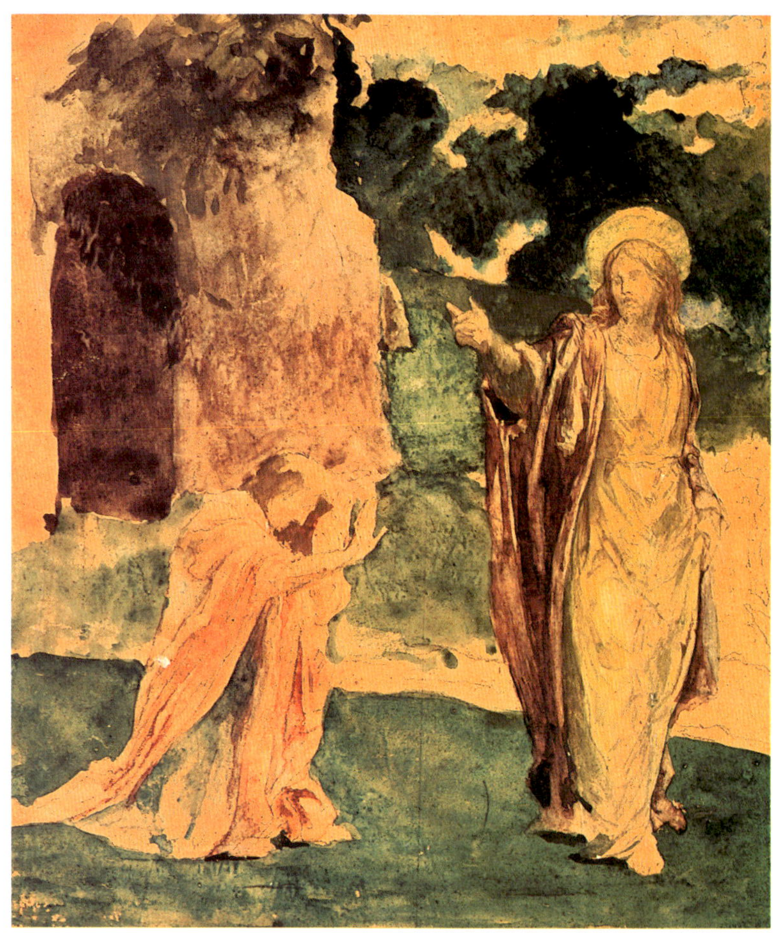

4

Saint James and the Risen Christ; Color Study for James C. Harrison Memorial Window, Trinity Church, Buffalo, c. 1884-1886.

Watercolor over graphite on thin tracing paper.
7 1/4 x 6 1/2 in. (18.0 x 15.7 cm.)
Private Collection.

5

Angel of Help; Color Study for Helen Angier Ames Memorial Window, Unity Church, North Easton, Massachusetts, 1884.

Watercolor and gouache on paper
11 1/2 x 6 1/2 in. (29.2 x 16.5 cm.)
Collection of Mr. and Mrs. Richard N. Carrell.

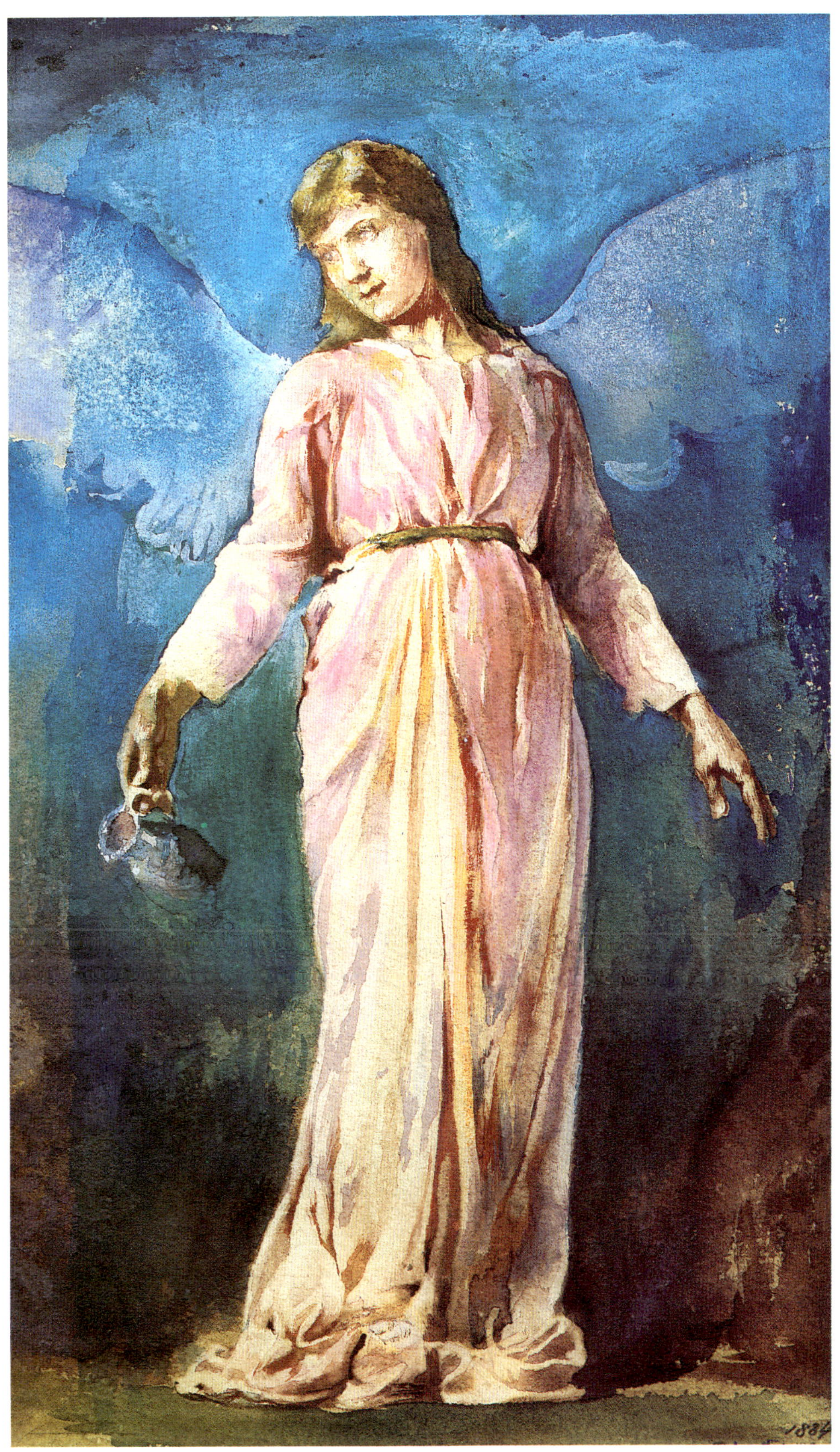

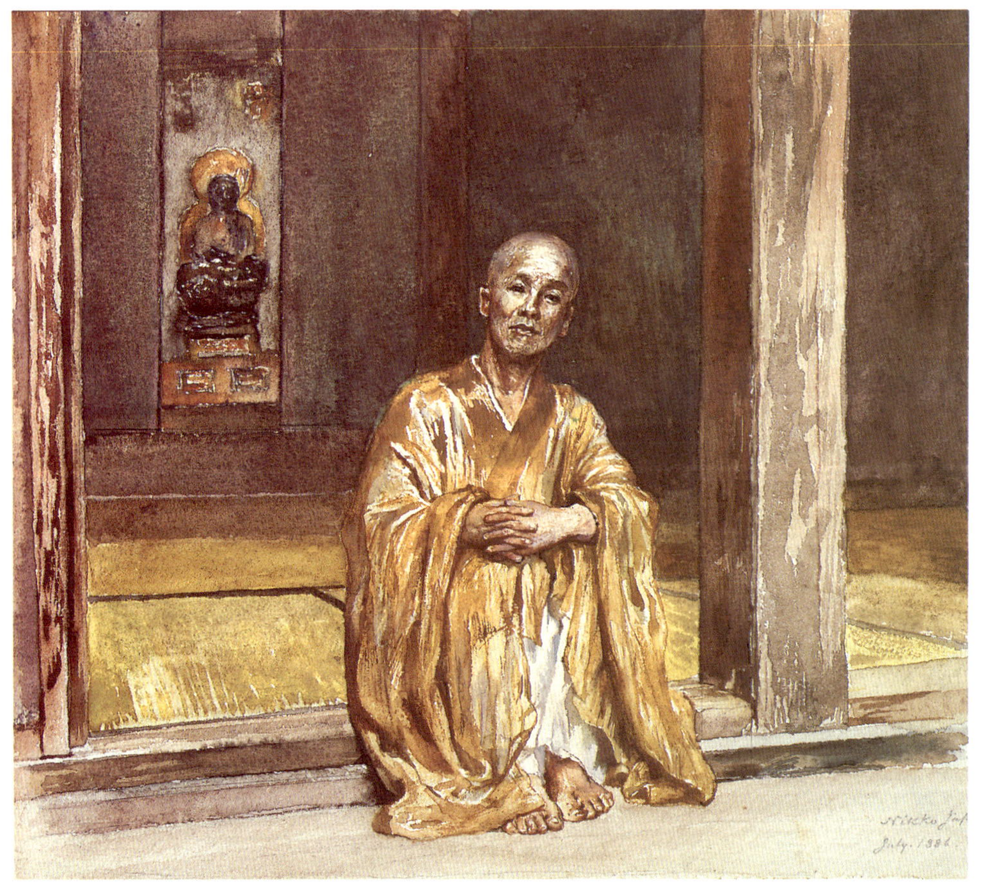

6

Portrait of Our Landlord, the Buddhist Priest Zenshin San, at the Door of the Clergy House, Iyemitsu Temple, Nikko (Portrait of Suzuki), 1886.

Watercolor and gouache over graphite on off-white, thick-wove paper. Sight: 8 3/4 x 9 3/4 in. (22.4 x 25.1 cm.). Collection of Mr. and Mrs. Willard G. Clark.

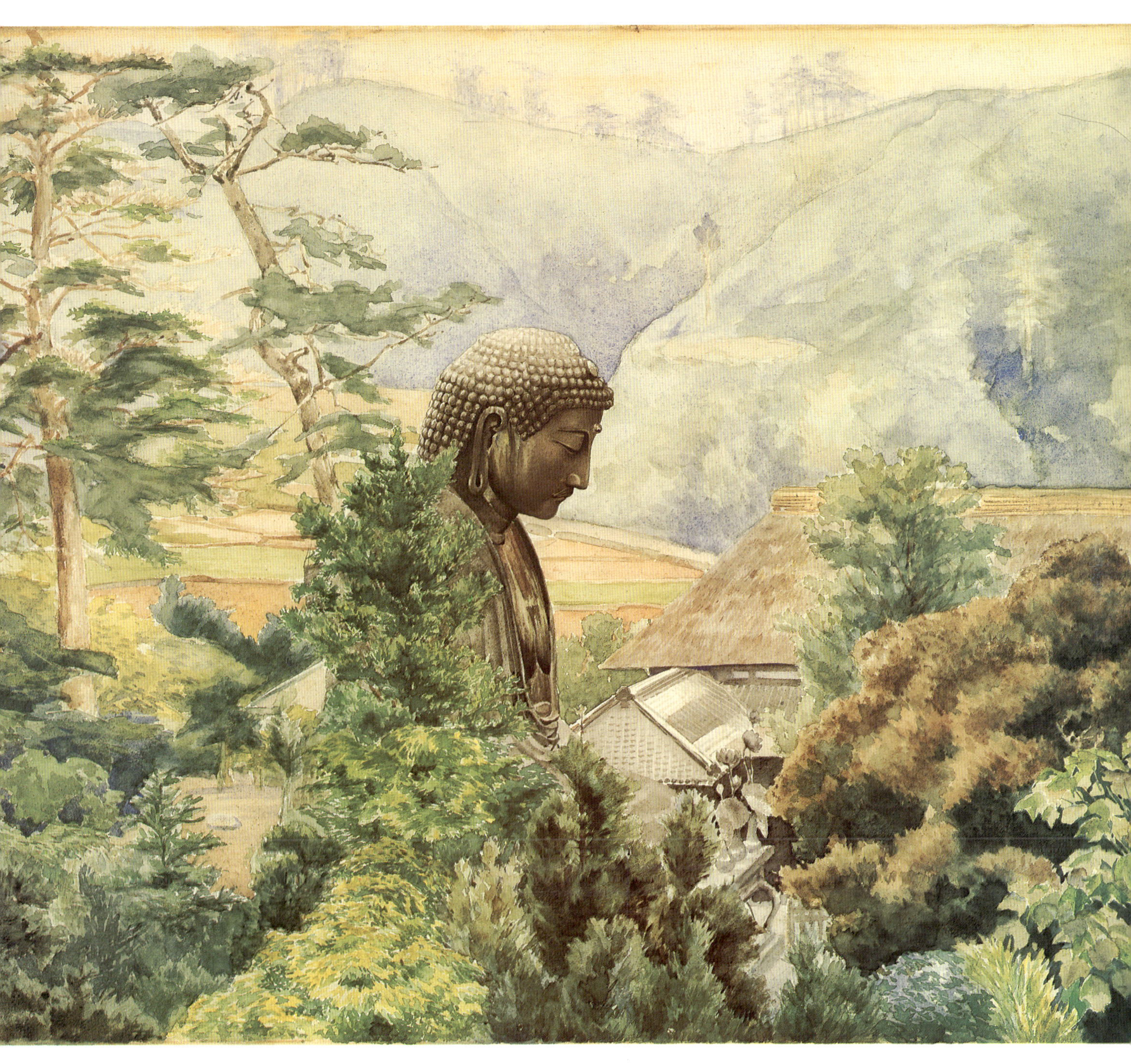

7

The Great Bronze Statue of Amida Buddha at Kamakura. Side View, c. 1887.

Watercolor over graphite on paper.
15 7/8 x 19 1/4 in. (39.3 x 48.5 cm.).
Achenbach Foundation for Graphic Arts, The Fine Arts Museums of San Francisco, Gift of Mr. and Mrs. John D. Rockerfeller 3rd.

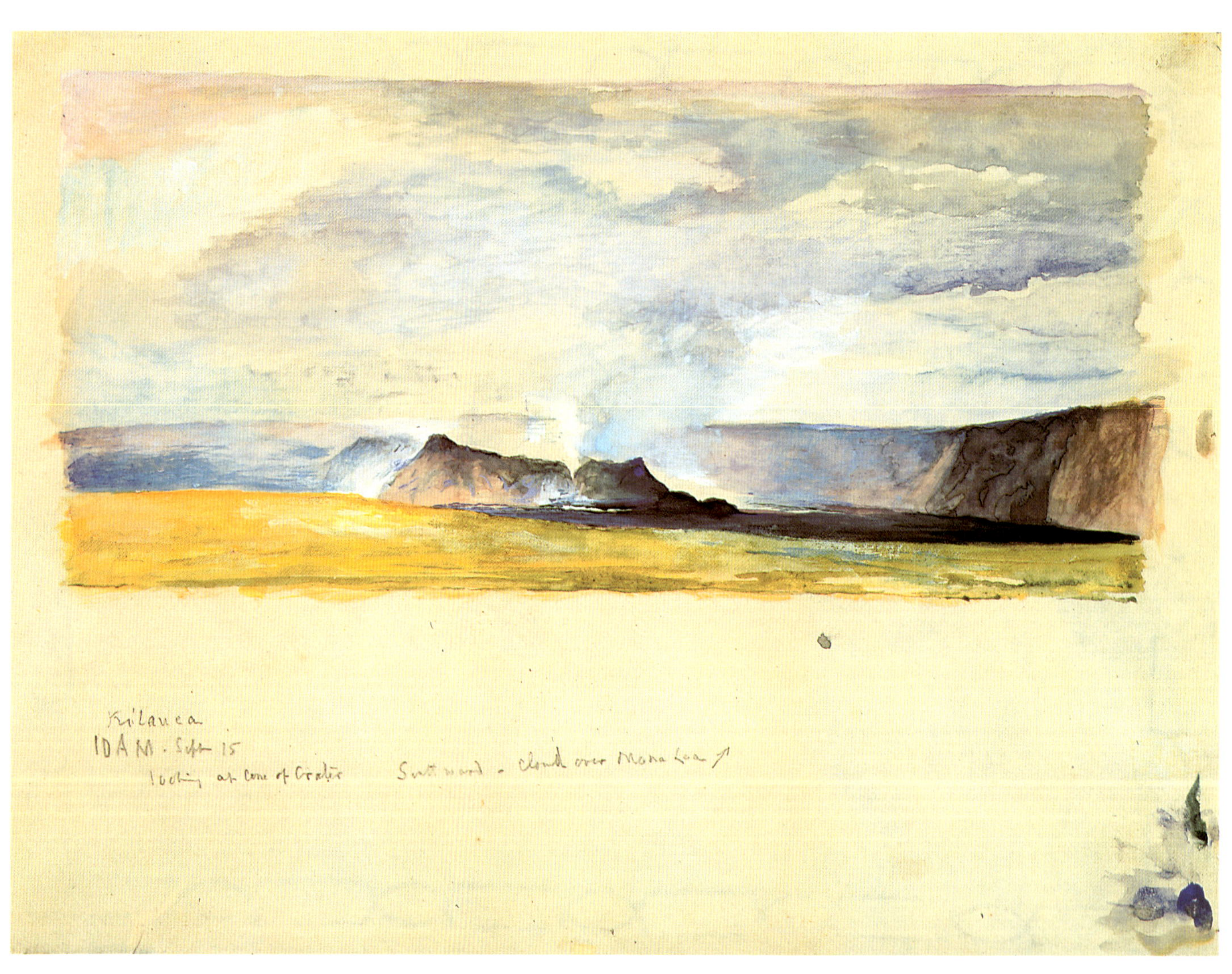

8

Kilauea, 10 a.m., Sept. 15th, 1890. Looking at Cone of Crater. Southward. Cloud over Mauna Loa, 1890.

Watercolor and gouache over graphite on laid paper.
Sheet: 7 7/8 x 10 1/2 in. (18.7 x 25.9 cm.).
Honolulu Academy of Fine Arts,
Gift of Admiral and Mrs. Henry S. Persons, 1988.

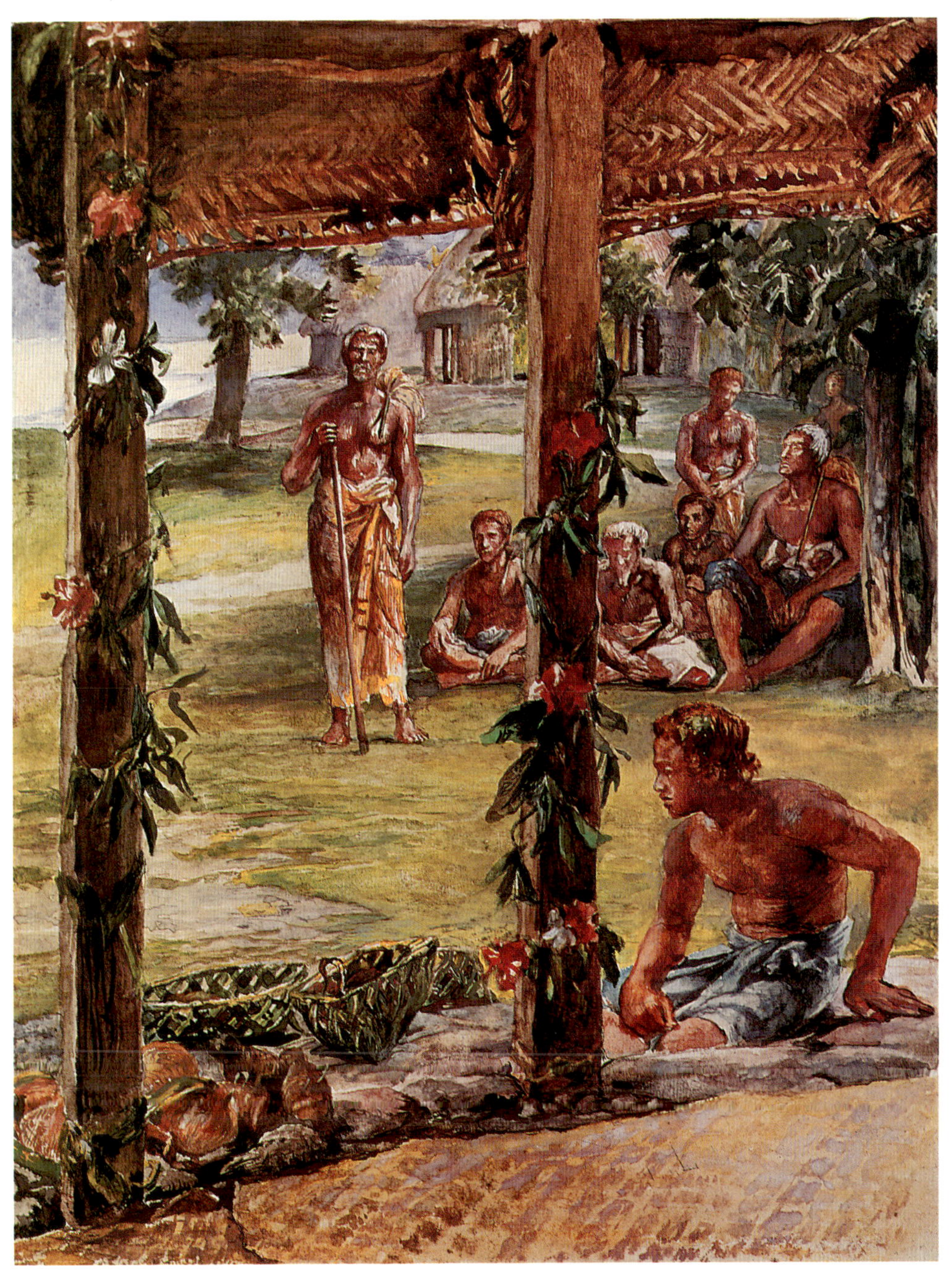

9

Presentation of Gifts of Food on Manono Island. Samoa, November 22, 1890, 1890.

Watercolor and gouache on paper.
11 3/8 x 8 3/4 in. (28.3 x 21.1 cm.).
Private Collection.

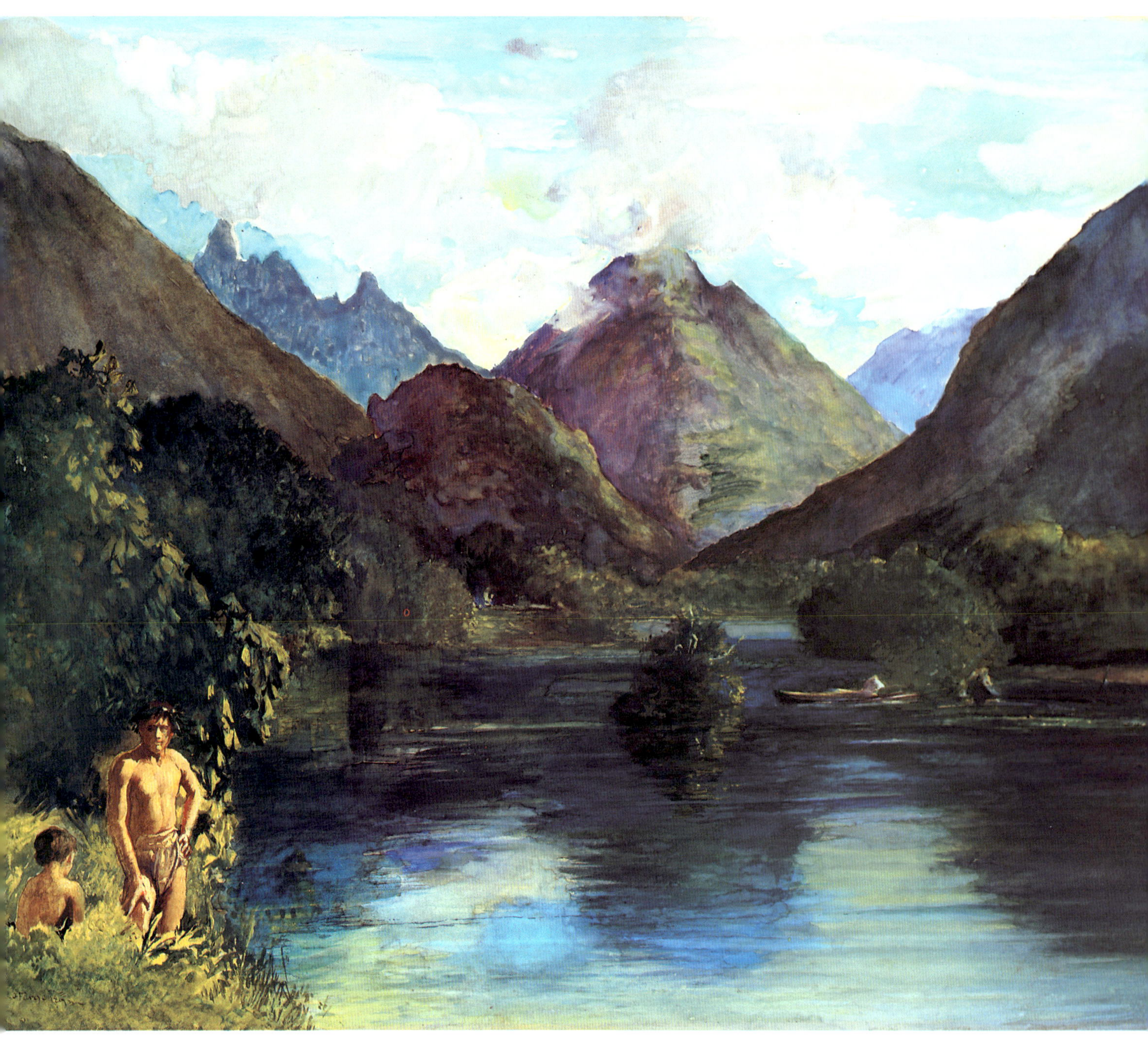

10

Entrance to Tautira River, Tahiti,
c. 1891.

Watercolor and gouache on paper.
13 3/8 x 21 3/8 in. (33.0 x 55.9 cm.).
Collection of Mr. and Mrs. Willard
G. Clark.

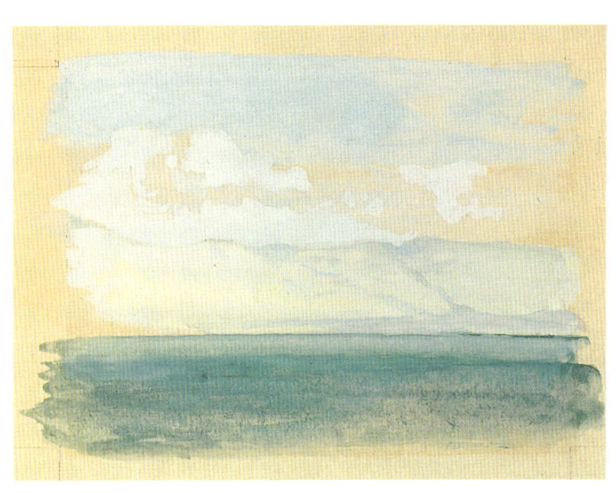

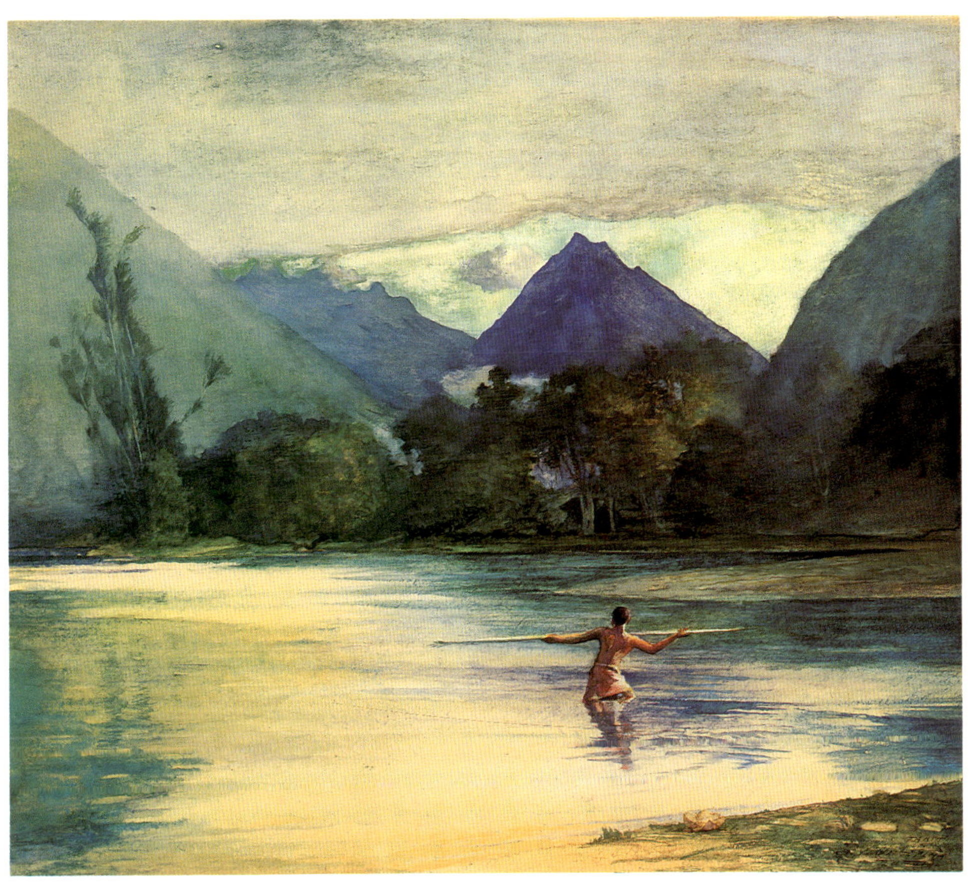

11

Entrance to the Vai-Te-Piha River. Cook's Anchorage, c. 1891.

Watercolor and gouache over graphite on heavy off-white paper.
16 x 18 1/4 in. (40.6 x 46.0 cm.).
Collection of Erving and Joyce Wolf.

12

Off Viti Levu. Sea and Desert Mountains. Fiji. Color Note, 1891.

Watercolor and gouache on tan laid paper.
Sight: 3 1/2 x 4 3/4 in. (8.1 x 10.9 cm.).
Private Collection.

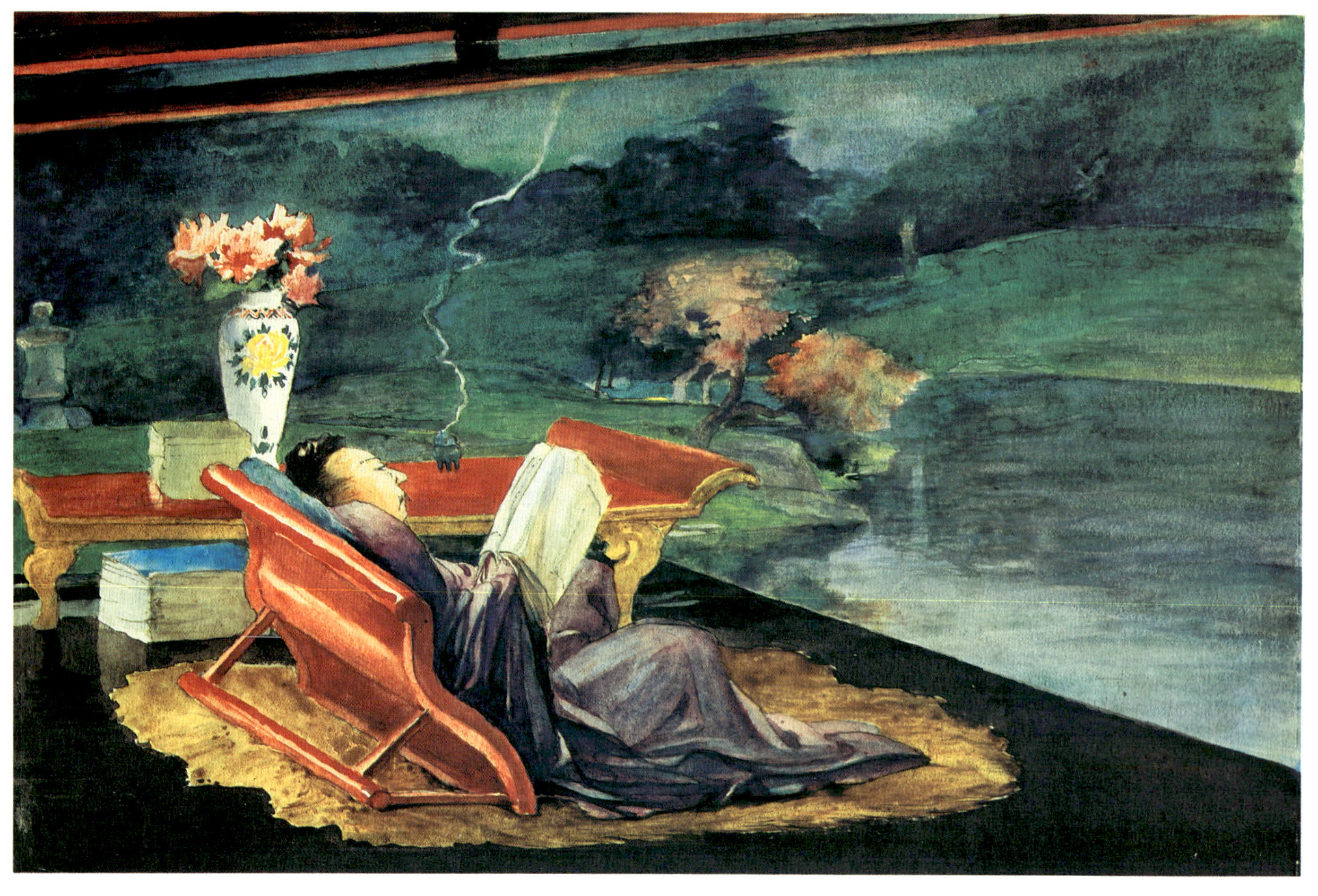

13

The Aesthete, 1898.

Watercolor, gouache, and pen and ink on paper.
10 x 14 1/2 in. (25.4 x 36.1 cm.).
Milton and Adrienne Porter.

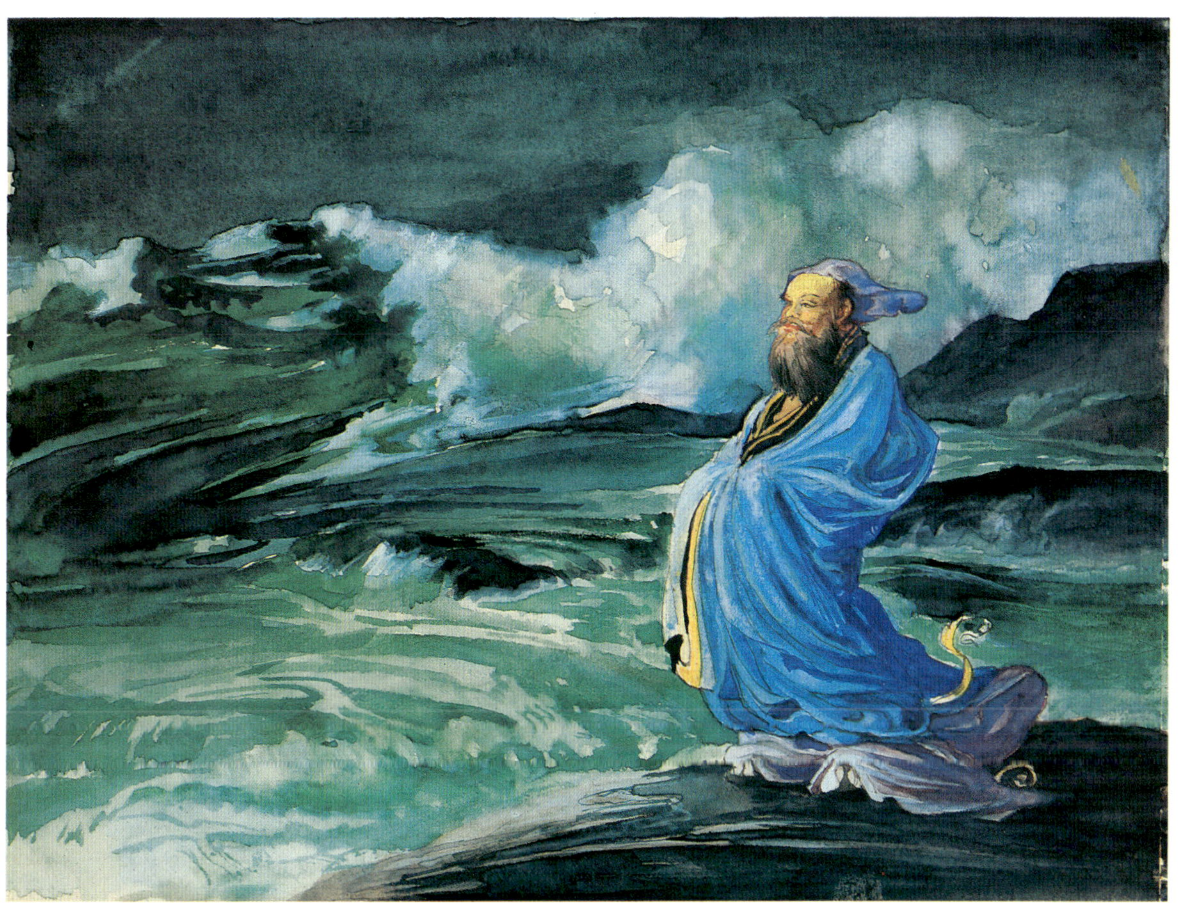

14

A Rishi Calling up a Storm, Japanese Folk Lore, c. 1897-1898.

Watercolor, gouache, and pen and ink over graphite on paper.
Sheet: 13 x 16 1/8 in. (33.0 x 40.4 cm.).
The Cleveland Museum of Art, Purchase from the J.H. Wade Fund.

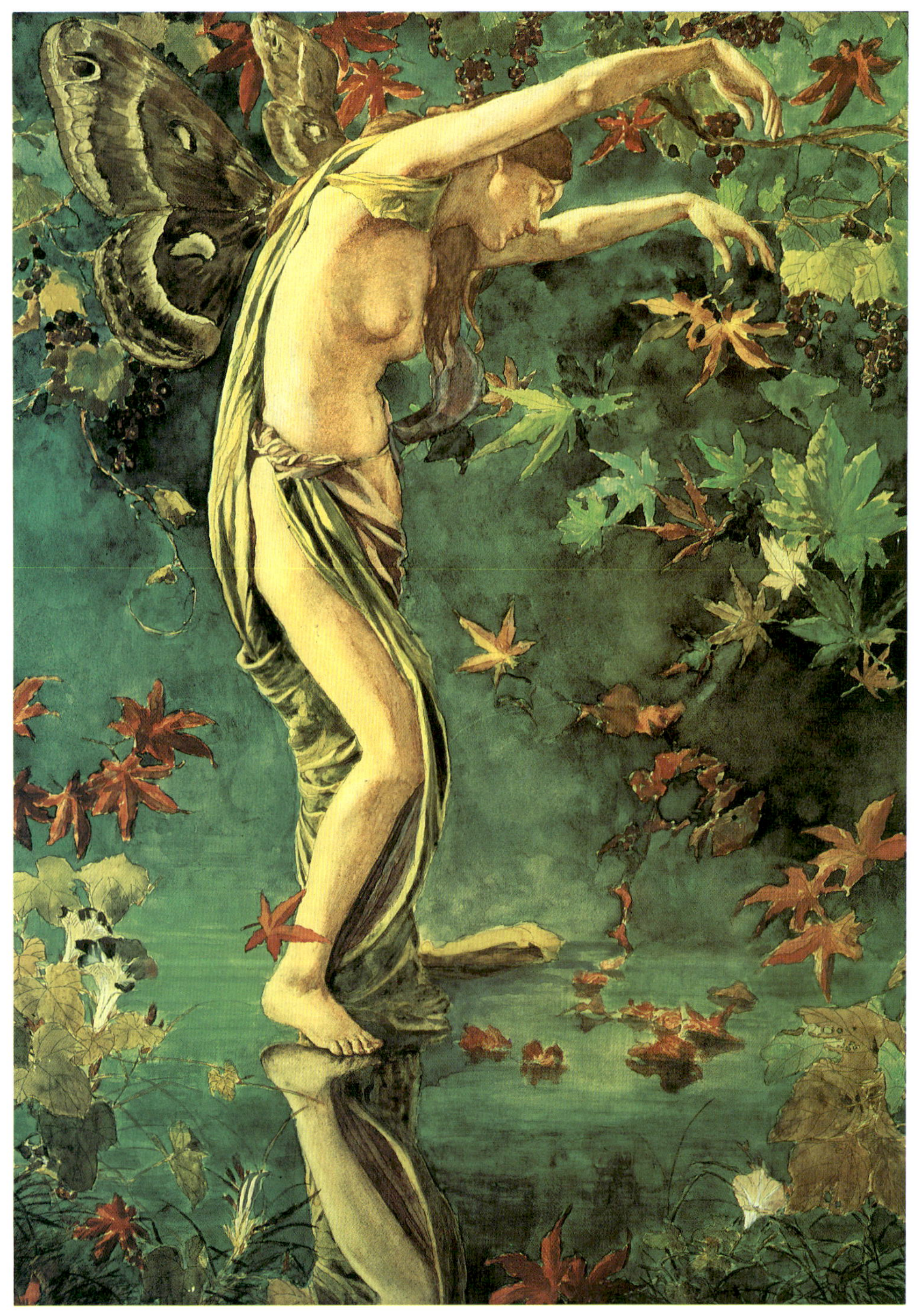

15

Autumn Scattering Leaves; Color Study for Window Intended for William C. Whitney House, Old Westbury, Long Island, New York, c. 1900.

Watercolor and gouache on paper. 18 1/4 x 13 1/4 in. (46.0 x 33.3 cm.). Private Collection.

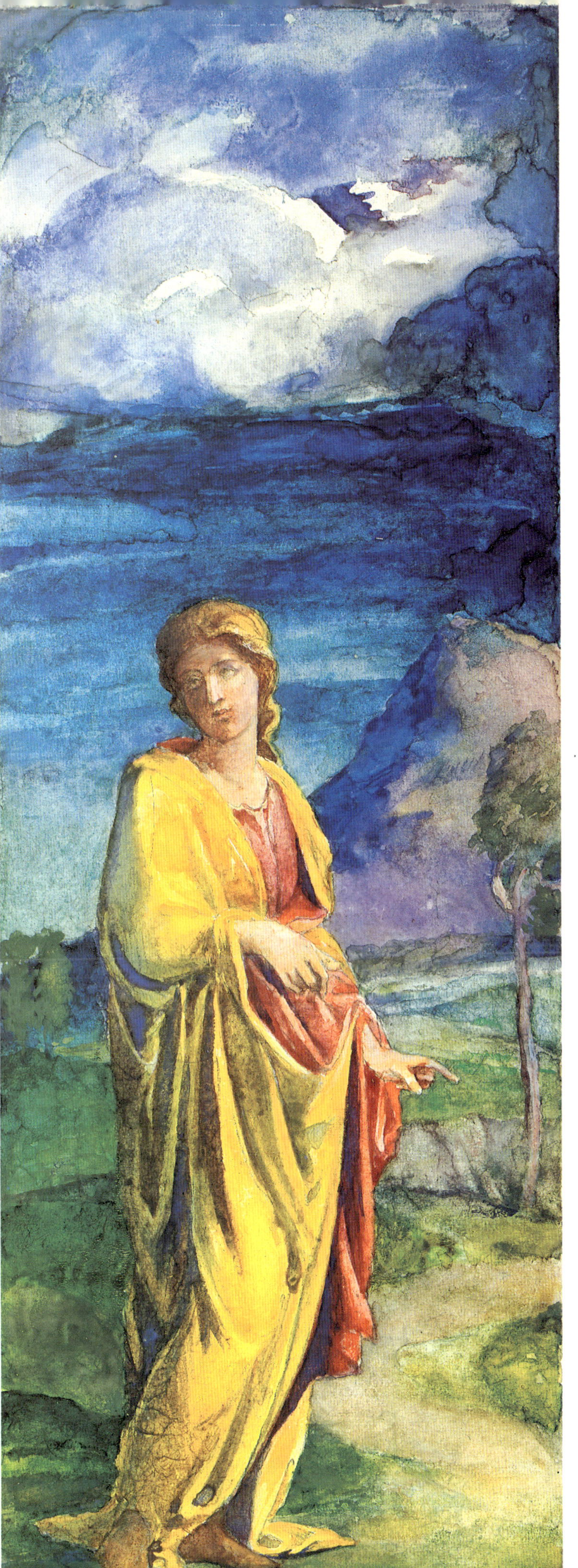

16

Semita Certe; Color Study for Helen A. Shafer Memorial Window, Wellesley College, Wellesley, Massachusetts, 1901.

Watercolor and gouache over graphite on grainy buff paper.
Sight: 15 1/4 x 5 1/2 in. (38.4 x 13.2 cm.).
Wellesley College Museum, Wellesley, Massachusetts.

Checklist and bibliography

CHECKLIST OF WORKS IN THE EXHIBITION

EARLY WORKS

1 *The Crucifixion of Saint Peter*; Study after a drawing by Michelangelo for a mural in the Pauline Chapel of the Vatican, Rome, 1856
Red chalk on grainy brown paper
7 1/4 x 10 in. (18.0 x 25.4 cm.)
Bowdoin College Museum of Art, Brunswick, Maine

2 *Christ and the Disciples at Emmaus. Copy of Rembrandt. July 1856*, 1856
Watercolor and gouache or ink wash over graphite and possibly red chalk on paper
13 x 17 1/2 in. (33.0 x 43.7 cm.)
Hood Art Museum, Dartmouth College, Gift of George Breed Zug, Class of 1920H

3 *Head of Boy*;
Copy after Couture's *Etude d'enfant*, 1856
Crayon and white chalk on paper
13 1/2 x 11 1/4 in. (34.3 x 28.2 cm.)
Collection of Matilda S. Dordet and Allen C. Davis

4 *House at St. Pol de Léon*, 1856
Graphite and white chalk on brown paper
8 3/4 x 7 3/4 in. (21.1 x 19.7 cm.)
Mead Art Museum, Amherst College

5 *Studies from the Nude*, 1857?
Graphite on paper
Sheet: 5 3/4 x 8 3/4 in. (14.4 x 22.1 cm.)
Courtesy of Indiana University Art Museum

6 *Frank La Farge*, 1857-1858
Chalk on tinted paper
13 3/16 x 9 9/16 in. (33.2 x 23.4 cm.)
The Pierpont Morgan Library, New York, Gift of Mr. Henry A. La Farge

THE NEWPORT PERIOD, 1859–1873

7 *John Chandler Bancroft*, 1863
Charcoal on paper
8 x 5 5/8 in. (20.3 x 14.3 cm.)
Redwood Library and Athenaeum, Newport

8 *John Chandler Bancroft*, 1863?
Soft graphite or black crayon on paper
6 x 3 7/16 in. (15.2 x 8.1 cm.)
Worcester Art Museum, Worcester, Massachusetts

9 *Thomas Sergeant Perry*, 1865
Graphite on paper
7 3/4 x 5 11/16 in. (19.7 x 14.5 cm.)
Redwood Library and Athenaeum, Newport

10 *Robert Gould Shaw*, 1863
Graphite on paper
4 3/4 x 3 1/4 in. (12.1 x 8.3 cm.)
Collection of Mr. and Mrs. Stuart P. Feld

11 *Lamplight Study*, 1865
Soft graphite or black crayon on thin Japanese paper
7 5/16 x 5 11/16 (18.4 x 13.7 cm.)
The Spencer Museum of Art,
William Bridges Thayer Memorial

12 *Mother and Child*, c. 1866
Graphite on Japanese mulberry vellum
Sight: 7 1/4 x 7 1/2 in. (18.3 x 18.9 cm.)
Lee-La Farge Collection, Mount Saint Mary's College, Emmitsburg, Maryland

13 *Father Isaac Thomas Hecker Reading Goethe*, 1866
Charcoal on rice paper, mounted
6 11/16 x 4 1/4 in. (16.2 x 10.8 cm.)
The Metropolitan Museum of Art, New York,
Gift of Mrs. Samuel M. Hamill, 1990

14 *Father Francis Aloysius Baker*, 1863
Soft graphite or black crayon on thin paper
5 7/8 x 4 in. (13.8 x 10.2 cm.)
The Art Museum, Princeton University, Princeton, New Jersey. Gift of Frank Jewett Mather, Jr.

15 *Design for a Coin* (Allegory of New York), 1859
Graphite on vellum
2 5/16 x 2 7/8 in. (5.4 x 6.0 cm.)
Sterling and Francine Clark Art Institute, Williamstown, Massachusetts. Gift of L. Bancel La Farge

16 *The Children*, 1864; published in Alfred Lord Tennyson, *Enoch Arden* (Boston, 1865)
Wood-engraving on paper
3 7/16 x 3 15/16 in. (8.7 x 10.0 cm.)
Private Collection

17 *The Lovers*, 1864; published in Alfred Lord Tennyson, *Enoch Arden* (Boston, 1865)
Wood-engraving on paper
3 15/16 x 3 1/8 in. (10.0 x 7.9 cm.)
Private Collection

18 *Philip and Annie in the Wood*, 1864; published in Alfred Lord Tennyson, *Enoch Arden* (Boston, 1865)
Wood-engraving on paper
3 15/16 x 3 15/16 in. (10.0 x 10.0 cm.)
Private Collection

19 *Shipwrecked*, 1864; published in Alfred Lord Tennyson, *Enoch Arden* (Boston, 1865)
Wood-engraving on paper
3 15/16 x 4 3/4 in. (10.0 x 12.6 cm.)
Private Collection

20 *The Island Home*, 1864; published in Alfred Lord Tennyson, *Enoch Arden* (Boston, 1865)
Wood-engraving on paper
3 13/16 x 3 1/4 in. (9.7 x 8.3 cm.)
Private Collection

21 *Enoch Alone*, 1864; published in Alfred Lord Tennyson, *Enoch Arden* (Boston, 1865)
Wood-engraving on paper
3 7/8 x 3 1/4 in. (9.8 x 8.3 cm.)
Private Collection

22 *The Solitary*, 1864; published in Alfred Lord Tennyson, *Enoch Arden* (Boston, 1865)
Wood-engraving on paper
3 15/16 x 3 3/8 in. (10.0 x 8.6 cm.)
Private Collection

23 *Enoch's Supplication*, 1864; published in Alfred Lord Tennyson, *Enoch Arden* (Boston, 1865)
Wood-engraving on paper
3 3/16 x 3 11/16 in. (8.1 x 9.4 cm.)
Private Collection

24 *The Seal of Silence*, 1864; published in Alfred Lord Tennyson, *Enoch Arden* (Boston, 1865)
Wood-engraving on paper
3 15/16 x 3 9/16 in. (10.0 x 9.5 cm.)
Private Collection

25 *The Pied Piper of Hamelin Town*, 1868; published in *The Riverside Magazine for Young People*, January 1868
Wood-engraving on paper
6 3/4 x 5 3/8 in. (17.2 x 13.7 cm.)
Private Collection

26 *The Wolf-Charmer*, 1867; published in *The Riverside Magazine for Young People*, December 1867
Wood-engraving on paper
6 5/8 x 5 5/16 in. (16.8 x 13.5 cm.)
Private Collection

27 *The Enchantress*, 1867
India ink on uncut woodblock
6 3/4 x 5 3/8 in. (16.0 x 13.1 cm.)
Private Collection

28 *The Fisherman and the Afrite*, 1868; published in *The Riverside Magazine for Young People*, July 1868
Wood-engraving on paper
6 3/4 x 5 3/8 in. (17.2 x 14.3 cm.)
Private Collection

29 *In the King's Garden*, 1868
India ink and Chinese white on uncut woodblock
5 3/4 x 4 3/16 in. (13.5 x 10.3 cm.)
Private Collection

30 *The Giant* (*The Giant and the Travelers*), 1869; published in *The Riverside Magazine for Young People*, July 1869
Wood-engraving on paper
7 x 5 1/2 in. (17.8 x 14.0 cm.)
Private Collection

31 *Midsummer Eve*, 1870; published in *The Riverside Magazine for Young People*, August 1870
Wood-engraving on paper
7 x 5 1/2 in. (17.8 x 14.0 cm.)
Private Collection

32 *The Spirit of the Water-Lily*, 1872; published in Abby Sage Richardson, *Songs from the Old Dramatists* (New York, 1873)
Wood-engraving on paper
5 1/4 x 3 1/2 in. (13.3 x 8.9 cm.)
Private Collection

33 *Songs of Feeling, Songs of Thought*, 1872; published in Abby Sage Richardson, *Songs from the Old Dramatists* (New York, 1873)
Wood-engraving on paper
5 1/4 x 3 1/2 in. (13.3 x 8.9 cm.)
Private Collection

34 *The Song of the Siren*, 1872; published in Abby Sage Richardson, *Songs from the Old Dramatists* (New York, 1873)
Wood-engraving on paper
5 3/4 x 3 9/16 in. (14.6 x 9.0 cm.)
Private Collection

35 *Songs of Sorrow*, 1872; published in Abby Sage Richardson, *Songs from the Old Dramatists* (New York, 1873)
Wood-engraving on paper
5 3/8 x 3 3/8 in. (13.7 x 8.6 cm.)
Private Collection

36 *Lotos Leaves*, 1874; published as frontispiece to *Lotos Leaves* (New York, 1875)
Wood-engraving on paper
5 1/2 x 3 1/4 in. (13.2 x 7.9 cm.)
Private Collection

37 *Water Lily and Linden Leaves*, 1872
Oil on panel
12 x 10 in. (30.5 x 25.4 cm.)
Mead Art Museum, Amherst College

38 *Study of Cloud Movement, Newport*, 1865
Graphite on paper
Sight: 6 3/4 x 3 15/16 in. (17.2 x 10 cm.)
Museum of Fine Arts, Boston, Gift of Major H.L. Higginson

39 *Study of Iris*, c. 1868?
Soft graphite or black crayon on paper
7 3/8 x 4 1/4 in. (19.5 x 10.4 cm.)
Private Collection

40 *Study of Flowers for Embroidery*, 1860
Watercolor, gouache, and gold leaf over graphite on graph paper
8 1/4 x 6 3/4 in. (21.0 x 17.0 cm.)
The Preservation Society of Newport County

41 *Pastoral Study.—Paradise, Newport, R.I.*, c. 1864-1865
Watercolor on paper
Sight: 7 x 9 in. (17.2 x 23.2 cm.)
Yale University Art Gallery, Bequest of John I.H. Downes, B.A. 1889

42 *Portrait of the Artist's Wife, Margaret La Farge*, c. 1865
Watercolor over graphite on watercolor paper
18 3/4 x 13 in. (47.6 x 33.1 cm.)
Private Collection

43 *Study for Salome's Dance*, c. 1872
Graphite and watercolor on grey paper
13 7/8 x 9 1/4 in. (33.9 x 23.1 cm.)
Museum of Fine Arts, Boston, Gift of Henry L. Higginson

44 *Epaminondas*; Study for Window, Memorial Hall, Harvard University, Cambridge, Massachusetts, 1874
Lithograph.
12 1/8 x 5 1/16 in. (30.6 x 12.8 cm.)
The Art Institute of Chicago, Chicago, Print Department Purchase

45 *Sir Philip Sidney*; Study for Window, Memorial Hall, Harvard University, Cambridge, Massachusetts, 1875
Watercolor on photomechanical reproduction of drawing
11 x 3 3/4 in. (27.9 x 8.4 cm.)
Private Collection

46 *Angel with Scroll*; Working Drawing for Mural, Trinity Church, Boston, 1876
Charcoal on squared paper
Sheet: 14 13/16 x 18 1/8 in. (11.0 x 45.8 cm.)
Sterling and Francine Clark Art Institute, Williamstown, Massachusetts. Gift of L. Bancel La Farge

47 *Angel*; Study for Trinity Church, Boston, 1876
Watercolor and gouache over graphite on coarse buff paper
Sight: 5 x 6 in. (12.7 x 14.9 cm.)
Yale University Art Gallery, Gift of Neva Bicknell Hecker

48 *Jeremiah*; Cartoon for Mural, Trinity Church, Boston, 1876
Charcoal and graphite on brown paper
28 x 14 in. (71.1 x 35.5 cm.)
Yale University Art Gallery, The Gherardi Davis Fund

49 *Nicodemus*, c. 1877
Graphite on heavy Whatman paper
14 x 10 in. (35.6 x 25.4 cm.)
Private Collection

50 *The Resurrection*; Design for Altarpiece, St. Thomas's Church, New York, 1877
Soft graphite or black crayon on grainy tan paper
6 x 11 in. (14.9 x 26.4 cm.)
Avery Architectural and Fine Arts Library, Columbia University

51 *The Three Marys*; Color Study for Altarpiece, St. Thomas's Church New York, 1877
Watercolor on paper
9 3/16 x 8 5/16 in. (23.0 x 20.6 cm.)
Private Collection

52 *The Dawn*; Design for Cornelius Vanderbilt II House, New York, 1880
Crayon on faded tan paper
13 x 13 in. (33.0 x 33.0 cm.)
Harvard University Art Museums, Fogg Art Museum, Cambridge, Massachusetts, Gift of the Family of the late Frederick A. Dwight

53 *Sketch for a Fountain*; Study for Glass, Cornelius Vanderbilt House, New York, c. 1881
Watercolor and graphite on thin paper, mounted
9 x 6 3/8 in. (22.9 x 15.6 cm.)
Museum of Fine Arts, Boston, Gift of Henry L. Higginson

54 *The Virgin Mary*; Cartoon for Barnabas Bates Memorial Window, Channing Memorial Church, Newport, c. 1881
India ink on paper
Sight: 32 x 13 in. (81.3 x 33.0 cm.)
Lee-La Farge Collection, Mount Saint Mary's College, Emmitsburg, Maryland

55 *Design for Ceiling, Brick Presbyterian Church, New York*, c. 1883
Graphite, watercolor, and gold leaf on light grey paper
11 1/8 x 7 3/8 in. (28.1 x 18.2 cm.)
Museum of Fine Arts, Boston, Gift of Henry L. Higginson

56 *Moon in Clouds*; Color Study for Glass, c. 1884-1885
Watercolor and pencil retouched with silver on paper
11 1/2 x 7 1/2 in. (29.2 x 18.3 cm.)
Private Collection

57 *Angel of Help*; Color Study for Helen Angier Ames Memorial Window, Unity Church, North Easton, Massachusetts, 1884
Watercolor and gouache on paper
11 1/2 x 6 1/2 in. (29.2 x 16.5 cm.)
Collection of Mr. and Mrs. Richard N. Carrell

58 *Saint James and the Risen Christ*; Design for James C. Harrison Memorial Window, Trinity Church, Buffalo, 1884?
Graphite on tracing paper
12 1/2 x 9 1/16 in. (31.0 x 22.9 cm.)
Museum of Fine Arts, Boston, Gift of Major H.L. Higginson

59 *Saint James and the Risen Christ*; Color Study for James C. Harrison Memorial Window, Trinity Church, Buffalo, c. 1884-1886
Watercolor over graphite on thin tracing paper
7 1/4 x 6 1/2 in. (18.0 x 15.7 cm.).
Private Collection

60 *The Maji and the Heavenly Sign*; Color Study for Jerry Radcliffe and Ariadne Webster Radcliffe Memorial Window. Trinity Church, Buffalo, c. 1885-1886
Watercolor, graphite, and gouache on paper
10 1/2 x 4 in. (26.7 x 10.2 cm.)
M. Lloyd

61 *Study of Female Figure. Intended to Illustrate a Verse of Isaiah*, 1882
Watercolor and gouache over graphite on coarse buff paper
13 x 9 3/4 in. (33.0 x 24.8 cm.)
Private Collection

62 *Female Figure in Blue, Reading*, c. 1883-1884
Watercolor and gouache over graphite on paper
7 1/2 x 3 1/2 in. (18.3 x 8.1 cm.)
M. Lloyd

63 *Female Figure in a Pink Dress with Blue Cloak, with Hand Extended.—Study for a Figure of Andromache*, c. 1883-1884
Watercolor and gouache on paper
8 1/4 x 4 1/8 in. (21.0 x 10.5 cm.)
Private Collection

64 *Marcella. Study of Seated Figure in Classical Costume*, 1883
Watercolor and gouache on paper
7 5/8 x 5 7/8 in. (18.4 x 13.8 cm.)
IBM Corporation

65 *Hollyhocks*, c. 1879-1882
Watercolor on paper
7 1/4 x 3 1/2 in. (18.0 x 8.1 cm.)
Private Collection, courtesy of Thomas Colville Fine Art, Inc.

66 *Flowers. In a Blue Chinese Vase, of Antique Shape*, c. 1879-1884
Watercolor and gouache on paper
6 3/4 x 8 1/8 in. (16.0 x 20.4 cm.)
Private Collection

67 *Camellias and Roses in Japanese Vase of Earthenware with Crackle Glaze*, 1879
Watercolor and tempera on paper
Sheet: 16 13/16 x 17 11/16 in. (41.5 x 43.9 cm.)
Museum of Art, Rhode Island School of Design, Providence, Gift of Mrs. Gustav Metcalf Radeke

68 *Roses in Blue Crackled Glass Pitcher*, c. 1879
Watercolor and gouache over graphite on paper
13 3/4 x 11 3/4 in. (34.9 x 29.8 cm.)
Private Collection

69 *Roses*, c. 1880
Watercolor and gouache over graphite on off-white paper
8 1/2 x 10 3/4 in. (21.6 x 27.3 cm.)
Private Collection

70 *Waterlily and Pads*, 1881
Watercolor and gouache on paper
Sight: 5 3/4 x 9 1/8 in. (14.6 x 22.9 cm.)
San Diego Museum of Art, Gift of Jesse Albert Locke

71 *Peacocks and Peonies*; Color Study for Window in Frederick Lothrop Ames House, Boston, c. 1882
Watercolor over graphite on paper
7 5/8 x 4 1/4 in. (18.4 x 10.4 cm.)
Private Collection

72 *Study of Autumn Flowers in Persian Glass Bowl with White Enamel Edge*, 1884
Watercolor on paper
11 x 13 1/2 in. (27.9 x 34.3 cm.)
Washington County Museum of Fine Arts, Hagerstown, Maryland, Museum Gift, 1951

73 *Hollyhocks*, 1885
Watercolor heightened with gouache on paper
11 x 7 5/8 in. (27.9 x 18.4 cm.)
Private Collection

74 *Study at Berkeley Ridge or Hanging Rock*, c. 1883-1884
Watercolor and gouache on paper
10 1/2 x 13 in. (26.7 x 33.0 cm.)
Museum of Fine Arts, Boston, Bequest of Mrs. Henry Lee Higginson

75 *The Fisherman and the Djinn (The Fisherman and the Afrite)*, 1883-1884
Watercolor and gouache on paper
14 x 10 in. (35.6 x 25.4 cm.)
Museum of Fine Arts, Boston, Bequest of Sarah Wyman Whitman

76 *Water-Fall of Urami-No-Taki*, 1886
Watercolor and gouache on paper
10 1/2 x 15 1/2 in. (26.7 x 39.4 cm.)
Addison Gallery of American Art, Phillips Academy, Andover, Massachusetts, Gift of Mr. and Mrs. Stuart P. Feld, 1985

77 *Temple Carving, Nikko*, 1886
Crayon on squared paper
Sight: 4 1/8 x 4 3/8 in. (10.3 x 10.5 cm.)
Museum of Fine Arts, Boston, Gift of Major H.L. Higginson

78 *Red Pagoda, Nikko*, 1886
Watercolor on paper
11 7/8 x 9 1/2 in. (30.1 x 24.2 cm.)
Albright-Knox Art Gallery, Buffalo, New York; bequest of Edmund Hayes, 1924

79 *Looking Over the Garden Wall and Steps Toward the Temple Enclosure of Iyeyasu*, 1886
Watercolor on paper
11 x 8 in. (27.9 x 20.3 cm.)
Whitney Museum of American Art, Gift of Susan and David Workman

80 *Corner of Water Tank or Sacred Font, Temple of Iyemitsu, Nikko*, 1886
Watercolor over graphite on paper
Sight: 7 x 6 1/2 in. (17.2 x 15.7 cm.)
Mathilda G. La Farge

81 *Sacred Font in the Temple of Iyemitsu, Nikko. From the Platform of the Second Gate*, 1886
Watercolor and gouache over graphite on paper, mounted
9 1/2 x 11 3/4 in. (24.1 x 29.8 cm.)
Collection of Mr. and Mrs. Richard N. Carrell

82 *Tokio Geisha, Dancing in the House of Our Neighbor, Nikko*, 1886
Watercolor and gouache over graphite on paper
13 1/4 x 8 7/8 (33.3 x 22.6 cm.)
Bowdoin College Museum of Art, Brunswick, Maine

83 *Portrait of Our Landlord, the Buddhist Priest Zenshin San, at the Door of the Clergy House, Iyemitsu Temple, Nikko* (Portrait of Suzuki), 1886
Watercolor and gouache over graphite on off-white, thick-wove paper
Sight: 8 3/4 x 9 3/4 in. (22.4 x 25.1 cm.)
Collection of Mr. and Mrs. Willard G. Clark

84 *The Great Bronze Statue of Amida Buddha at Kamakura. Side View*, c. 1887
Watercolor over graphite on paper
15 7/8 x 19 1/4 in. (39.3 x 48.5 cm.)
Achenbach Foundation for Graphic Arts, The Fine Arts Museums of San Francisco, Gift of Mr. and Mrs. John D. Rockerfeller 3rd

85 *Sunset in Fog Over Kiyoto*, 1886
Watercolor on paper
6 7/8 x 11 3/4 in. (18.1 x 29.8 cm.)
Private Collection

86 *Mountain of Fuji-San from Fuji-Kawa*, 1886

Watercolor on paper
Sheet: 10 3/4 x 14 15/16 in. (26.2 x 36.5 cm.)
Georgia Museum of Art, University of Georgia, Athens, Georgia, Eva Underhill Holbrook Memorial Collection of American Art, Gift of Alfred H. Holbrook

87 *The Sower and the Reapers*; Color Study for Glass, c. 1887-1890

Watercolor, gouache, and pencil on paper
9 1/4 x 8 1/4 in. (23.4 x 21.0 cm.)
Private Collection

88 *Tattooed Jinrikisha Boy*, c. 1888

India ink on paper
13 7/16 x 10 7/16 in. (33.5 x 25.8 cm.)
Bowdoin College Museum of Art, Brunswick, Maine

89 *Fisherman. (Sunlight.)*, c. 1888-1889

Watercolor on paper
Sight: 4 1/2 x 4 in. (10.7 x 10.2 cm.)
The William A. Farnsworth Library and Art Museum, Rockland, Maine

90 *Ancient Japanese Woman*, c. 1888

Wood-engraving on paper
7 3/8 x 5 7/8 in. (19.5 x 13.8 cm.)
Private Collection

91 *The Great Pali*, 1890

Watercolor and gouache on paper
16 1/8 x 11 5/8 in. (42.9 cm. x 29.5 cm.)
Private Collection

92 *Kilauea, 10 a.m., Sept. 15th, 1890. Looking at Cone of Crater. Southward. Cloud over Mauna Loa*, 1890

Watercolor and gouache over graphite on laid paper
Sheet: 7 7/8 x 10 1/2 in. (18.7 x 25.9 cm.)
Honolulu Academy of Fine Arts, Gift of Admiral and Mrs. Henry S. Persons, 1988

93 *Presentation of Gifts of Food on Manono Island. Samoa, November 22, 1890*, 1890

Watercolor and gouache on paper
11 3/8 x 8 3/4 in. (28.3 x 21.1 cm.)
Private Collection

94 *Presentation of Gifts of Food on Manono Island, November 22, 1890*, c. 1895

India ink on paper
16 x 12 in. (40.6 x 30.5 cm.)
Private Collection

95 *Faase and her Duenna, Samoa, 1891*, c. 1891

Watercolor and gouache on paper
Sheet: 23 1/16 x 17 3/8 in. (58.5 x 43.6 cm.)
Collection of Rita and Daniel Fraad

96 *A Samoan Lady*, 1891

Watercolor and gouache on paperboard
9 1/16 x 5 3/4 in. (22.0 x 13.5 cm.)
The Brooklyn Museum, Brooklyn, Gift of Daniel and Rita Fraad Collection

97 *Another Standing Dance*, 1890

Watercolor and gouache on paper
Sight: 8 1/2 x 11 in. (21.6 x 27.9 cm.)
Collection of Mr. and Mrs. Willard G. Clark

98 *Sivà Dance* (Triptych of Seated Single Figures), 1890

Watercolor on paper
Each: 11 1/8 x 9 1/4 in. (28.2 x 23.1 cm.)
Private Collection courtesy of Jordan–Volpe Gallery, Inc.

99 *Samoan Girls Wrestling*, 1890

Watercolor and gouache on paper
12 x 12 1/2 in. (30.5 x 31.0 cm.)
The Peabody Museum of Salem, Gift of Francis Lee Higginson III

100 *Sivà Dance, Two Girls*, 1890

Watercolor and gouache on paper
16 x 21 1/2 in. (40.6 x 54.6 cm.)
Santa Barbara Museum of Art, Museum Purchase

101 *Sivà with Siakumu Making Kava in Tofae's House*, c. 1891-1895

Watercolor on Japanese mulberry vellum
Sheet: 18 9/16 x 23 3/4 in. (46.3 x 59.2 cm.)
Sterling and Francine Clark Art Institute, Williamstown, Massachusetts. Gift of L. Bancel La Farge

102 *Man in Canoe, Samoa*, 1890
Watercolor and gouache on paper
9 1/2 x 13 3/8 in. (24.1 x 34.0 cm.)
Private Collection

103 *View from Our Hut, At Vaiala, in Upolu. Bread Fruit Tree, War Drums and Canoe. November 19, 1890*, 1890
Watercolor and gouache over graphite on paper
10 1/2 x 13 1/2 in. (26.7 x 34.3 cm.)
Gift of Alice Hanszen, Collection of McNay Art Museum, San Antonio, Texas

104 *In Front of Our Gate, Papeete, Tahiti, 1891. Morning*, 1891
Watercolor and gouache over graphite on paper
10 1/4 x 8 7/8 in. (21.3 x 21.2 cm.)
Private Collection

105 *Diadem Mountain at Sunset, Tahiti*, c. 1899-1900
Watercolor, gouache, and mixed media on paper
Sheet: 16 3/4 x 22 3/16 in. (41.4 x 56.1 cm.)
The Brooklyn Museum, Brooklyn, Gift of Frank L. Babbott

106 *Himene at Papara In Front of Tati Salmon's, The Chief's House. February 26th, 1891*, 1891
Watercolor and gouache over graphite on paper
6 1/4 x 12 3/4 in. (15.9 x 32.4 cm.)
Private Collection

107 *Landscape. Evening. Tahiti. Pass and Peak of Vaiaroa, Taiarapu*, 1891
Watercolor and gouache on rice paper
Sight: 14 1/2 x 21 3/8 in. (36.1 x 53.7 cm.)
Private Collection

108 *Afterglow. March 30th, 1891. From Tautira Looking Towards the Mainland of Tahiti; in the Distance Orhena Peaks and the Aorai*, 1891
Watercolor and gouache on Japanese paper
5 5/16 x 10 1/8 in. (13.5 x 25.7 cm.)
Private Collection

109 *Entrance to Tautira River, Tahiti*, c. 1891
Watercolor and gouache on paper
13 3/8 x 21 3/8 in. (33.0 x 55.9 cm.)
Collection of Mr. and Mrs. Willard G. Clark

110 *Entrance to the Vai-Te-Piha River. Cook's Anchorage*, c. 1891
Watercolor and gouache over graphite on heavy off-white paper
16 x 18 1/4 in. (40.6 x 46.0 cm.)
Collection of Erving and Joyce Wolf

111 *Spearing Fish, Samoa*, c. 1891
Watercolor and gouache on paper
13 3/8 x 29 3/8 in. (33.0 x 74.6 cm.)
Addison Gallery of American Art, Phillips Academy, Andover, Massachusetts, Addison Purchase Fund

112 *Edge of the Aorai Mountain, Tahiti, May 1891*, 1891
Graphite on laid paper
7 1/2 x 4 7/8 in. (18.3 x 11.0 cm.)
Private Collection

113 *Hitiaa. Tahiti. June 4, 1891. Looking Towards Tiarapu and Neck of Isthmus, Upper Part Lost in Cloud*, 1891
Watercolor and gouache on paper
9 x 11 1/2 in. (22.9 x 29.2 cm.)
Private Collection

114 *Study on Reef at Tautira, Tahiti*, 1891
Watercolor and gouache on paper
7 9/16 x 13 3/8 in. (18.3 x 33.0 cm.)
Private Collection

115 *The Island of Moorea Looking Across the Strait from Tahiti*, 1891
Watercolor and gouache on paper
7 1/16 x 12 7/16 in. (17.8 x 30.9 cm.)
The Metropolitan Museum of Art, New York, Bequest of Susan Dwight Bliss, 1966

116 *The End of Cook's Bay. Island of Moorea. Society Islands. 1891. Dawn*, 1891
Watercolor and gouache on paper
14 1/2 x 22 in. (36.1 x 55.9 cm.)
New Britain Museum of American Art, Helen Russell Stanley Fund

117 *Study of Tongan Girl. With a Fan*, 1891
Watercolor and gouache on paper
Sight: 9 x 7 3/8 in. (23.2 x 18.2 cm.)
Eleanor S. Lunde

118 *Chiefs in War Dress Seated After a Dance. Islands of Fiji*, c. 1899-1901
Watercolor, gouache, and tempera on paper mounted on illustration board
9 1/2 x 21 in. (24.1 x 53.3 cm.)
The Phillips Collection, Washington, D.C.

119 *Off Viti Levu. Sea and Desert Mountains. Fiji. Color Note*, 1891
Watercolor and gouache on tan laid paper
Sight: 3 1/2 x 4 3/4 in. (8.1 x 10.9 cm.)
Private Collection

120 *At Naiserelangi, from Ratu Jonii Mandraiwiwi's "Yavu". July 14th, 1891*, 1891
Watercolor, gouache, and graphite on paper
Sight: 10 1/4 x 8 1/4 in. (26.0 x 20.0 cm.)
The Huntington Museum of Art, Huntington, WV, Daywood Collection

121 *Fruit of the Mangosteen. Java*, 1891
Watercolor and gouache on Japanese vellum
4 1/4 x 7 1/2 in. (10.8 x 19.1 cm.)
Private Collection

122 *Village Dancing Girls at Garoet in the Preanger Regency, Java*, 1891
Watercolor and gouache on paper
6 1/16 x 4 1/2 in. (15.4 x 11.4 cm.)
Yale University Art Gallery, Gift of Mrs. John Hay Whitney

123 *Colossal Statue of Ananda, near the Ruined City of Pollanarua. Ceylon, 1891*, 1891
Watercolor and gouache on paper, mounted on board
9 7/8 x 7 in. (25.1 x 17.8 cm.)
Private Collection

124 *Fayaway* (*Girl in Bow of Canoe Spreading Out Her Loin-Cloth for a Sail*), c. 1895-1896
Watercolor and gouache over graphite on thin Japanese paper laid down on thick, cream-surfaced artist's board
15 3/16 x 21 3/16 in. (38.6 x 55.4 cm.)
The Corcoran Gallery of Art, Museum Purchase

125 *Uatea Dancing the Seated Sivà*, c. 1895
Wood-engraving on paper
8 1/8 x 6 1/2 in. (20.6 x 16.5 cm.)
Private Collection

126 *Sifa Dancing the Sitting Sivà*, c. 1895
Wood-engraving on paper
8 1/8 x 6 1/2 in. (20.6 x 16.5 cm.)
Private Collection

127 *Adoring Angels*; Color Study for Mural, Church of the Ascension, New York, c. 1887-1888
Watercolor and gouache over graphite on paper
Sight: 8 1/4 x 5 3/4 in. (20 x 14.6 cm.)
Museum of Fine Arts, Boston, Gift of Mary W. Bartol, John W. Bartol, and Abigail Clark

128 *Color Study for a Rose Window*, c. 1887-1888
Watercolor over graphite on brown paper, mounted
9 5/8 x 7 7/8 in. (23.2 x 20.0 cm.)
Museum of Fine Arts, Boston, Gift of Henry L. Higginson

129 *Angel Sealing the Servant of God*; Design for Anna Margaret Sherman and Gertrude Van Daltsen (so-called "Watson") Memorial Window, Trinity Church, Buffalo, 1889
Graphite on thin rice paper
Sheet: 21 3/4 x 16 in. (54.1 x 40.6 cm.)
The Metropolitan Museum of Art, New York, Bequest of Flora E. Whiting, 1970

130 *Angel Sealing the Servant of God*; Design for Anna Margaret Sherman and Gertrude Van Daltsen (so-called "Watson") Memorial Window, Trinity Church, Buffalo, 1889
Graphite on thin brown tracing paper
Sheet: 16 3/8 x 8 in. (41.0 x 20.3 cm.)
The Brooklyn Museum, Brooklyn, Gift of George D. Pratt

131 *Angels of the Resurrection*; Color Study for Emily Martin Southworth Memorial Window, Church of the Ascension, New York, c. 1889
Watercolor and gouache on paperboard
Sheet: 11 1/4 x 9 7/8 in. (28.2 x 23.7 cm.)
Harriet B. Lidgerwood

132 Studio of John La Farge, *Color Study for Interior Decoration of Church of St. Paul the Apostle, New York*, c. 1896-1899
Watercolor and gouache over graphite on paper
20 1/4 x 15 7/8 in. (51.1 x 39.0 cm.) (irregular)
Cooper-Hewitt. National Museum of Design, Smithsonian Institution

133 *Angel of the Annunciation*; Color Study for Emma Knox Cain and Amanda Knox Jennings Memorial Window, The Presbyterian Church of Sewickley, Sewickley, Pennsylvania, c. 1896-1899
Watercolor and graphite on paper
Sheet: 25 1/4 x 15 3/4 in. (63.8 x 38.9 cm.)
Collection of Stuart Pivar

134 *On the Tower of Ivory*; Color Study for Angie Lacey Peck Memorial Window, Wellesley College, Wellesley, Massachusetts, 1900
Watercolor and graphite on paper
7 3/4 x 4 3/4 in. (19.7 x 11.5 cm.)
The Art Museum, Princeton University, Princeton, New Jersey. Gift of Frank Jewett Mather, Jr.

135 *Semita Certe*; Color Study for Helen A. Shafer Memorial Window, Wellesley College, Wellesley, Massachusetts, 1901

Watercolor and gouache over graphite on grainy buff paper
Sight: 15 1/4 x 5 1/2 in. (38.4 x 13.2 cm.)
Wellesley College Museum, Wellesley, Massachusetts

136 *Spring*; Color Study for Window Intended for William C. Whitney House, Old Westbury, Long Island, New York, 1900

Watercolor and gouache over graphite on paper
7 1/4 x 5 11/16 in. (18.4 x 13.4 cm.)
Detroit Institute of Arts, Detroit, Gift of the Founders Society, Merrill Fund, 1947

137 *Autumn Scattering Leaves*; Design for Window Intended for William C. Whitney House, Old Westbury, Long Island, New York, c. 1900

Graphite on tracing paper mounted on Japanese tissue
10 1/2 x 7 1/4 in. (26.7 x 18.4 cm.)
Museum of Fine Arts, Boston, Gift of Major H.L. Higginson

138 *Autumn Scattering Leaves*; Color Study for Window Intended for William C. Whitney House, Old Westbury, Long Island, New York, c. 1900

Watercolor and gouache on paper
18 1/2 x 13 1/2 in. (47.0 x 32.4 cm.)
Private Collection

139 *Autumn Scattering Leaves*; Color Study for Window Intended for William C. Whitney House, Old Westbury, Long Island, New York, c. 1900

Watercolor and gouache on paper
18 1/4 x 13 1/4 in. (46.0 x 33.3 cm.)
Private Collection

140 *Fortune on Wheel*; Design for Window, Frick Building, Pittsburgh, 1901

Graphite on paper
Sheet: 10 15/16 x 7 7/8 (27.8 x 20.0 cm.)
The Cleveland Museum of Art, Gift of William G. Mather

141 *The Resurrection*; Color Study for Mary Love Boott Welch Memorial Window, Trinity Church, Boston, c. 1902

Watercolor and gouache on paper
Sight: 13 1/2 x 4 1/2 in. (33.5 x 10.7 cm.)
William Varieka Fine Arts, Newport, Rhode Island

142 *The Resurrection*; Color Study for Mary Love Boott Welch Memorial Window, Trinity Church, Boston, c. 1902

Watercolor and gouache on paper
15 x 7 1/2 in. (38.1 x 18.3 cm.)
The Cleveland Museum of Art. In memory of Ralph King. Gift of Mrs. Ralph King, Ralph T. Woods, Charles G. King, and Frances King Schafer

143 *Christ and the Woman of Samaria at the Well*; Design for Harriet Whiton and William R. Storrs Memorial Window, Westminister Presbyterian Church, Scranton, Pennsylvania, c. 1903

Graphite on paper
11 x 11 in. (27.9 x 27.9 cm.)
The Toledo Museum of Art; Gift of Edward Drummond Libbey

144 *Christ and the Woman of Samaria at the Well*; Color Study for Harriet Whiton and William R. Storrs Memorial Window, Westminister Presbyterian Church, Scranton, Pennsylvania, c. 1903

Watercolor, gouache, and graphite on thin paper
9 x 10 1/2 in. (22.9 x 25.9 cm.)
Museum of Art, Rhode Island School of Design, Providence, Gift of Mr. and Mrs. Gilman Angier

145 *Madonna and Child*; Design for Altarpiece, Emmanuel Chapel, Saint Luke's Cathedral, Portland, Maine, c. 1903

Graphite on thin paper, mounted
11 x 7 15/16 in. (27.9 x 18.7 cm.)
The Toledo Museum of Art; Gift of Edward Drummond Libbey

146 *Seated Woman*; Design for *Saint Paul Preaching at Athens* Window, Columbia University Chapel, New York, c. 1906

Graphite on yellowed wove paper
Sheet: 10 1/16 x 8 1/16 in. (25.6 x 20.4 cm.)
Harvard University Art Museums, Fogg Art Museum, Bequest of Arthur Mansfield Brooks

147 *Mother and Child*, 1888

Watercolor and gouache on paper
7 5/8 x 7 1/4 in. (17.8 x 18.5 cm.)
Lee-La Farge Collection, Mount Saint Mary's College, Emmitsburg, Maryland

148 *Mother and Child*, c. 1888

Watercolor and gouache over graphite on off-white paper
7 3/8 x 7 3/8 in. (19.5 x 19.5 cm.)
Private Collection

149 *The Escape, Japan*, 1895

Watercolor and gouache on Japanese laid mulberry paper
Sheet: 7 3/4 x 10 3/4 in. (18.5 x 26.2 cm.)
Schenectady Museum Collection, Schenectady, New York, Art Committee Purchase

150 *Spirit of the Storm. Japanese Folk Lore*, 1897

Watercolor and ink wash on Japanese paper
15 3/8 x 10 3/4 in. (39.0 x 27.3 cm.)
The Toledo Museum of Art; Gift of Edward Drummond Libbey

151 *The Aesthete*, 1898

Watercolor, gouache, and pen and ink on paper
10 x 14 1/2 in. (25.4 x 36.1 cm.)
Milton Porter, Pittsburgh

152 *A Rishi Calling up a Storm, Japanese Folk Lore*, c. 1897-1898

Watercolor, gouache, and pen and ink over graphite on paper
Sheet: 13 x 16 1/8 in. (33.0 x 40.4 cm.)
The Cleveland Museum of Art, Purchase from the J.H. Wade Fund

153 *Robed Female Figure*, c. 1903

Soft graphite or black crayon on oriental paper
8 5/8 x 5 11/16 in. (22.0 x 14.5 cm.)
The Art Museum, Princeton University, Princeton, New Jersey. Gift of Frank Jewett Mather, Jr.

154 *The Woman in Red*, c. 1903

Watercolor and gouache on paper
8 3/4 x 5 1/4 in. (21.1 x 13.0 cm.)
Private Collection

SELECTED BIBLIOGRAPHY

This selected bibliography cites only sources referenced in the footnotes. A more complete bibliography of La Farge's work, including a detailed chronology and a full listing of exhibitions, is found in the first book listed below.

BOOKS ON JOHN LA FARGE

Adams, Henry, Kathleen A. Foster, Henry A. La Farge, H. Barbara Weinberg, Linnea H. Wren, and James L. Yarnall, *John La Farge* (New York: Abbeville Press, 1987).

Cortissoz, Royal, *John La Farge: A Memoir and a Study* (Boston and New York: Houghton Mifflin and Co., 1911).

Waern, Cecelia, *John La Farge, Artist and Writer* (London: Seeley and Co.; New York: Macmillan and Co., 1896).

Weinberg, H. Barbara, *The Decorative Work of John La Farge* (New York: Garland Press, 1977).

BOOKS ON RELATED TOPICS

Adams, Henry, *Tahiti: Memoirs of Araii Tamai e Marama of Eimeo, Teriinere of Tooarai, Terrenui of Tahiti, Taurraatua i Amo* (Washington, D.C.: Privately Printed, 1901).

Adams, Henry, John Caldwell, John R. Lane, Kenneth Neal, and Elizabeth A. Prelinger, *American Drawings and Watercolors in the Museum of Art*, Carnegie Institute (Pittsburgh: Museum of Art, Carnegie Institute, 1985).

Bachelder, John B., *Popular Resorts and How to Reach Them* (Boston: John B. Bachelder, Publisher, 1875).

Boime, Albert, *The Academy and French Painting in the Nineteenth Century* (New York: Phaidon Publishers, Inc., 1971).

___, *Thomas Couture and the Eclectic Vision* (New Haven, Connecticut: Yale University Press, 1980).

Brougham, John, and John Elderkin, eds., *Lotos Leaves, Original Stories and Essays* (Boston: William F. Gill and Company, 1875).

Brooks, Van Wyck, *Fenollosa and his Circle* (New York: E.P. Dutton and Co., Inc., 1962).

Chazeaux, Evelyne de, translator and introduction, *Lettres des Mers du Sud* (Paris: Publication de la Société des Océanistes, no. 34, 1974).

Edel, Leon, *Henry James Letters*, 2 vols. (Cambridge, Massachusetts: Belknap Press of Harvard University, 1974).

Gannon, Robert I., S.J., *Up to the Present: The Story of Fordham* (Garden City, New York: Doubleday and Co., 1967).

Hendy, Philip, *Isabella Stewart Gardner Museum Catalogue of Exhibited Paintings and Drawings* (Boston: For the Trustees, 1931).

Howe, Julia Ward, *Reminiscences: 1819-1899* (Boston and New York: Houghton Mifflin and Company, 1899).

La Farge, John, *An Artist's Letters from Japan* (New York: Century Company, 1897).

___, *Hokusai: A Talk about Hokusai, The Japanese Painter, at the Century Club, March 28, 1896* (New York: William C. Martin Printing House, 1897).

___, *Reminiscences of the South Seas* (Garden City, New York: Doubleday, Page and Co., 1912).

La Farge, John, S.J., *The Manner is Ordinary* (New York: Harcourt, Brace and Co., 1954).

Levenson, J.C., Ernest Samuels, Charles Vandersee, and Viola Hopkins Winner, eds., *The Letters of Henry Adams*, 6 vols. (Cambridge, Massachusetts, and London, England: Belknap Press of Harvard University, 1982-1988).

Lewis, R.W.B. and Nancy Lewis, eds., *The Letters of Edith Wharton* (New York: Charles Scribner's Sons, 1988).

Melville, Herman, *Typee* (New York: Dodd, Mead and Co., 1951).

Mount Saint Mary's College, *Catalogue of the Officers and Students of Mount Saint Mary's College, Emmitsburg, Maryland, for the Academic Year 1854-1855* (Emmitsburg, Maryland: Mount Saint Mary's College, 1855).

O'Brien, Frederick, *Atolls of the Sun* (New York: The Century Company, 1922).

Richards, Laura E. and Maud Howe Elliott, *Julia Ward Howe 1819-1910*, 2 vols. (Boston and New York: Houghton Mifflin Company, The Riverside Press Cambridge, 1916).

Rowland, Benjamin, *The Art and Architecture of India, Hindu, Jain* (New York: Penguin Books, 1967).

Stedman, Arthur, notes and introduction to Herman Melville, *Typee: A Real Romance of the South Seas* (New York: United States Book Company, 1892).

Strickler, Susan, ed., *American Traditions in Watercolor* (New York: Abbeville Press, 1987).

Taaba, Pamela S., "The Great Boston Collectors: The Copley Square Years," *The Great Boston Collectors* (Boston: Museum of Fine Arts, Boston, 1984).

Warner, Charles D., ed., *Library of the World's Best Literature*, (New York: H.A. Hill and Co., 1902).

Wilson, Richard Guy, Dianne H. Pilgrim, and Richard N. Murray, *The American Renaissance: 1876-1917* (New York: Pantheon Books, 1979).

Adams, Henry, "A Fish by John La Farge," *Art Bulletin* 62 (Jun. 1980): 269-80.

___, "John La Farge and Japan," *Apollo* 119 (Feb. 1984): 120-29.

___, "John La Farge's Discovery of Japanese Art," *Art Bulletin* 67 (Sept. 1985): 449-85.

"Art and Artists," *Boston Evening Transcript*, 16 Apr. 1884: 6.

"Artist La Farge Arrested," *New York World*, 20 May 1885: 2.

"Art Notes," *Critic and Good Literature* 4 (31 May 1884): 258.

"An Atelier," *Boston Daily Transcript*, 24 May 1883: 6.

Bullard, E. John, "John La Farge at Tautira, Tahiti," *National Gallery of Art Reports and Studies in the History of Art* 2 (1968): 146-54.

"The Chronicle of Arts," *New York Tribune*, 24 Feb. 1895: 24.

Clement, Clara Erskine, "Later Religious Painting in America," *New England Magazine* 12 (Apr. 1895): 131-54.

"Debts May Eat Up La Farge's Estate," *New York Times*, 28 Dec. 1910: 3.

"Editor's Table," *Appleton's Journal* n.s. 2 (May 1877): 473.

"The Fine Arts," *Boston Daily Advertiser*, 19 Apr. 1884: 4.

"The Fine Arts: Exhibition of South Sea Islands and Japan. Pictures by John La Farge," *Boston Weekly Transcript*, 25 Mar. 1898: 5.

Foster, Kathleen M., "The Still-Life Painting of John La Farge," *American Art Journal* 11 (Jul. [Summer] 1979): 4-37.

"A Glimpse of John La Farge's Work, as shown at the Montross Gallery," *New York Mail and Express Illustrated Saturday Magazine*, 9 Feb. 1901: 4.

Higginson, Thomas Wentworth, "Julia Ward Howe," *Outlook* 85 (26 Jan. 1907): 167-78.

Humphreys, Mary Gay, "The Cornelius Vanderbilt House. Decorations of the Dining-Room, Water-Color Room, and Smoking Room," *Art Amateur* 8 (May 1883): 135-36.

___, "John La Farge, Artist and Decorator," *Art Amateur* 9 (Jun. 1883): 12.

"Inspired by Faith, Catholic and Colorist, John La Farge, Heralded by Puritan Boston, a Type of Catholic Imagination in Art," *Republic* 24 (5 Mar. 1904): 5.

Jarvis, Robert, "Pictures by La Farge and Inness," *Art Amateur* 11 (Jun. 1884): 12-13.

"John La Farge" [obituary], *New York Times*, 26 Jun. 1858: 5.

"John La Farge: Flame of Inspiration," *Mount Alumnus* 1 (Spring 1952): 8, 27-28.

"John La Farge's Story," *New York Daily Tribune*, 30 Jan. 1909: 7.

"La Farge Embroideries," *Art Amateur* 8 (Jan. 1883): 49.

"The Lafarge [sic] Exhibition," *Critic and Good Literature* 4 (16 Apr. 1884): 198.

La Farge, Henry A., "The Early Drawings of John La Farge," *American Art Journal* 16 (Spring 1984): 4-37.

___, "John La Farge and the 1878 Auction of his Works," *American Art Journal* 15 (Summer 1983): 4-34.

___, "John La Farge's Work in the Vanderbilt Houses," *American Art Journal* 16 (Autumn 1984): 30-70.

La Farge, John, "An Artist's Letters from Japan" (serialized): "An Artist's Letters from Japan," 39 (Feb. 1890): 483-91; "From Tokio to Nikko," 39 (Mar. 1890): 712-20; "The Shrines of Iyeyasu and Iyemitsu in the Holy Mountain of Nikko," 39 (Apr. 1890): 859-69; "An Artist's Letters from Japan: Iyemitsu," 40 (Jun. 1890): 195-203; "An Artist's Letters from Japan: Sketching," 40 (Aug. 1890): 566-74; "An Artist's Letters from Japan: Sketching," 40 (Sept. 1890): 751-59; "An Artist's Letters from Japan," 40 (Oct. 1890): 866-77; "Tao: The Way," 42 (Jul. 1891): 442-48; "Bric-a-Brac," 46 (Jul. 1893): 419-29; "An Artist's Letters from Japan: Yokohama-Kamakura," 46 (Aug. 1893): 571-76.

___, "A Fiji Festival," *Century Magazine* 67 (Feb. 1904): 518-26.

___, [Letter to the Editor], *New York Times*, 5 Feb. 1909: 6.

___, "The Making of the Ascension," *New York Herald*, 5 Apr. 1903: 6.

___, "Passages from a Diary in the Pacific: A First Day in the South Seas," *Scribner's Magazine* 29 (Jun. 1901): 670-84.

___, "Passages from a Diary in the Pacific: Hawaii," *Scribner's Magazine* 29 (May 1901): 537-46.

___, "Passages from a Diary in the Pacific: Tahiti," *Scribner's Magazine* 30 (Jul. 1901): 69-83.

___, "Son of Bancroft" [Letter to the Editor], *New York Times Saturday Review of Books and Art*, 17 Aug. 1901: 581.

___, "Tahitian Literature" in Charles D. Warner, ed., *Library of the World's Best Literature*, (New York: H.A. Hill and Co., 1902) 24: 14389-398.

"La Farge Left $599 Here," *New York Times*, 14 Jun. 1914: 1.

La Farge, Mabel, "John La Farge: The Artist," *Commonweal* 22 (3 May 1935): 7-10.

La Farge, O.H.P., "Schoolboy Letters between John La Farge and his Father," *United States Catholic Historical Society Historical Records and Studies* 18 (Mar. 1928): 74-120.

"The La Farge Sale," *New York Times*, 15 Apr. 1884: 5.

"La Farge Shades His Fling at Architects," *New York World*, 31 Jan. 1909: 1.

"La Farge's Bad Break," *American Art News* 7 (6 Feb. 1909): 4.

"La Farge's Medal Comes Late," *Boston Evening Transcript*, 30 Jan. 1909: 2.

"Late for a Medal, Says John La Farge," *New York Times*, 30 Jan. 1909: 1.

Mather, Frank Jewett, "John La Farge—An Appreciation," *World's Work* 23 (Mar. 1911): 14085-100.

"Mr. La Farge's Arrest," *New York World*, 21 May 1885: 1.

"Mr. La Farge's Health" [Letter to the Editor], *New York Daily Tribune*, 28 Oct. 1908: 7.

"Mr. La Farge's Troubles," *New York Commercial Advertiser*, 25 May 1885: 1.

"Our Artistic Library," *Boston Sunday Herald*, 17 Feb. 1895: 13.

"Passengers Sailed . . . in the Steamship Fulton," *New York Times*, 7 Apr. 1856: 8.

"[Review of] An Artist's Letters from Japan," *Art Interchange* 27 (Nov. 1897): 320.

Richardson, Charles F., "A Book of Beginnings" [Letter to the Editor], *Nation* 91 (1 Dec. 1910): 520-21

Shinn, Earl, "The Growing School of American Water-Color Art," *Nation* 28 (6 Mar. 1879): 172-73.

"Studies of the Artists," *New York Times*, 5 Feb. 1879: 5.

Sturgis, Russell, "John La Farge," *Scribner's Magazine* 26 (Jul.1899): 3-19.

Thompson, D. Dodge, "John La Farge's masterpieces in stained glass," *The Magazine Antiques* (Mar. 1989): 708-17.

Weitenkampf, Frank, "John La Farge, Illustrator," *The Print-Collector's Quarterly* 5 (Dec. 1915): 472-94.

"Works by John La Farge," *Boston Evening Transcript*, 25 Mar. 1914: 9.

Yarnall, James, "John La Farge and Henry Adams in Japan," *American Art Journal* 21 (1989): 40-77.

___, "John La Farge and Henry Adams in the South Seas," *American Art Journal* 20 (1988): 51-109.

___, "John La Farge's *Paradise Valley Period*," *Newport History* 55 (Winter 1982): 1-25.

___, "John La Farge's *Portrait of the Painter* and the Use of Photography in his Work," *American Art Journal* 18 (1986): 4-20.

___, "New Insights on John La Farge and Photography," *American Art Journal* 19 (1987): 52-79.

___, "Tennyson Illustration in Boston, 1864-1872," *Imprint, Journal of the American Historical Print Collectors Society* 7 (Fall 1982): 10-16.

American Art Association, New York, *Catalogue of the Art Property and Other Objects Belonging to the Estate of the Late John La Farge*, 24-31 Mar. 1911.

Art Institute of Chicago, Chicago, *Catalogue. Paintings, Studies, Sketches and Drawings, Mostly Records of Travel 1886 and 1890-91, by John La Farge*, 26 Jan.-21 Feb. 1897.

Doll and Richards, Boston, *Catalogue of Drawings, Watercolors, and Paintings by Mr. John La Farge on Exhibition and Sale*, 25 Jan.-6 Feb. 1890.

___, *Catalogue of Drawings, Watercolors, and Paintings by Mr. John La Farge on Exhibition and Sale*, 25 Mar.-6 Apr. 1892.

___, *Catalogue of Water Color and Oil Paintings by Mr. John La Farge on Exhibition and Sale*, 10-22 Mar. 1893.

___, *Exhibition and Private Sale of Paintings in Water Color Chiefly from South Sea Islands and Japan by Mr. John La Farge*, 18-30 Mar. 1898.

___, *Exhibition and Private Sale of Paintings in Water Color and Oil from the South Sea Islands and Japan*, 14-20 Feb. 1895.

___, *Exhibition and Private Sale of Pictures, Drawings and Sketches by Mr. John La Farge*, 26 Feb.-16 Mar. 1904.

Durand-Ruel Galleries, New York, *Paintings, Studies, Sketches and Drawings, Mostly Records of Travel 1886 and 1890-91 by John La Farge*, 25 Feb.-5 Mar. 1895.

Durand-Ruel Galleries, Paris, *Exposition des Peintures et Sculptures d'Artistes Américains*, Jun. 1891.

Gallery of the Picture Exhibition Society, Cleveland, *Catalogue. Paintings, Studies, Sketches and Drawings, Mostly Records of Travel 1886 and 1890-91, by John La Farge*, 23 Dec. 1896-5 Jan. 1897.

Leavitt and Co., Auctioneers, New York, *Catalogue of Pottery & Porcelain, Japanese Lacquers, Bronzes, Jades . . . from the Collections of Messrs. W.L. Andrews, Sam. Colman, John La Farge, Russell Sturgis, and two other Amateurs*, 31 Mar.-2 Apr. [1879].

Leavitt Art Galleries, New York, *The La Farge Collection. Oriental Porcelains, Bric-a-Brac. . . . belonging to John La Farge, Esq., of this City*, 22-23 Dec. [1880].

Leavitt, Strebeigh & Co., Auctioneers, New York, *Catalogue of the Private Library of John La Farge, esq., (who will shortly depart for Europe) . . .*, 18-19 Dec. 1866.

Leonard's Gallery, Boston, *The Drawings, Water-Colors, and Oil-Paintings by John La Farge. To Be Sold at Auction*, 18-19 Dec. [1879].

Moore's Art Gallery, New York, *Catalogue of a Collection of Oil and Water Color Paintings by John La Farge*, 26-27 Mar. [1885].

Ortgies and Co., New York, *Important Collection of Oil and Water Color Paintings, by John La Farge of This City. To Be Sold at Auction*, 14-17 Apr. [1884].

___, *Supplementary Catalogue of Water Colors, by John La Farge. To Be Sold at Auction*, 14-17 Apr. [1884].

Reichard and Co., New York, *Catalogue of Drawings, Water Colors, and Paintings by Mr. John La Farge*, 15 Apr.-1 May 1890.

Saint Louis Exposition, Saint Louis, Missouri, *Catalogue of the Art Collection of the St. Louis Exposition and Musical Hall Association. Seventh Annual Exhibition*, [Sept.] 1890.

Saint Louis Museum of Fine Arts, Saint Louis, Missouri, *A Group of Paintings, Studies, and Sketches, Records of Travel 1886, 1890, and 1891, by John La Farge*, 5-20 Mar. 1897.

Salon of 1874, Paris, *Salon de 1874*, Mar.-Apr. 1874.

Salon of 1895, Champ de Mars, Paris, *Etudes, esquisses, dessins: Souvenirs et notes de voyage (1886 and 1890-91) par John La Farge, traduction du catalogue américain*, Mar.-Apr. 1895.

Society of French Artists, London, *Seventh Exhibition of the Society of French Artists*, [Fall] 1873.

Sotheby's Arcade Auctions, New York, *American 19th and 20th Century Paintings, Drawings and Sculpture*, 20 Jan. 1987.

UNPUBLISHED MATERIAL

Adams, Henry, "John La Farge, 1830-1870: From Artist to Amateur" (Ph.D. dissertation, Yale University, 1980).

Covell, Virginia Galvin, "A Critical Examination of the Town and Country Club of Newport, Rhode Island" (Master's Thesis, University of Rhode Island, 1964).

Doll and Richards, Boston, "List of Pictures by Mr. John La Farge sold by Doll & Richards, Inc., Boston" (Typescript, Henry A. La Farge Papers, New Canaan, Connecticut, 1874-1910).

Katz, Ruth Berenson, "John La Farge as Painter and Critic (Ph.D. dissertation, Radcliffe College, 1951).

La Farge, Henry A., "Catalogue Raisonné of the Works of John La Farge" (unpublished manuscript, Henry A. La Farge Papers, New Canaan, Connecticut, 1974-1985; an earlier version of this catalogue [1932-1934] is housed in the La Farge Family Papers [Yale]).

La Farge, John, "An Artist of Japan: Lecture Delivered Before the Architectural League of New York (With Illustrations), June 1893" (Manuscript, La Farge Family Papers [Yale], 1893).

___, "[Reply to] the questions asked by Mr. Bing regarding my work and my ideas, so as to include a notice of the same in his report to the French Government" (Typescript, La Farge Family Papers [Yale], c. 1894).

Lefor, Patricia Joan, "John La Farge and Japan: An Instance of Oriental Influence in American Art" (Ph.D. dissertation, Northwestern University, 1978).

Murakata, Akiko, "William Sturgis Bigelow" (Manuscript, Henry A. La Farge Papers, New Canaan, Connecticut, 1972).

Siegel, Louise, "John Chandler Bancroft (1835-1901)" (Manuscript, National Museum of American Art, Smithsonian Institution, Washington, D.C., 1969).

Yarnall, James L., "The Role of Landscape in the Art of John La Farge" (Ph.D. dissertation, University of Chicago, 1981).

MANUSCRIPT COLLECTIONS

Archives of American Art, Smithsonian Institution, Washington, D.C.

Archives du Louvre, Paris.

Cortissoz, Royal, Papers, Beinicke Rare Book and Manuscript Library, Yale University, New Haven, Connecticut.

Isabella Stewart Gardner Museum Archives, Isabella Stewart Gardner Museum, Boston.

La Farge Family Papers, Division of Manuscripts and Archives, Sterling Memorial Library, Yale University, New Haven, Connecticut.

La Farge Family Papers, New-York Historical Society, New York.

La Farge, Henry A., Papers, New Canaan, Connecticut.

Massachusetts Historical Society, Boston.

Mount Saint Mary's College Archives, Hugh Phillips Memorial Library, Mount Saint Mary's College, Emmitsburg, Maryland.

Perry, Thomas Sergeant, Papers, Colby College, Waterville, Maine.

Private Archives, New Canaan, Connecticut.

Private Archives, Ploujean, Finistère, France.

Private Archives, Princeton, New Jersey.

Saint-Gaudens Correspondence, Dartmouth College Library, Hanover, New Hampshire.

Scudder, Horace, Papers, Houghton Library, Harvard University, Cambridge, Massachusetts.

Vose Galleries Papers, Boston.

PUBLIC DOCUMENTS

Middletown Town Hall, Middletown, Rhode Island, Public Land Records.

Newport Town Hall, Newport, Rhode Island, Land Evidence Books.

New York City Municipal Archives, Department of Records and Information Services

New York City Surrogate Court, New York, Probate Records.

ACKNOWLEDGEMENTS

For those of us who participated in this exhibition, one of the greatest joys has been working with guest curator James Yarnall. Jim is a consummate scholar and his enthusiasm, professionalism and generosity have added immeasurably to the project at every step of the way, from allowing me to participate in selecting works of art for the exhibition to providing materials well in advance of deadlines. I would also like to thank Mrs. Henry La Farge for her continual support and enthusiasm for the project.

I would like to add my thanks to Mark Ouderkirk, former Registrar of the Museum, and to Liese Hilgeman, former Curator of Exhibitions, and Bernadette M. Sigler, Associate Curator and Acting Registrar, who put in long hours editing the manuscript, arranging transportation of the works and making the exhibition and the catalogue come together. Special thanks should be made to Scott Atkinson, Curator of the Terra Museum of American Art in Chicago, and to Paul Schweizer, former Director of the Munson–Williams–Proctor Institute in Utica, New York, for agreeing to take the exhibition.

The Museum would also like to thank Stephen Lovette for his generosity in supporting this publication.

Barbara Bloemink

I wish to acknowledge the generosity and help of the following individuals: the late Henry A. La Farge, whose unpublished Catalogue Raisonné of the Works of John La Farge is the source of much of the factual information in this book; his widow, Mary A. La Farge, whose magnanimous support of and enthusiasm for the catalogue raisonné has been invaluable in furthering her late husband's life work; Amy B. Werbel, Francine Corcione, and Lisa Stutman, the research staff of the catalogue raisonné, who contributed immeasurably to the material utilized in this book; Susanne O. Koenig, who edited the manuscript and made many valuable suggestions for writing it; Catherine Hoover Voorsanger, who provided help and information from her personal research files; and Maureen C. O'Brien, who first suggested the idea for an exhibition that evolved into the present show. I owe in addition a great debt to the present and former staff of The Hudson River Museum, who worked with great diligence and cheerfulness on a large and difficult project, particularly: Barbara J. Bloemink, Bernadette M. Sigler, Liese Hilgeman, Robert Workman, and Mark Ouderkirk.

The monetary conversions throughout were provided by Stephen M. Lovette, Manager of Policy Implementation, Division of Banking Supervision and Regulation, Board of Governors of the Federal Reserve System, Washington, D.C. He adjusted calculations for tax equivalency and inflation using the implicit price index of the Gross National Product through 1970 and the implicit price deflator from 1970 through 1989. Due to inflation, conversions for some values published herein are greater than conversions published several years ago for the same values.

James L. Yarnall

LENDERS TO THE EXHIBITION

The Achenbach Foundation for Graphic Arts, The Fine Arts Museums of San Francisco, California

Addison Gallery of American Art, Phillips Academy, Andover, Massachusetts

Albright–Knox Art Gallery, Buffalo, New York

The Art Institute of Chicago, Illinois

The Art Museum, Princeton University, Princeton, New Jersey

Avery Architectural and Fine Arts Library, Columbia University, New York

Mr. and Mrs. Fred D. Bentley, Sr.

Bowdoin College Museum of Art, Brunswick, Maine

The Brooklyn Museum, New York

Mr. and Mrs. Richard N. Carrell

Sterling and Francine Clark Art Institute, Williamstown, Massachusetts

Mr. and Mrs. Willard G. Clark

The Cleveland Museum of Art, Ohio

Thomas Colville Fine Arts, Inc.

Cooper–Hewitt, National Museum of Design, Smithsonian Institution

Corcoran Gallery of Art, Washington, D.C.

Detroit Institute of Arts, Michigan

Mrs. Matilda S. Dordet and Allen C. Davis

The William A. Farnsworth Library and Art Museum, Rockland, Maine

Mr. and Mrs. Stuart P. Feld

Mrs. Diane Moore Field

Dr. Thomas C. Folk

Mrs. William H. Forsyth

Daniel and Rita Fraad

Georgia Museum of Art, Athens, Georgia

Fogg Art Museum, Harvard University, Cambridge, Massachusetts

Honolulu Academy of Arts, Honolulu, Hawaii

Hood Museum of Art, Darmouth College, Hanover, New Hampshire

Huntington Museum of Art, West Virginia

IBM Gallery, New York

Indiana University Art Museum, Bloomington, Indiana

Jordan–Volpe Gallery, Inc.

Mathilda G. La Farge

Harriet B. Lidgerwood

Margaret H. Lloyd

Mrs. Eleanor S. Lunde

The Marion Koogler McNay Art Museum, San Antonio, Texas

Mead Art Museum, Amherst College, Amherst, Massachusetts

The Metropolitan Museum of Art, New York

Mount Saint Mary's College, Emmitsburg, Maryland

Museum of Art, Rhode Island School of Design, Providence, Rhode Island

Museum of Fine Arts, Boston

The New Britian Museum of American Art, New Britain, Connecticut

The Peabody Museum of Salem, Massachusetts

The Phillips Collection, Washington, D.C.

The Pierpont Morgan Library, New York

Stuart Pivar

Milton and Adrienne Porter

Preservation Society of Newport County, Newport, Rhode Island

Private Collections (23)

Redwood Library and Athenaeum, Newport, Rhode Island

San Diego Museum of Art, California

The Santa Barbara Museum of Art, California

Schenectady Museum, New York

The Spencer Museum of Art, Lawrence, Kansas

The Toledo Museum of Art, Ohio

William Vareika Fine Arts, Newport, Rhode Island

Washington County Museum of Art, Hagerstown, Maryland

Wellesley College Museum, Wellesley, Massachusetts

The Whitney Museum of American Art, New York

Erving and Joyce Wolf

Worcester Art Museum, Massachusetts

Yale University Art Gallery, New Haven, Connecticut

STAFF AND TRUSTEES OF THE HUDSON RIVER MUSEUM

SUPPORTERS OF THE HUDSON RIVER MUSEUM

The list below reflects gifts received
from July 1, 1989 through June 30, 1990

$10,000 AND ABOVE

Louis & Anne Abrons Foundation, Inc.
National Endowment for the Arts
New York State Assembly
New York State Senate
New York State Council on the Arts
New York State Department of Parks, Recreation and Historic Preservation
Safe Flight Instrument Corporation
Texaco Inc.
Westchester County
City of Yonkers
Anonymous

$5,000 TO $9,999

Auxiliary of The Hudson River Museum
Chemical Bank
CIBA-GEIGY Corporation
General Foods Corporation
Jewish Communal Fund of New York
IBM Corporation
Mr. Stephen M. Lovette
The Pope Foundation
Sarah I. Schieffelin Residuary Trust
John Sloan Memorial Foundation, Inc.
Mr. John Bond Trevor, Jr.
Carl Zeiss, Inc.

$2,500 TO $4,999

Citibank, N.A.
Fuji Photo Film U.S.A., Inc.
Mr. and Mrs. Howard D. Harlow
Peoples Westchester Savings Bank
Pepsi Cola Bottling Company of New York, Inc.
Reader's Digest Association Inc.

$1,000 TO $2,499

Mr. and Mrs. Joseph C. Abeles
Mr. and Mrs. Robert H. Abplanalp
Mr. and Mrs. Norman Adler
American Express
American Savings Bank
Mr. and Mrs. George E. Austin
Mr. and Mrs. Andrew J. Balint
Mr. and Mrs. Edward B. Berninger
Rhoda and Gerald Blumberg
Mr. and Mrs. David Boccio
The Charlpeg Foundation
Chase Communications Group, Ltd.
Chase Manhattan Bank
Mr. and Mrs. Harry B. DeMaio
Mr. and Mrs. David Durst
Mr. and Mrs. Ronald Emerson
Friends of the Bronxville Library
The Glickenhaus Foundation
Mr. and Mrs. Marvin Goodless
L. Grand Printing Company, Inc.
Dr. and Mrs. Leonard M. Greene
The Victor Herbert Foundation
The Hudson River Museum Foundation
The Hudson Valley National Foundation, Inc.
The Junior League of Bronxville, New York
Mr. and Mrs. Robert W. Koo
The Lederer Foundation
Mr. and Mrs. Jerome Le Shaw
Mr. and Mrs. Matthew L. Lifflander
The Mandel Foundation
M. Tech Printing, Inc.
Philip Morris Management Corporation
Polychrome Corporation
Schulman Realty Group
Mr. and Mrs. Stephen W. Small
Mr. Gregory Smayda
Mr. Howard I. Stein
Mr. and Mrs. Frederick J. Stock
Mr. and Mrs. Jeff Tamarin
Union Carbide Corporation
Ms. Kate Washton
Theodore & Renee Weiler Foundation
Mr. and Mrs. George Zeno

$500 TO $999

Altman-Stiller Foundation
Mr. and Mrs. Edward V. Atnally
Balint & Associates, Inc.
Mr. and Mrs. John Balint, Jr.
The Bank of New York
Mr. and Mrs. Anthony J. Caputo
Charina Foundation
Mr. George V. Comfort
Mr. and Mrs. Joseph B. DeBlasi
Dorman & Wilson
Mr. and Mrs. Harold Drimmer
Emjay Arts Corp.
Mr. Dean J. Grandin, Jr.
Graphite Metallizing Corporation
Mrs. Maitland L. Griggs
Mr. and Mrs. Daniel J. Houlihan
Mr. and Mrs. Leslie E. Klein
Mr. and Mrs. Eric Lagercrantz
Mr. and Mrs. Richard Maass
Rolf and Elisabeth Meyer
Mr. and Mrs. Ira Millstein
Mr. and Mrs. James Milne
Mr. and Mrs. Stephen B. Morris
Mr. and Mrs. Morris W. Offit
Honorable Richard L. Ottinger
Mr. and Mrs. Howard M. Pack
Palisades Realty Group, Inc.
Pepsi-Cola Company
Mr. and Mrs. Frederick P. Rose
Rose Associates, Inc.
Szoke Koo Associates
Mr. William Wulfing

$250 TO $499

Bennett, Kielson & Company
Mr. and Mrs. Peter Bertine
Mr. John R. Carhuff
Ms. Karen Cochrane
Mr. and Mrs. Paul Elston
Mr. and Mrs. Bernard Fein
Mrs. Sidney Friend
Mr. and Mrs. Peter J. Gallagher
Mr. and Mrs. R. Leigh Glover
Mr. William A. Hall
Mr. and Mrs. Robert F. Heins
Mr. and Mrs. Charles G. Herbermann
Mr. and Mrs. Leonard Jacobson
Stuart Kolbert Consulting, Inc.
Lasberg Construction Associates
Dr. and Mrs. Gerson Lesnick
Mr. and Mrs. Tristram W. Metcalfe, Jr.
Roger & Barbara Michaels Family Fund
National Westminster Bank, USA
Mr. and Mrs. Robert B. Oresman
Mr. and Mrs. Gideon Rabin
Mr. and Mrs. Stanley E. Redka
Mr. and Mrs. David Rockefeller
Mr. and Mrs. Rodman Rockefeller
Rosenberg-Diamond Development Corp.
Mr. and Mrs. Joel Sachs
Martin & Betty Schwab Foundation, Inc.
Mr. and Mrs. Ernest Schwartz
Mr. Richard J. Schwartz
Mrs. J. Walter Severinghaus
Mr. and Mrs. Ernest Shapiro
Mr. and Mrs. David A. Shulman
Mr. and Mrs. Samuel Silberman
Simone Development
Lawrence & Alice Valenstein Fund, Inc.
Mr. and Mrs. David Zealand

COLOPHON

JOHN LA FARGE: Watercolors and Drawings

This catalogue was produced on a Macintosh SE computer. The typeface is Caslon 540—a contemporary redrawing of an 18th century typeface designed by William Caslon, an English printer and type designer. The cover was printed on Strathmore Esprit, the images were printed on Centura Dull, and the text pages are Passport. The type was output at Typogram in New York City on a Mergenthaler Linotronic printer.

September, 1990